*The Religious Dimension
in Hegel's Thought*

Emil L. Fackenheim

The Religious Dimension in Hegel's Thought

The University of Chicago Press
Chicago and London

The University of Chicago Press, Chicago 60637
The University of Chicago Press, Ltd., London

89 88 87 86 85 84 83 82   1 2 3 4 5

Library of Congress Cataloging in Publication Data

Fackenheim, Emil L.
   The religious dimension in Hegel's thought.

   Includes bibliographical references.
   1. Hegel, Georg Wilhelm Friedrich, 1770–1831—Religion.
I. Title.
B2949.R3F3 1982   193   81-21914
ISBN 0-226-23350-2 (pbk.)   AACR2

For Rose, Michael, Susan, and David

Contents

Preface

The religious thought of classical German idealism has long vanished into the past. Yet it is not of concern to historians only, but still speaks to present philosophers and theologians. It speaks indirectly, mainly through the mediation of existentialism. It also speaks directly, by virtue of its own profundity.

These are convictions at which I arrived two decades ago. About ten years ago they ripened into a plan to produce a one-volume work which would trace the relation between religion and philosophy from Kant to Kierkegaard. The work was to address itself to scholars in the field, but also to philosophers and theologians who are interested in the past only where it has a bearing on the present.

The original plan broke down because of Hegel. Hegel's philosophy shatters the context of German idealism; it is as much a response to Aristotle and Spinoza as to Kant, Fichte, and Schelling. Moreover, in the case of all the other thinkers, religious thought can more or less be isolated from the rest of their philosophy; this is impossible in Hegel's case, for his philosophy exemplifies his assertion that "the Whole is the Truth." As a result of this breakdown, the present work is offered as one of two independent (although, it is hoped, mutually illuminating) companion volumes. The second volume (which I hope to offer in the near future) will be composed of essays on Kant, Fichte, Schleiermacher, and Schelling.

One feature of the original plan remains unchanged: this volume is addressed to scholars, on the one hand, philosophers and theologians, on the other. Hence the text is kept as free as possible of technical terminology; also, matters of purely scholarly interest— such as documentation, argument with alternative interpretations, crucial but esoteric points of doctrine—are confined to the notes and appendices. For this reason these are more extensive than is usual.

It remains only to offer thanks. A John Simon Guggenheim Memorial Fellowship enabled me to devote the year 1957–58 wholly to this study. I have enjoyed the fellowship of a group of Jewish thinkers united in their commitment to Judaism, and of the members of the University of Toronto philosophy department who are open to every form of philosophizing; this fellowship has helped me endure the ever-present tension between religious immediacy and philosophical reflection. Mrs. Jean Reoch, senior secretary of my department, typed the manuscript, undeterred by illegible scribblings and complex notes. Finally, the members of my family (to whom this work is dedicated) are a constant revelation that there is, as Hegel believed, a philosophical blessing in the fact that the philosopher, inclined or even obligated to "walk on his head" during the "speculative Sunday," is compelled to "stand on his feet" during the "workaday week."

Toronto   E. L. F.
April 1967

We see that thought moves to begin with
[i.e., in the Middle Ages] within Christianity, accepting
it as absolute presupposition. Later,
when the wings of thought have grown strong
[i.e., in the modern world] philosophy
rises to the sun like a young eagle, a bird of prey
which strikes religion down. But it is the last development
of speculative thought to do justice to faith
and make peace with religion.

Einl. Gesch. Phil., pp.190 ff.*

Philosophy is seen [by Hegel] as the consummator . . .
of what was promised by revelation.
Nor does philosophy exercise this office only sporadically
or at the height of its career; but in every moment,
with every breath it draws, it automatically
confirms the truth predicated by revelation.
Thus the old quarrel seems to have been composed,
heaven and earth reconciled.

FRANZ ROSENZWEIG, *Der Stern der Erloesung*
(Frankfurt: Kauffman, 1921), p.12.

Why did Hegel not become for the Protestant world
something similar to what Thomas Aquinas
was for Roman Catholicism? How could it come to pass
that, very soon after Hegel's death . . .
it was exactly his achievement which began to be
looked upon, with a pitying smile,
as representing something which was . . .
already superseded? This happened, though the same
people who pitied his achievement were still
secretly drawing intellectual sustenance from certain isolated
elements of his thought . . . . Was not Hegel
he who should come as the fulfiller
of every promise, and was it worth waiting for
another after he had come?

KARL BARTH, *From Rousseau to Ritschl*
(London: SCM Press, 1959), pp.268 ff.**

* Abbreviations are listed on pp.245 ff.

** Published in the United States as *Protestant Thought: From Rousseau
to Ritschl* (New York: Harper & Row, 1959).

*The Religious Dimension
in Hegel's Thought*

CHAPTER ONE

Introduction

According to a legend of great longevity, the Hegelian philosophy is not and never was to be taken seriously. It is a dogmatic rationalism which undertakes a priori deductions of empirical fact by some strange thesis-antithesis-synthesis method, or even a panlogism which denies the empirical altogether. It is an absolutist thought system divorced from, and blind to, the contingencies of life. It intellectualizes art and religion and thus destroys them. It deifies history so as to identify might with right, and the history thus deified culminates in the Prussian state. And it ex-

presses all these absurdities in a barbarous and well-nigh unintelligible language.

This legend was never credible. As early as 1844 (when Hegel's
philosophy was already widely declared dead) his biographer Karl
Rosenkranz observed that if this were the case, "one would have to
be astounded by the vehemence with which it is attacked precisely
by those who declare it dead."[1] His point is well taken. It is astonishing that anti-Hegelianism should have been an indispensable
part of the thought of such strange nineteenth-century bedfellows
as Marx and Kierkegaard, and that the ghost of Hegel should
once again haunt such twentieth-century figures as Tillich and
Rosenzweig, Heidegger and Sartre. Nothing, in fact, could be
more astonishing—except that thinkers of such stature should
waste their strength on a philosophy which is manifestly absurd.

The Hegel legend, though dying hard, has in recent decades
shown signs of fading away. Serious students could never ignore
facts which no amount of juggling can fit into the legend: to name
but a few, that sections of the *Phenomenology of Spirit* are every
bit as existential as anything in Kierkegaard, Heidegger, or Sartre;
that the *Philosophy of Nature* does not replace but on the contrary
presupposes empirical science; that the *Philosophy of History* ends
with the present, not because it ends all history but because philosophy cannot transcend present history; and that the entire
Hegelian philosophy, far from denying the contingent, on the
contrary seeks to demonstrate its inescapability. If facts such as
these did not at once smash the Hegel legend, and indeed until
this day have not destroyed it, it is because they seemed to replace
a caricature, not with a clear and true picture, but rather with an
impenetrable mystery. Hegel, after all, *does* put forward an absolute philosophy, that is, an all-comprehensive and therefore final
system of an all-comprehensive and therefore infinite Reason. How
can he do so and yet take existence seriously? Or admit the contingent in either nature or history? Or limit his philosophy—whatever the nature of this limitation—to his finite historical present?

It is no accident that Hegel's philosophy fragmented itself into right- and left-wing schools among his own disciples, that serious continental scholars have long held that it collapses in internal contradiction, and that some of the most penetrating studies have been produced, not by objective academic expositors, but rather by partisans who tear fragments from the Hegelian whole.

It is tempting to dispose of the Hegel mystery by means of a genetic explanation, and the temptation to do so has greatly increased ever since early Hegel manuscripts, hitherto unpublished, have become available in print in recent decades. The so-called *Early Theological Writings* antedate the completion of the Hegelian system. But they fully reflect dialectic and conflict: between outmoded institutions and revolutionary social forces, between a merely positive external religion and living religious spirit, between throbbing life as a whole and abstract, lifeless thought. What is more natural than to regard the later system-tendency as hopelessly at war with a youthful dialectic opposed to all system? It has become fashionable to do just this and, what is more, to exalt a "young" Hegel at the expense of an "old." The "young" Hegel is a vigorous thinker and a straightforward if not elegant writer; and he may be viewed as a proto-Marxist, or proto-Nietzschean, or proto-existentialist, and in any case as a revolutionary. The "old" Hegel, the author of the *Logic*, the *Encyclopedia of Philosophical Sciences*, and above all of the late Berlin lectures, is an obscure and tortuous writer, and a lifeless and sterile thinker; a conservative if not reactionary who—worst of all—has taken refuge in some sort of orthodox Christianity. Between these two extremes falls the *Phenomenology*, still full of the life of the "young" Hegel yet already burying it in the end in the absolute knowledge of the "old." A new Hegel legend is rapidly replacing the old.

For that this *is* a legend can be doubted by no student serious enough to seek more than a neat disposal of the Hegel mystery. Four major considerations remove all doubt.

First, though a prolific writer, Hegel did not publish his first book—the *Phenomenology*—until he was thirty-seven years of age. In 1806 his friend Schelling, five years his junior, was the celebrated author of ten books; Hegel himself was an obscure lecturer. Throughout his life he refused to rush into print, and he published only four books in his entire lifetime. How then can one deprecate these books which he published in favor of early manuscripts which he did not publish?

Refusing to do so, one will suspect, secondly, that if the style of the published books is difficult (and doubtless often obscure and tortuous) it is not without good reasons. Hegel *could* write fairly straightforwardly even in his later years. As for the style of his four books, this reflects labor, not lack of labor. Hegel is a compact writer and—still more important—a thinker of incredible complexity, and he tortures language to make it say at once what must be said at once. One is almost tempted to say: he *must* torture language. For as one tries to say differently exactly what Hegel says one often ends up either by saying much less, or else reverting to his own words. (The present work, which has pedagogic as well as expository purposes, for the most part deliberately says much less.) It is thus not wholly perverse to say that the mature Hegel is a master of philosophical style. And it is not perverse at all to say that he could have written with the elegance of a Schopenhauer only if he had shared that thinker's superficiality, and with the passion of a Nietzsche only if he had let go of his determination to see all truths, above all the truths of passion, in perspective.

Thirdly, while slow in reaching his mature position Hegel did not significantly alter that position after having reached it. Doubtless he changed even in the mature years, and these changes cannot be ignored. But the emphasis in these years is entirely on systematic explication and elaboration. Nor did Hegel's energies falter in his last years. (These years were mainly devoted to his

Berlin lecture cycles. These works are second in importance only to Hegel's four published books, and they are to be taken seriously despite the inadequate form in which they were posthumously published.) The "old" Hegel is not free of "resignation," although signs of resignation are by no means absent from his earlier works. But the resignation is there, not because of a lapse from the earlier philosophic vigor but precisely because there is no such lapse: because a radical thought which claims to stay with—not flee from—the world must realistically confront such aspects of the world as may make resignation necessary.

The final consideration is most important of all and, indeed, includes all the others. The mature Hegelian system has not simply abandoned the earlier "revolutionary"—and proto-Marxist, proto-Nietzschean or proto-existentialist—tendencies. Whether or not the modern interpreter (presumably himself no lover of system) likes it, it has incorporated and superseded these tendencies. This is, indeed, what *makes* it mature and a system: one which seeks to do justice to all (including philosophical) fragmentation.

Three conclusions follow from these considerations. First, the *Early Theological Writings* are important for Hegel's intellectual biography; they add little to the understanding of his mature thought, beyond confirming that, if such thinkers as Marx and Kierkegaard attack Hegel, it is not because he is irrelevant or absurd, but rather because he is too close for comfort. Next, the Hegelian philosophy, more than perhaps any other, requires systematic rather than genetic exposition. Finally, there is no legitimate way of circumventing the fundamental mystery of the mature system.

But can one still seriously hope to contribute to the solution of that mystery, after well over a century of Hegel scholarship and much recent literature? Two interrelated failings of the more recent interpreters may here be noted. The Hegelian philosophy is thoroughly contextual. Such terms as "Idea," "Spirit," "Freedom,"

"God," "World" and—perhaps above all—"Reason" are not externally brought to experience; they are seen as emerging from experience and, in their final significance, from *all* of it. Hence they can be fully grasped and appraised, not at the beginning, but only at the end. Here it is not only vulgar polemicists who fail to do Hegel justice. These latter will attack Hegel's "Reason rules the World" without any prior attempt to understand his concept of "Reason" or, for that matter, "ruling" and "World." Even serious students will often judge Hegel on the basis of abstract initial definitions, misled by the fact that the rationalism of Hegel's *Logic* has already passed through the process by which Reason emerges from experience whereas they themselves have yet to pass through that process.

Some scholars grasp this vital requirement admirably. They still fail when they do not give due weight to *all* of experience as Hegel understands it. In Hegel's clearly and unequivocally stated view, human life has an essential religious dimension; and without it men could not have risen to philosophical thought anywhere in history. Moreover, without the Christian dimension of modern life his own philosophy could not have reached its all-comprehensive goals; without the Christian dimension Reason could not be complete in the modern world. And without that completeness the Reason which is Hegelian thought would remain hopelessly fragmented. These crucial assertions were well remembered by Hegel's own left-wing disciples, who found it necessary to begin their attacks on him with an attack on religion. For whatever reason, most recent expositors have forgotten it.

Perhaps it is more accurate to say: they misunderstand Hegel or make light of him. They misunderstand him when they view his religion as no more than, so to speak, philosophy for the masses, that is, an exoteric picture-thinking simply swept aside by philosophical thinking if and when this latter comes on the scene. (Why, in that case, would any philosophy presuppose religion at all, and Hegel's own, modern Christianity?) They make light of

Hegel when they characterize his philosophy as "secularized Christianity." In a sense, to be sure, this characterization is correct enough. But it is correct only when so qualified as to contain Hegel's double-barreled assertion that the Christianity which is philosophically comprehended is *un*secularized Christianity (interrelated, to be sure, with the modern secular world), and that his philosophy which does the comprehending transcends all confessional limitations. When Hegel's philosophy is viewed simply as secularized Christianity it is all too easily disposed of—by Christians as pseudo-Christianity, and by philosophers as Christian ideology.

The relation between the religious life which is to be comprehended and the comprehending activity which is Hegel's philosophy is the central theme of the following exposition. That theme demands heavy concentration on the *Lectures on the Philosophy of Religion*, the only mature work wholly and explicitly devoted to the subject. But the exposition would fall radically short of its objective were it to confine its attention to that work alone. Hegel holds the actual existence of religious life to be an indispensable condition, not only (as is obvious) of his philosophical comprehension of religion, but also (as is far from obvious) of his philosophy as a whole. It is the larger claim, not the smaller one only, which our exposition seeks to grasp. And this cannot be done without an interpretation of the entire Hegelian system. Only a selective interpretation may be attempted: we must suppress all desires to enter into such subjects as art, history, the state, and even the details of the *Logic* except insofar as they bear on our objective. This selective interpretation, however, must be substantial: too often have neat summaries passed blithely over questions on which, by its own confession and insistence, the fate of Hegel's philosophy as a whole depends. How can Hegel's philosophy need the Christian religion and yet have the autonomy of a rational system? And how can it—with or without the help of the Christian religion—be an *all*-comprehensive thought system and yet recognize the persistent reality of the contingent, fragmented and finite?

Our answers to these questions can become intelligible only in the course of our actual exposition. Yet, following Hegel's own practice in his introductions, we may here attempt an anticipating summary. And we may rely on Karl Barth's apt formulation that Hegel seeks to do for the modern Protestant world what St. Thomas Aquinas has done for the Catholic Middle Ages. This formula, however, becomes even rudimentarily intelligible only when interwoven with Hegel's conceptions of philosophy, Christianity, and the ancient, medieval, and modern worlds.

First, not only Hegel's but all philosophy is a rise of thought to absoluteness or divinity, and philosophies which do not recognize themselves as such, too, are phases of such a rise. Moreover, in ancient pagan Greece this rise was already accomplished and, indeed, in a sense complete.

Ancient pagan philosophy was in principle incomplete, however, in that it could rise to the Divine only by means of flight from the contingent world. It could not preserve or reinstate but only help destroy the ancient pagan world from which it had arisen, thus creating a rift between the thinker who had fled from the world and the man who must live in it. And yet it could not heal this rift which it had created.

It was healed in principle when God in Christ entered into the world, but throughout the Middle Ages this healing existed in the world in principle only. As for the ancient philosophical flight from the world, it was not then reversed at all. Redeemed in the sight of God, the medieval Christian remained unfree in the sight of feudal princes, and medieval philosophy could reconcile a Catholic heaven with a feudal earth only by keeping the two neatly apart. The incursion of Christ into the world had begun to invert the world; only in the modern world could the ancient philosophical flight from the world be reversed.

In the modern Protestant world, the medieval peace of distance has given way to what may be called a war of proximity. On the one hand, the Christian God has descended from a Catholic heaven into a Protestant heart on earth. On the other hand, secular man on earth has smashed medieval fetters and acquired an infinite self-confidence, which makes him aspire to heaven. This self-confidence is manifest in his life—his science, technology, morality, and political constitutions, all of which are inspired by the revolutionary demand for autonomy. This self-confidence is also manifest in his philosophy, which begins with the revolutionary self-assertion of an omnipotent Reason which has destroyed all authorities. However, this very war gives rise to a peace which is without precedent. The realities manifest in modern Protestant faith and modern secular life are not *two* realities; they are two aspects of *one* Reality which are already implicitly united. And the philosophy which *recognizes* the one Reality in these two aspects makes the implicit explicit. That philosophy—it is Hegel's own—rises, like the Greek, to divinity. But unlike the Greek it can unite the "knowledge of God" with the "wisdom of the world," and indeed, with the world itself. It does not flee from but stays with the modern world. The comprehended world is not destroyed by it but rather preserved and reinstated. Reason exists *in* the modern world, in the midst of that very contingency without which there is *no* world. And the philosophic Reason which is Hegelian thought recognizes both Reason in the modern world and the modern world itself, even though, to be such a recognition, it must rise above all contingency.

The summary just given is grossly inadequate. But it suffices to show, first, that what we have called the Hegel mystery is not an accidental inconsistency in the Hegelian philosophy but part and parcel of its innermost historical self-understanding; and, secondly, that this self-understanding resolves the mystery. Hegel's thought takes itself to be, and is, a synthesis without parallel in the history of philosophy. It involves these three main elements: a modern religious confidence in an infinite God who, transcendent of the finite world, has fully entered into it and redeemed it; a modern secular self-confidence, immanent in the infinite aspirations of modern culture; and the confidence in a philosophical thought to make radically intelligible what is already actual.

No wisdom is required today for the insight that the Hegelian synthesis, if ever a genuine possibility, has broken down beyond all possible recovery. Shortsighted academic critics may focus their criticism even now on the Hegelian system, taken in isolation from the world which it seeks to comprehend. Prophetic non-academic critics such as Marx and Kierkegaard focused their criticism, even in the nineteenth century, on that modern world which Hegel could still view with so colossal an optimism. Today, no prophetic insight is needed for the perception of universal fragmentation. The sins of colonialism have come to visit Hegel's modern Europe. America—Hegel's "land of the future"—has lost its innocence at Hiroshima and Nagasaki. Hegel's own countrymen—in his view permanently raised above their original barbarism by a Christian culture originally alien to them—have shown at Auschwitz a depravity unequaled in all history. Modern secular self-confidence, if surviving at all, has lost its titanic quality, and the God who speaks to present-day faith speaks ambiguously if He is not wholly silent. This writer—a Jew committed to Judaism—woud in any case be at odds with the Hegelian synthesis, which, after all, is Christian or post-Christian. In the world of today, no one can accept this synthesis—Christian, post-Christian, or non-Christian.

Nor could Hegel, were he alive today, remain with his own nineteenth-century synthesis. For if a truly modern philosophic thought must stay with the world rather than flee from it, then a twentieth-century Hegelianism would have to stay with a fragmented world. Protests against any contemporary synthesis such as the protests implicit in the work of Barth and Buber, Sartre and Heidegger are therefore wholly in accord with Hegelian teaching, and it is entirely safe to say that Hegel, were he alive today, would not be a Hegelian.

And yet, such is the power of Hegel's philosophy that it speaks as directly to the fragmented world of the present age as do that world's own fragmented philosophies. This is not only because it discloses that what Hegel failed to achieve cannot be achieved: compared to Hegel's system, all subsequent attempts at system and synthesis are feeble. Nor is it only because, even if the Hegelian system collapses, we are still left with countless invaluable fragments. Most importantly of all, it is because neither post-Hegelian modern life nor post-Hegelian philosophical thought can remain in *sheer* fragmentation. Thus modern faith may well directly contradict Hegel on the ultimate issue; asserting, after all, a radical incommensurability between the Word of God and the word of man, it may begin with a radical "No!" to the modern world, said in behalf of the Word of God. But modern faith cannot remain with this sheer "No!"; and if it does so remain, it shrinks into a worldless pietism turned upon itself: a faith whose nemesis is a secularism which would appropriate the life of faith itself. Again, modern secularity may seek to withdraw into a finite sphere, i.e., into a humanism simply innocent of divinity. But it cannot return to agnostic innocence; beginning with affirming the life of the human, it ends up affirming the death of the Divine. Even less than life can philosophical thought remain with sheer fragmentation. For to philosophize at all—even within the severely drawn limits of an existential here-and-now or a specific mode of linguistic discourse—is inevitably to transcend these self-drawn limits. Part of the human quality of human life, and part of its suffering, is to seek and partially achieve transcendence of fragmentation even while remaining confined to it. Philosophy can do no less; incapable of achieving the speculative goal, aimed at from Parmenides to Hegel, of becoming divine, it must even in these post-Hegelian days remain human. Too long—since Nietzsche on the one hand and positivism on the other—a philosophers' fashion has been to wallow without purpose and direction in one of the fragments of the disrupted modern world. It is time for sober transcending reflection to seek such unity, purpose, and direction as may be found even in the midst of the present disruption. A philosophy which assumes this burden may well become, not only (as Hegel wrote) the owl of Minerva, but also (as he is reported to have said) the cock which announces the coming of a new day.

CHAPTER TWO

Human Experience and Absolute Thought: The Central Problem of Hegel's Philosophy

The decision to philosophize casts itself purely
into thinking . . . as into an ocean without
beaches; all bright colors, all mainstays have vanished,
all friendly lights otherwise present are extinct.
Only one star still shines, the inner
star of Spirit . . . . It is natural that, thus alone,
Spirit is assailed . . . by dread; it is as yet unknown where
everything leads, where one will end.
Among the things vanished are many which one would
not surrender at any price. But in this solitude they have
not yet been reconstituted. And it is uncertain
whether they will be found again and given back.

Bln. Schr., pp.19–20*

1. *Comprehensive System and Radical Openness*

The philosophy of G. F. W. Hegel claims to comprehend all philosophy. One of his earliest published writings seeks to unite the thought of his immediate predecessors—Fichte and Schelling—in a larger whole.[1] In the mature Hegelian writings, the tendency to philosophic comprehensiveness has itself become comprehensive. Thus whereas Fichtean idealism is opposed, and opposes itself, to dogmatic realism, Hegelian idealism may be regarded as a synthesis of the idealism of Kant and Fichte with the realism of

* Abbreviations are listed on pp.245 ff.

Spinoza—according to Fichte, the archdogmatist of them all. Again, Hegel may understand his thought as the completion of modern philosophy. He by no means simply rejects the thought of the ancients. His only complete account of his entire system ends with a quotation from Aristotle's *Metaphysics*.[2]

But one does not begin to grasp the Hegelian claim to comprehensiveness if one sees it as extending to other *philosophies* only. Such indeed is the limit of pre-Kantian metaphysics. That metaphysics seeks to grasp either a highest reality or else a universal structure of all reality, thus leaving for lesser type of knowledge, respectively, lower realities and contingent particulars; moreover, being theoretical knowledge only, it remains simply distinct from what is not knowledge, e.g., practical life with its varied concerns. The Hegelian philosophy, in contrast, seeks to grasp a Reality which *lives in* the particulars, by means of a thought which *passes through* and *encompasses* them. Moreover, it is not a theory *beside* practical life but rather an activity which moves through both theory and practice, being in a sense neither and in a sense both.

All this is because the Hegelian philosophy has carried to a radical and unsurpassable conclusion the Kantian revolution in philosophy. For Kant, all theoretical knowledge has become phenomenal, and philosophy has become the discipline which recognizes this phenomenal character. In Hegel's view, Kant's philosophy is a half-way house. First, phenomenal knowledge is not divorced from Reality but rather a partial grasp of it. Secondly, such partial grasps are obtained, not in the detached theoretical observation of objects only, but rather throughout the length and breadth of human life and experience. Thirdly, radically to recognize this partiality—i.e., to philosophize—is to transcend it.

There is, then, a sharp contrast between pre-Kantian and Hegel's post-Kantian metaphysics. For the pre-Kantians, metaphysics differs from other forms of knowledge by virtue of its object, and from all practical forms of human life by virtue of its theoretical relation to its object. For Hegel, the difference between philosophy (it is doubtful whether the term "metaphysics" should still be used[3]) and the whole remainder of human life (*both* theoretical and practical) is one of standpoint. All other human activities are truly in contact with Reality, but reach partial truths only because they are limited to finite standpoints. Philosophy—or at any rate the true or final philosophy—rises to an infinite or absolute standpoint, and to encompass and transfigure the partial truths of the finite standpoints into a Truth no longer partial is its sole aim.

Hegel's philosophy is thus a system whose claims exceed all previous philosophical systems not only in degree but also in principle. But the word "system" is wholly misunderstood unless the usual connotation of closedness is brought into immediate clash with a notion of total openness.[4] Hegel's system is by its own admission and insistence a closed circle, but it is also totally open, by virtue of a claim to comprehensiveness which makes it the radical foe of every form of one-sidedness. It is fashionable among contemporary empiricists to describe closed systems as attitudes toward reality, unverifiable and irrefutable because they *are* attitudes, and in conflict with other attitudes because they are one-sided, and yet naively to imagine that such attitudes can survive the exposure of their one-sidedness. Hegel encountered this kind of doctrine (and in a much more profound form) in contemporary romanticism, which gloried in the plurality and indeed conflict of *Weltanschauungen*. But though briefly involved with romanticism he quickly emancipated himself from it. His mature system, far from being a *Weltanschauung*, on the contrary spells the death of all mere *Weltanschauungen*—precisely by exposing their one-sidedness. Nor does it cure their flaw merely by uniting them into one *Weltanschauung*, *all*-comprehensive because it somehow demonstrates its comprehensiveness. The demonstrated unity and necessity of such a system would still be confronted with a world which is not united and necessary but on the contrary shot through with disunion and brute chance.

When thus confronted, to be sure, some Hegelians—F. H. Bradley comes to mind—dissipate conflict and chance into mere

unreality, on the authority of a system and a Reason which, presupposed from the start, do not expose themselves to the world.
Hegel himself is not among these Hegelians. His system, to be
sure, will seek to demonstrate itself as being comprehensive of the
world. But, in his view, if the system, hugging itself, denied the
world in order to save itself, it would not comprehend the world
but rather be in flight from it.* The system can *be* comprehensive
of the world only by means of total self-exposure to it. In his inaugural lecture at the University of Berlin Hegel said: "The decision to philosophize casts itself purely into thinking . . . as into an
ocean without beaches; all bright colors, all mainstays have vanished, all friendly lights otherwise present are extinct. Only one
star still shines, the inner star of Spirit . . . . It is natural that, thus
alone, Spirit is assailed . . . by dread; it is as yet unknown where
everything leads, where one will end. Among the things vanished
are many which one would not surrender at any price. But in this
solitude they have not yet been reconstituted. And it is uncertain
whether they will be found again and given back."[5]

2. *Spirit*

The characteristic of the Hegelian system just described has always been recognized, with varying degrees of clarity, as being at
the core of all that is baffling about the Hegelian philosophy. Initially the student, fastening on the incredibly high claims made

---

* In Hegel's view it is the decisive advantage of his own completion of
modern (Christian) philosophy over the Neoplatonic completion of ancient
(pagan) philosophy to be able to stay with the world. (See ch. 6, sects. 3–6.)
In case it should nevertheless be forced into flight from the modern world
(See ch. 7, sect. 3.), this occurrence would, therefore, have to be viewed as
contrary to its innermost intentions, and as of devastating consequence.
As an example of a philosophy-in-flight, the absolute idealism of F. H.
Bradley, already referred to, begins with the mere external assertion that the
contradictory cannot be real, and hence has as its nemesis a contradiction-free
"Experience" which is itself merely asserted, i.e., which is no one's actual
experience. See ch. 7, sect. 4.

by Hegel in behalf of Reason, will assume that he already knows the meaning of this word, and Hegel will then appear to him as the arch-rationalist of all time. His work will seem an attempt, made in the teeth of all facts, to deduce reality from a priori principles and, indeed, as the final *reductio ad absurdum* of all such attempts ever made, but the serious student cannot long remain with this caricature. For he soon finds that Hegel asserts an Understanding which confronts, analyzes, and keeps separate facts, not merely *beside* a Reason which speculatively unites them but rather—of incomparably greater consequence—*within* a Reason empty without it. And he discovers that Hegel not only *admits* contingency *in addition* to a necessity free of it but rather—again of incomparably greater consequence—insists that contingency *enters into* the necessity which in turn consists of nothing but its conquest. Hegel is so far from denying the reality of contingency as actually to be the only speculative philosopher in history to attempt a demonstration of its inevitability.[6] Other speculative philosophers kept at least the Divine free from chance. But it was Hegel—not Nietzsche—who first asserted that God is dead.[7]

Taking our cue from the passage cited at the end of the previous section, we may seek to cope with the enigma of the Hegelian system by turning to its fundamental affirmation. *Reality is Spirit.* This, however, merely seems to shift the enigma. For Hegelian Spirit, though opposed to Matter, cannot be *simply* opposed to it: a spiritualism which denied Matter would be, in Hegel's view, as false and one-sided as a materialism which asserted the opposite. Hegel's Spirit—which is free internal self-development—*includes* Matter, which is unfree externality, brute givenness, and chance. But how can Matter be *included* in Spirit and yet, real in its own right, be and remain *opposed to* Spirit? It may well seem that Hegel's philosophy must either, as Marx believed, after all be a one-sided spiritualism or else dissolve itself into so radical an openness to the world as to cease to be a philosophical system of any kind.

The turn to Spirit nevertheless takes us a few decisive steps further, in that it gives us an inkling of the realities behind the Hegelian enigma, as well as of the central problems these raise for Hegelian thought.

The enigma concerning Spirit appears because Hegel asserts—for the present this is a bare assertion—that Spirit has the power of what he calls overreaching.[8] Spirit, first, tolerates the other-than-Spirit *beside* itself. Secondly, it can and does overcome this side-by-sideness, by absorbing the other-than-Spirit. Thirdly—this must not be overlooked—it reconstitutes the other in its otherness even while absorbing it. If in absorbing the other Spirit simply destroyed its otherness—if the "union" which is the "result" did not preserve the "process" throughout which there is "nonunion"—the philosophy affirming this result would be a one-sided monism opposed by an equally one-sided pluralism. If it failed to absorb the other-than-Spirit there would be no Spirit but at best only spirits, side-by-side, and immersed in, what is *not* Spirit. The upshot is that only *if* Spirit has overreaching power can there be an all-comprehensive, yet radically open system, rather than either a one-sided system opposed by other one-sided systems, or else so radical an openness to the world as to dissipate all philosophy into it.

But how does one know that Reality *is* overreaching Spirit? Spirit can hardly be a category of *thought* only, brought to life in an attempt to interpret it. Life would testify too loudly against such an interpretation—against a Spirit *inclusive of* Matter in behalf of spirits remaining *immersed in, limited by,* and *opposed to* it. Thought itself would thus become a merely one-sided enterprise, its one-sidedness exposed by human existence as a whole. Thus the Hegelian philosophic strictures against one-sidedness would turn against his own philosophy, and indeed, against all philosophy. For philosophy, having failed to comprehend life, would be disclosed in this failure as being comprehended *by* life. It is no accident that post-Hegelian philosophers such as Marx and Nietzsche who considered the Hegelian system a failure should have proclaimed the end of speculative philosophy.[9]

This destructive consequence can be avoided only if Spirit is *not* a category brought to life by thought *only, if its overreaching power is already manifest in life, for man, prior to and apart from all philosophizing.* But the problem will not settle itself easily even then. If the absence of a manifestation of Spirit in life will make philosophy impossible will not its presence in life make philosophy unnecessary? Hegel defines what philosophical thought *is* in terms of what it *does.* But if the Truth of Spirit is already manifest in life what remains to be done for philosophical thought?

This question may seem susceptible of a ready answer. Even if a Spirit inclusive of Matter is in fact manifest somewhere in life, spirits immersed in and limited by Matter indisputably exist in life as well. May not to philosophy fall the task of *demonstrating* the inclusiveness of Spirit, over against the spirits whose very finitude is a testimony against it? But the problem does not dissipate itself so readily. No simple escape is in sight from the dilemma that, if in life finite spirit testifies successfully against a Spirit manifesting its all-inclusiveness, a philosophic demonstration to the contrary remains a one-sided assertion of thought over against life; whereas, if Spirit in life already demonstrates its all-inclusiveness over the protests of finite spirits philosophy is, once again, left without function. As might have been suspected—and as Hegel himself certainly warns often enough—no solution, or even adequate comprehension, of the central issues of the Hegelian philosophy can be achieved by a thought which, rather than immersing itself in that philosophy, tries to spare itself such labor by means of some abstract a priori argument.

Our turn from Hegel's concept of philosophy to its central assertion has nevertheless served to make two disclosures. First, the togetherness of comprehensive system with radical openness depends on a Reality which is itself one and yet radically open, i.e., so hospitable to plurality of every kind as to eject nothing—no discord, evil, chance, brute fact—into the limbo of unreality. Secondly, Hegelian philosophy cannot be a mere theory *of* life which is merely *over against* life. Its truth of thought must be also—and already—a truth manifest in life. In a companion volume to the present work, we intend to exhibit, in the thought of Hegel's idealistic predecessors from Kant on, an intimate, intricate, and indispensable interconnection between human life and philosophical thought. We shall try to show that a truth of life—such as moral duty, religious feeling or aesthetic creation—supports a truth of philosophical thought, even as in turn it receives support from philosophy. In the present volume, our task is to show that, here as elsewhere, Hegel radicalizes tendencies manifest in his predecessors. These exalt one standpoint of life at the expense of others, and the philosophy bound up with the exalted standpoint is in simple opposition to all other philosophies. In the case of Hegel, the "life" in question is *all* of life, not one of its standpoints onesidedly exalted; and the philosophy he puts forward does not so much oppose other philosophies but encompass and transfigure them.[10] The problem of the relation between comprehensive system and radical openness thus transforms itself into the problem of the relation between all of human life and an all-comprehensive philosophical thought. This is the central problem of the whole Hegelian philosophy.

3. *Religious Life and Philosophic Thought*

Possibly the last statement in the preceding paragraph is an exaggeration. The exaggeration is justified, however, in the context of this exposition, the central theme of which is the relation between religion and philosophy in Hegel's thought. For if for Hegel the truth of Spirit is already disclosed in life the disclosure is found —or found decisively—in *religious* life, reaching its fullness in modern Protestant Christianity. In the Hegelian system, religion appears as one among other forms of spiritual life. This must under no circumstances obscure the fact that *it is also the basis, and the condition of the possibility, of the system in its entirety.* The Hegelian problem concerning the relation between life and philosophical thought therefore specifies itself into a problem concerning the relation between *religious* life and philosophic thought. It is a central Hegelian doctrine that the true religion already is the true "content," lacking merely the true "form" of speculative thought; that philosophy could not reach truth unless its true content preexisted in religion; that philosophic thought therefore requires religion as its basis in life, and that the true philosophy, in giving the true religious content its true form of thought, both transfigures religion and produces itself. The purpose of our entire concern with Hegel is, in the end, but to expound that doctrine.

Toward this purpose, it is essential to face up from the start to the fact that, whereas Hegel's mature thought is unwaveringly committed to the doctrine just stated he nowhere systematically expounds it. More precisely, while the doctrine calls for an exposition composed of two stages Hegel himself gives only the second.

The first stage would be to *describe* how Truth is present in a religious life *philosophically uncomprehended*, i.e., for *religious self-understanding*, thus bringing to light the basis, in life, of the true philosophy. The second stage would be to produce the philosophical comprehension, i.e., a thought which absorbs and transfigures its religious basis and rises above it. Of these two tasks, Hegel explicitly accomplishes only the second in all the three major works in which religion has a central role. His *Phenomenology of Spirit* (1807) "hands the ladder" to all—including religious—standpoints, to the standpoint of absolute knowledge; but in so doing it has itself already assumed the standpoint of absolute knowledge.[11] *The Encyclopedia of Philosophical Sciences* (first ed., 1817; second ed., 1828; third ed., 1830) reenacts in thought all natural and spiritual—including religious—reality; but the thought reenacting it is already philosophical.* The *Lectures on the Philosophy of Religion* (delivered in 1821, 1824, 1827, and 1831 and published posthumously) are, unlike the other two works, entirely confined to religion. But this work too does not first describe religious life in its self-understanding, in order then to show the possibility, necessity and effect of its transfiguration into speculative thought. In this work religious life is already speculatively transfigured.[12]

No doubt this Hegelian practice has done much to foster the widespread view that his philosophy is a barren system of abstract thought externally and arbitrarily *imposed on* life when in fact it *arises from* life in order only then to attempt to rise above it. Admittedly, Hegel's gigantic attempt may fail. His thought may, after all, remain bound to the life above which it seeks to rise, unable to live up to its vast speculative pretensions. Or it may, after all, rise only at the cost of loss of foothold in life, thus becoming in fact the dogmatic rationalism it is so widely thought to be. But if Hegelian thought suffers in fact either failure—including and indeed especially the last-named—this is against its innermost intentions. What so often has been regarded as a thesis dogmatically asserted at the start is at worst a conclusion emerging at the end, despite bitter struggles against it. And whether it does in fact emerge is not a foregone conclusion. It is the question most in need of examination.

In order to carry out this examination we have no choice but to depart boldly, in decisive respects, from Hegel's own exposition. In handing a ladder *to* the standpoint of absolute thought, the *Phenomenology* already adopts that standpoint; we must ask whether, and if so how, this prior adoption can be justified. The *Encyclopedia* reenacts the actual world in absolute thought, claiming that no loss has occurred in the reenactment. We must focus all attention on this last-named claim, bearing in mind that reality re-

---

* This is why it can begin with pure *Logic*, although "logical Idea," "Nature," and "Spirit" are each mediated by the other two, see ch. 4, sect. 4.

mains shot through with contingency even while absolute thought rises above it. The *Philosophy of Religion* grasps, first, a speculative Notion of religion, and then, existing religions as the necessary process of its actualization, a process completed in Christianity. Here we must proceed in two stages. The first is a descriptive account of the philosophically unreenacted religion which is the alleged basis of both the Hegelian philosophy of religion and the Hegelian philosophy as a whole, i.e., Christianity. The second is an account of Hegel's speculative comprehension of that religion, i.e., of how in "encompassing" that religion "in its own being" Hegelian thought can hope to produce itself as the all-comprehensive philosophy.

4. *Schellingian and Hegelian Absolute Idealism*

In a future work already repeatedly referred to, we intend to consider the religious thought of Hegel's idealistic predecessors—Kant, Fichte, Schleiermacher and Schelling. Here we must pause for a brief comparison of Hegel's absolute idealism with that of F. W. J. Schelling, his immediate predecessor, erstwhile close friend and subsequent rival. This comparison will serve three systematic purposes in the present context. It will identify the stage in the development of German idealism at which Hegel's philosophy comes on the scene. It will corroborate, in terms of that stage of development, the major points already made in the preceding pages. And it will show that Hegelian thought calls for a systematic comprehension which concentrates on his mature works. The last-named point has already been made. A comparison of Hegel and Schelling will confirm it. Schelling's philosophy, which shifts from standpoint to standpoint, calls for a genetic exposition. Hegel's dissent from Schelling's various positions, his absolute idealism included, concerns precisely those aspects which make restless shifts on Schelling's part a seemingly endless necessity. And it is against Schelling, more than against any other philos-

opher, that Hegel asserts that philosophy must assume system
and finality. The interpreter may not ignore or minimize this
Hegelian assertion. He must understand it.

Commentators often belittle Hegel's debt to Schelling. One cannot belittle it. It was Schelling who in 1801 first reached the standpoint of absolute idealism. It may briefly be described as the
standpoint of an infinite or divine Thought which has relativized,
and thereby exposed as merely phenomenal, all those hard-and-
fast distinctions which remain hard-and-fast for a merely finite
or human thought. Hegel comes to share the standpoint reached
by Schelling in 1801. Indeed, whereas Schelling quickly abandons
absolute idealism Hegel remains with it to the end.*

He is able to do so, however, only because he is critical of
Schelling's *kind* of absolute idealism from the start. Indeed,
while his criticism deepens as his thought develops his basic objection to Schelling's position actually antedates Schelling's statement of it. As early as in 1800 Hegel writes: "Life is the union of
union *and nonunion.*"[13] For the Schelling of 1801, nonunion is
mere appearance, taken for real by finite standpoints but not by
a thought risen to the absolute standpoint. It is Hegel's life-long

---

* Even as knowledgeable a student as G. E. Müller refers to Schelling as
Hegel's "evil genius" (*Hegel: Denkgeschichte eines Lebendigen* [Bern and
Munich: Francke, 1959], pp.170 ff.). Hegel's relation to Schelling (which
was one of intimate philosophical cooperation in his formative years) came to
an end with the appearance of the *Phenomenology,* whose preface contained
an attack on Schelling's followers and possibly on Schelling himself. The erstwhile friends would have become philosophically estranged in any case, for
Schelling was even then moving away from absolute idealism. (This subject
will be dealt with in "The God Within." A selection from the Schelling-
Hegel correspondence may conveniently be found in Walter Kaufmann,
Hegel [New York: Doubleday, 1965], pp.300 ff.) But it is noteworthy that
in Hegel's late *Lectures on the History of Philosophy* Schelling's absolute
idealism still appears as the penultimate position, i.e., next to Hegel's own.
(This is beyond doubt even though some of the manuscript material on which
the posthumously published version of the *Lectures* is based dates back as far
as 1805–1806.)

For a careful account of the alienation between Schelling and Hegel,
which occurred gradually rather than abruptly, see F. W. J. Schelling, *Briefe
und Dokumente,* I, ed. H. Fuhrmans (Bonn: Bouvier, 1962), pp.451 ff.

objection that reality *itself* includes nonunion and that, unless a thought aspiring to absoluteness can recognize and preserve it as such it dissipates both reality and itself into mere shadows.

A negative outcome of just this kind was to lead Schelling—in his overall endeavors no less concerned to preserve the realities of life from dissipation into abstract thought—to abandon absolute idealism for what finally turned out to be an existentialist position. If Hegel's absolute idealism is sometimes seriously strained but in the end never threatened, it is because of two interrelated—but not identical—convictions, arrived at by the time of philosophical maturity and never subsequently abandoned. One is that Reality is dialectical. The other is that the true philosophical thought is dialectical.

One must hesitate to make general pronouncements of any sort about Hegelian dialectic. There has been and can be no greater misunderstanding of Hegel's thought than the ascription to it of a dialectical method separable from all content, deriving its validity one knows not whence, and indiscriminately applied one cannot say by what justification. The error owes much of its inspiration to the same kind of positivistic thinking which concludes that, inasmuch as Hegel's thought is obviously not inductive it must somehow be deductive; and it acquires a touch of comedy whenever the triumphant discovery is made that the dialectical method has broken down because general characteristics, mistakenly ascribed to it to begin with, do not fit a particular application.[14] The truth is that Hegelian dialectic—the dialectic of both Reality and philosophical thought—is inseparable from content, and that only a thought which actually labors with reality can come upon either. For this reason our present merely introductory observations cannot go far beyond corroborating what has already been said.

First, Reality is dialectical in that the finite at once points to an Infinity which contains it while yet retaining its own reality. For Hegel, as for the Schelling of 1801, "the ideality of the finite is the main principle of philosophy."[15] But to Schelling this means that the finite merely appears real at finite standpoints and is seen as absorbed in infinity at the absolute standpoint. To Hegel it means that the finite is overreached by the Infinite, and that it must be real as well as "merely ideal,"[16] if the overreaching Infinite is not itself to suffer loss of all reality. It is this conviction which forces Hegel to recognize the partial truth of finite thought— e.g., natural science—when Schelling can merely oppose or ignore it.[17] It is this conviction, too, which produces his charge that Schellingian thought reduces the Absolute to a "night in which all cows are black"[18]—a charge made in behalf of a "labor of thought"[19]— which must take place, so to speak, in the daylight of multicolored life. It is this, finally—and for our purpose most importantly—which makes the mature Hegel confront seriously the actual Christianity of historical tradition. For a brief period early in his career—more precisely, before his career had begun in earnest—he had embraced a religious romanticism which exalts ecstatic moments in which the finite human spirit seems simply to become one with the Divine.[20] The mature Hegel is forced to take seriously the Christian claim that the Easter which reconciles the human with the Divine can occur only after a Good Friday which exhausts the whole agony of their discord. Hegel's mature confrontation of orthodox Christianity has often been viewed as a lapse into reaction, and this view has received renewed impetus by the absurd recent fashion to exalt the *Early Theological Writings*—never intended by Hegel for publication—at the expense of the published works of his maturity.* The truth is that the confrontation with orthodox Christianity is but part of Hegel's mature thought as a whole, as this exposition will seek to show, an integral and indeed indispensable part.

So much, for the present, for the dialectic of Reality. What of the dialectic of philosophic thought? Only a finite thought remains

* Nothing is wrong, of course, with studies which treat *Early Theological Writings* as a phase in the genesis of Hegel's thought and nothing more.

confronted by Reality, as its limiting other, and Hegel's absolute idealistic thought aspires as much to infinity as that of Schelling. Philosophical thought claims to be infinite Spirit in its ultimate form, and it does not confront Reality but rather is one with it. The Schelling of 1801, however, merely asserts this identity, in the teeth of all forms of finite existence and thought which deny it, an assertion which, as Hegel puts it, comes "shot from the pistol."[21] Hegel's own thought, in vast contrast, can absorb and transfigure Reality only after first of all confronting it in its otherness. Rather than assert its claim *over against* finite experience and thought—and indeed over against conflicting philosophic thought—it *arises from* all these or, more precisely, *has* so arisen, and it must preserve the "process" of rising in the "result" of having risen. In other words, just as infinite Spirit in life overreaches the finite—finite spirit and all of Matter—so the infinite Spirit which is the true philosophic thought appears on the scene by manifesting overreaching power. But what *makes* it the true philosophic thought is that it overreaches all else.

Ten years after Hegel's death Schelling reemerged from philosophical obscurity to proclaim that philosophic thought cannot, after all, reach the titanic goals to which absolute idealism had aspired; that his own earlier absolute idealism, while grasping essence, had all along been eluded by existence; and he called for what in effect was an existential philosophy.[22] For the twentieth-century student it is all too easy to side with Schelling's existentialism and dispose, without real examination, of Hegel's philosophy as a mere essentialism.[23] But it has already been stated that Schelling and Hegel share an overall determination to guard against dissipating finite realities into an absolute thought reduced to mere shadows.[24] In Schelling's case, this determination is manifest in the restlessness with which he moves from position to position, and in his final arrival at a "positive" philosophy which has reduced his earlier absolute idealism to a necessary but merely "negative" preliminary. But Hegel's absolute idealism is not Schelling's, and in his case the loyalty to finite realities manifests itself in the steadfast persistence in a position believed capable of doing them justice. Whether or not Hegel is right in this belief cannot be decided by Schelling's strictures on *his* earlier absolute idealism but only by the study of Hegel's own. And such a study must take seriously his steadfast persistence in his position. It must comprehend and appraise his philosophy as it was intended to be comprehended—as a systematic, all-comprehensive whole.

CHAPTER THREE

The "Ladder" to the Standpoint of Absolute Knowledge: On the *Phenomenology of Spirit*

> That natural consciousness immediately entrusts
> itself to science is an attempt—attracted by it
> knows not what—to walk for a change on its head; and
> to compel it to adopt this unaccustomed
> posture and to move in it is to expect it to do itself
> a violence which is as unprepared as it
> must seem unnecessary.
>
> *Phän.*, p.25 (*Phen.*, p.86)*

> Man is what he does.
>
> *Enz.*, sect. 140

> I raise myself in thought to the Absolute . . . thus
> being infinite consciousness; yet at the same
> time I am finite consciousness . . . . Both aspects
> seek each other and flee each other . . . . I am
> the struggle between them.
>
> *Werke*, XI, p.64 (*Phil. Rel.*, I, p.65)

1. *Introduction*

The times, Hegel asserts in the preface to the *Phenomenology of Spirit*, are ripe for the "elevation of philosophy to the level of science."[1] Six years earlier Fichte had used the identical expression; more importantly, Schelling had in that year actually tried to produce "science."[2] But in Hegel's view Schelling had merely stated, and stated inadequately, the "scientific" program. In order to *be* science, philosophy must be the systematic grasp of absolute

---

* Abbreviations are listed on pp.245 ff.

Reality somehow inclusive—not exclusive or destructive—of all finite realities. And in order to achieve such a grasp, it must have risen to a standpoint of absolute knowledge somehow inclusive—not exclusive or destructive—of all standpoints falling short of absoluteness. Schelling's programmatic fragments had failed on both scores. As for his first failure, this is to be remedied in the Hegelian system, of which the *Encyclopedia of Philosophic Sciences* is the sole complete statement.[3] As for the second, this is remedied in the *Phenomenology*—an introduction to "science" because it shows all finite standpoints to be encompassed by the absolute standpoint. Hegel's work hands "the individual"—and it is not yet clear but does not yet matter who this individual is[4]—the "ladder" to the standpoint of "science," by "showing him that standpoint as it is in him."[5] Schelling's *My System* of 1801, in contrast, had merely *asserted* its standpoint *against* one and all standpoints, thus coming, as it were, "shot from the pistol." But such a bare and barren assertion, were philosophy forced to remain with it, would suffice to invalidate its claim to absoluteness, and indeed destroy all hope for its elevation to the level of science.

Hegelian "science" is marked by an unprecedented presumptuousness. The *Encyclopedia* is no mere conceptual philosophical system inclusive of other conceptual philosophical systems and related to Reality as its external object. Reality itself is included in the system, and what grasps and includes it are no ordinary concepts. The same presumptuousness is in evidence in the *Phenomenology*, and indeed, is there unmistakable even for the most careless of readers. For until one reaches the last ten pages of the more than 500-page work, one searches in vain for direct confrontations of the Hegelian with alternative philosophies.[*] The

---

[*] Not counting the Preface. (In Hegel's view, introductions to philosophical works can make no philosophical assertions in their own right since, in order to be philosophical, these assertions must be established—a task belonging to the work itself. Introductions are summary anticipations of the whole.) One must distinguish philosophies taken as such from philosophies insofar as they are taken as reflections and articulations of ways of nonphilosophic life. Confrontations with philosophies taken in this latter sense occur throughout the *Phenomenology*.

individuals who are handed the ladder to the Hegelian philosophic standpoint include the percipient of sensuous objects, the slave in fear of his master, the scientist engaged in the rational conquest of nature, the French revolutionary, and religious believers of various kinds. They do not include philosophers. But where else could one find a philosophic thought which in all seriousness labored to encompass and supersede, not merely alternative types of philosophic thought but also nonphilosophic human life? For that Hegel *is* serious in this labor is beyond all doubt. Marx's attempt to turn the Hegelian philosophy from its head to its feet may or may not be a valid piece of philosophic criticism. But it is Hegel—not Marx—who first recognizes the prima facie absurdity of his own demand that "natural consciousness . . . walk for a change on its head."[6]

But if Hegelian "science" is marked by an unprecedented philosophical presumptuousness it is also marked by an equally unprecedented philosophical humility, and only if both are seen together is there any hope of doing justice to either. Philosophical science is possible only when the times are ripe for it. The events which have made them ripe include not only events in the history of philosophy, such as Kant's *Critique of Pure Reason*, Fichte's *Science of Knowledge* of 1794, and Schelling's *My System* of 1801. They also include—and for our purpose this is far more important—such events in the history of nonphilosophic life as the Age of Enlightenment, the French revolution and, perhaps above all, the Protestant Reformation.[7] Hegel climbs to the pinnacle of philosophic pride with his claim that the complete philosophic thought does not leave behind but somehow includes and absorbs the nonphilosophic thought and life above which it rises; he plumbs the depths of philosophic humility with his admission, built into every aspect of his thought, that philosophic thought could not reach its climactic goal—indeed, it will turn out, *any* goal—were it not for indispensable aid furnished by nonphilosophic life. What speculative philosopher before Hegel considered it "absurd to fancy that a philosophy can transcend its contemporary world?"[8]

And yet as one absorbs oneself in the *Phenomenology* (to which the remainder of this chapter is exclusively devoted) the Hegelian humility may well seem to show itself a mere mock humility, with all traces of genuineness devoured by the Hegelian presumptuousness. Indeed, such may seem to be the case *necessarily*, if the work is to reach its goals. But is not then Hegelian "science" as nakedly self-assertive over against standpoints of nonphilosophic life as its Schellingian counterpart, and the phenomenological introduction *to* "science," in the end so much wasted labor?

It is true that the *Phenomenology* will not judge consciousness in the light of presupposed standards, a procedure which would be based on the dogmatic assertion that it *is* "science" when in fact it is merely the road to it. Instead, it will watch "consciousness examine itself," a process in which each finite standpoint, which is fragmentary because it is finite, will point to one higher because it is less fragmentary, until finally, at the standpoint of absolute knowledge, all fragmentariness is transcended. At the same time, the fact, or at any rate the full meaning, of this self-examination is known only to the watching philosopher. "The Absolute . . . [even if] present with us from the start" (i.e., with the most primitive human consciousness) is known *as* Absolute and present only to the true philosophy. As for all other forms of human consciousness, the self-examination in which they are engaged "goes on, as it were, behind their backs." But what is a philosophic humility before nonphilosophic human life which claims so vast a superiority over it?[9]

The *Phenomenology* would cease to be a road to "science" if it did not insist on this vast superiority. To do otherwise would be to confess that nonphilosophic life, rather than making the times ripe for goals yet to be reached by science, has already reached such goals as are humanly attainable, and that science, left without function, vanishes into nothingness. The phenomenological road to science can be a road only if it is *already* scientific. Phenomenological thought must already *be* at the absolute standpoint if it

is to "hand the individual the ladder" to it. And while this individual has "the right to demand" this ladder, any suggestion
that "unscientific consciousness be instructed in science" must be
rejected.[10]

And yet Hegel's phenomenological humility can be no mere
mock humility. There can be no total and unbridgeable dualism
between a self-examination occurring in nonphilosophic life, and
a philosophic thought in exclusive possession of all criteria for recognition of both the fact and the meaning of this self-examination.
If there were such a dualism, how could *any* individual—in Hegel's
own time any more than in any other—ascend the ladder to the
absolute standpoint, handed him by a philosopher who himself is
already—quite inexplicably—at that standpoint? He would have
no choice but to assert his own standpoint *against* that of a thought
making a pretense to absoluteness, and this would be enough to
shatter the pretense.

The entire phenomenological introduction to "science," then,
must be a mere elaborate failure unless the dualism between the
absolute thought which does the observing and the nonphilosophic
life whose self-examination is observed is somehow and somewhere bridged even while it is preserved. Human life cannot have
done the work yet to be done by philosophic thought. Yet what
life can do and *has done* is indispensable for what is yet *to be* done,
not by life but by philosophic thought, and the philosopher who
has risen to the absolute standpoint from the start must come to
recognize at the end that, had it not been for what life has done,
he could not himself have risen to that standpoint. Only thus
can one period in nonphilosophic history be riper for science than
any other. Hence everything in the end depends on this question:
*Can there be a form of nonphilosophic human life which makes
the rise to the scientific standpoint on the one hand possible and
on the other still necessary, and if so, what justifies Hegel's claim
that in the nineteenth century that form of life has become actual?*

To cope with this question is our sole purpose with the *Phenom-*

enology. We could not in any case hope here to do justice to its incredibly rich, complex, and difficult content. (While firmly on the road to science, Hegel cannot resist the temptation to dwell at length on standpoints which are stations on the road, and it has plausibly been argued that the work, though purportedly a mere introduction to science, already contains in one of several possible forms virtually the whole content of science.) Further, our special purpose would not be served if, rather than ask the stated question of the *Phenomenology*, we summarized its content with no special question in mind.[11] * Our overall objective is to understand the relation between religion and philosophy in Hegel's thought. But it will be seen that in that relation the question we presently ask of the *Phenomenology* comes to a head.

To make progress with our question we must depart from the *Phenomenology*'s own progression. Hegel on his phenomenological road to science views all standpoints as necessarily pointing beyond themselves to absolute knowledge, and only as he reaches absolute knowledge does he justify the standpoint from which he has done his viewing. The confrontation which occurs in the *Phenomenology* only at the end must be enacted by us at every turn.

This enactment, however, poses a methodological difficulty. To adopt Hegel's viewing standpoint would be, not to lead up to the absolute standpoint but rather to be at it from the start. To remain with any of Hegel's viewed standpoints would be to take them as final, i.e., to take them as they take themselves. We must, as it were, hover *between* the viewing and the viewed standpoints, and we can do so only by borrowing—at least for a while—one Hegelian doctrine: "The self is what it does,"[12]—a self-constituting process. The viewed standpoints do not know this truth, not at any rate in its full Hegelian significance, for if they did they would not take themselves as final and unalterable. The viewing standpoint, in contrast, knows this truth in its final form and, indeed, *produces* it.

* See the appendix to this chapter, pp.73 ff.

We on our part must tentatively assume it and grope from its minimal toward its maximal significance.*

But we may borrow this assumption *as* assumption only for a while. For as we ask our question of the *Phenomenology* the gap between viewing and viewed standpoints must gradually narrow; as it is closed, our assumption must cease to be an assumption, and the question we ask of the *Phenomenology* must find its answer.

2. *Of Individual Selfhood and Its Dialectic*

The modern world, Hegel thinks, is free in idea if not (or not yet) in actual fact.[13] Modern science has freed itself from medieval fetters. Modern Christian faith has moved from external, Catholic authorities into an inward Protestant heart. Modern states have smashed slavery and feudalism and recognized the rights and duties of men as men, i.e., belonging to them simply because they are human. To the modern consciousness, therefore, a true state is a free state, which recognizes the human rights of all its citizens, and is in turn recognized by them as their state, to which they owe duties of citizenship. And a true religion is a free religion—one whose God recognizes the humanity of his human worshipers, and is worshiped by them as recognizing it.**

No true state and no true religion are ever *simply* externally imposed. Thus in ancient China, only one was free. The Emperor had all the rights and no duties, and his subjects, all duties and no rights. Yet these subjects *recognized* the rights of the Emperor

---

* We single out this assumption (i) because it makes possible countless simplifications and, for our purposes, inevitable shortcuts; (ii) because it makes possible a clear grasp of central notions which usually remain both obscure and arbitrarily asserted rather than philosophically grasped—notably that of Spirit; (iii) above all, because it will lead most directly to our central theme: the relation between rational self-activity and religious receptivity to the Divine, and the relation of philosophical self-activity to both.

** "Freedom" is one of many terms whose meaning can emerge only in the context of discourse and must therefore here remain undefined. See especially ch. 6, sects. 2(c) and 5.

and their own duties toward him, and their humanity *was* this recognizing. The Emperor, on his part, *was* his being-recognized, and this was his freedom. Even the most primitive but genuine human society in history differs in principle from a heap of ants in nature. Still, much has had to happen between the beginnings of history which recognized the mere arbitrary freedom of one man, and the modern age, which recognizes—to repeat, in idea, however inadequately and fragmentarily in external fact—that men are free simply because they are human.[14]

What is this modern freedom and how has it arisen? What is modern, one may reply, is merely a state of consciousness which at length recognizes what exists whether or not it is recognized: that man is born free, having natural rights and duties as part of a given substance. The true natural science, religion, and political constitution, it may be held, are timelessly true, merely dropping from heaven, as it were, when their respective truths are recognized. All this not only *may* be said, but from some limited perspectives—philosophical or nonphilosophical—it *must* be said. For whereas the self makes and has made itself, it "forgets" that it has done so, mistaking its selfhood for a substance, ready-made by some force other than itself—and therefore fixed and unalterable. A true philosophic inquiry into the nature of modern freedom, however, is inseparable from an inquiry into its genesis, and it is not thorough unless it inquires into the *being* of the modern self even as it inquires into its self-knowledge. Since—for the present *ex hypothesi*—the self is a self-constituting process the self's *recognition* of its freedom and its *production* of that freedom are mutually inseparable.*

---

* The gravest error in the interpretation of the presently considered section of the *Phenomenology* is to take its dialectic as encompassing the self's self-consciousness only, to the exclusion of its being—a view wholly oblivious to the existential character of this most existential of all Hegelian texts. To dispose of this error as clearly as possible from the start has been one of our purposes in our initial concentration on the doctrine of self-making.

Such an inquiry must remain incomplete unless it pursues the double process of self-making and self-knowing back to its pristine origins. Were it to stop with a self already made it could not but take this self for a ready-made substance, thus showing the inadequacy of the perspective from which it has done its taking. The inquiry must go back to a point at which there is as yet no made self but only a pure power of self-making.

It cannot, however, go beyond this point, to a realm lacking this power, i.e., to the realm of nonhistorical, natural life. Animals are parts of a larger natural whole in their activities of feeding, reproducing, and protecting their young. They may seem to achieve a higher whole when they live, as do bees and ants, in organized "societies." These latter, however, are quasi-societies only because animals in principle lack the power of self-making. This is at most foreshadowed in animal desire—an urge to appropriate the desired which, when acted out, becomes a self-asserting against it. Animal desire, however, is merely for this or that *part* of nature, and the acting out of it, a mere *expression* of nature. Thus the animal is part of the natural whole but never comes to know itself as such a part, nor to transcend *being* a mere part which such knowledge would entail.

To be a genuine power of *self*-asserting, human desire must be not for this or that part of nature but rather for nature *as a whole*—a desire which, when acted out, does not express the natural whole but rather *tears itself loose from* it. The human power of self-making can be no less if an actual self is ever to have made its appearance. Also, it can be no more. A self already *actually* independent from nature would be a self already self-made.[15]

The desire now uncovered* must have the possibility of satis-

---

* By philosophic thought (here only preliminarily), not by the self in life. A desire as yet unsatisfied would not yet know its true object, and a satisfied desire takes its selfhood as ready-made, not as the result of a self-making process—a limitation which the self comes close to transcending only when it has become "Spirit certain-of-itself," see sect. 5 of this chapter.

faction. Without this possibility, the desiring human, though potentially a self, would even now be an actual animal, filled with
the ache of an unsatisfiable yearning and unconscious, moreover,
of its true object. (For to know this latter as selfhood he would
already have to possess selfhood.) Yet the uncovered desire can
find no *direct* satisfaction. A self already made might negate nature
in the realm of thought, putting up with its physical need of nature
and yet asserting its independence *as self* from this need. But a
self as yet unmade is not one which is self and has desires; it *is*
desire and as yet nothing else. To satisfy this desire *directly* would
require the physical negation of nature as a whole, and of this,
man is no more capable than the animal.

The human power of self-making would be foredoomed to eternal frustration were it not for the possibility of *indirect* satisfaction.
The desire can be satisfied, not by the negation of nature as a
whole, but by the negation of another desire to negate nature as a
whole, i.e., another man. Thus even in its pristine origins the human self is dependent for selfhood on other selves. It is *one*
dependence which it will never transcend.*

Directly, then, this negating is of another desire to negate nature. Indirectly, however, it is of nature *itself*, for each seeks to
take the life of the other while risking his own. Moreover, the
negating of nature is not itself an expression of nature, which it
would be if it were for purposes of life such as food and sex. This
taking and risking of life is a killing for the sake of killing, a risk
for risk's sake, hence a negating—albeit indirectly—of nature *as a
whole*. Taken in both its direct and its indirect aspects, it is a prestige battle, fought by two selves whose selfhood is *in* the battle
and its prestige and as yet nowhere else. The two selves *are*
selves—torn loose from nature—only if each *actually* risks his life
for the sake of prestige. They *know* themselves as selves and *have*
the prestige, only if each is *recognized* by the other as in fact risk-

---

* It ceases to be *mere* dependence, however, by virtue of the reality of
Spirit, see especially sects. 3 and 5 of this chapter.

ing his life for the sake of prestige. So savage, according to Hegel, are the primitive origins of human selfhood.[16] *

But the moments of this self's selfhood are short-lived. In the actual combat there is mutual recognition and through it self-recognition. Both vanish when the combat is ended. The slain can neither recognize nor be recognized. And the surviving victor is a *mere* survivor once the flush of the moment of victory has passed. If incapable of rising above so primitive a selfhood, the self would forever alternate, like some barbaric prehistoric Faust, between actual battles in which selfhood is achieved and times between battles in which selfhood, having been lost without result, would be dissolved into a dark longing for renewed battle.**

It can pass beyond this condition because not all those desiring to negate nature risk life to satisfy their desires. The killer of the foe gives way to the master of a slave; the self which *is* a risking of life not surviving the act of risk, to a self which *has* risked life and *is* this having-risked. For the "result" of the "process" survives in the recognition received from the slave.

The master's selfhood is the actual process of being recognized. As such it extends over the slave, whose being is his activity of recognizing of the master. It extends, as well, over nature; for,

---

* Kojève has rightly laid stress on the prestige-battle, although his over-emphasis has provoked the surely unjustified charge of turning Hegel into a fascist from left-wing quarters. It must be stressed that Hegel's "fascist" self is the most primitive self, and even then it is torn out of its social context. (See sect. 3 of this chapter.) We are in no doubt that Hegel would have viewed twentieth-century fascism as a form of nihilistic decadence—one vast prestige-battle devoid of all higher purpose not because no such purposes exist but because the prestige lies in the accomplishment of their destruction. Hegel might have found traces of such nihilistic decadence in the Western democracies as well. The hero of the great motion picture, *Rebel Without a Cause*, having discovered that he likes the antagonist with whom he is about to engage in a mortal prestige-battle, nevertheless goes on with the battle, on the grounds that "you've got to do something."

** Goethe's Faust exclaims: "From desire I rush to satisfaction and in satisfaction I yearn after desire." It may be said in passing that the Faust motif, while present in the *Phenomenology*, is far from being its central motif, as has been maintained by some Goethe idolizers.

belabored by the slave at the master's behest, nature is reduced to an object of his enjoyment.

Yet the slave, not the master, first attains *free* selfhood. The master's self is his dominating of the slave and his enjoyment of nature. He needs a slave to dominate and a nature to enjoy. This double dependence—on the human other and on nature—is in the end dependence on nature. For this human other is the master's slave only so long as he is nature's slave—so long as he lives in fear of losing his life. It is dependence on nature which is the self's unfreedom.

The process of slavery results in emancipation from this dependence. The master does a double chaining—of the laboring slave to nature and of the nature belabored to the slave. The slave is doubly chained—by the master to the belaboring of nature and to the master by nature, i.e., by his own fear of death. This latter is the ultimate chain, and he is bound by it because he has shrunk from the risks of selfhood into mere riskless life. Yet a human desire which has shrunk from selfhood into life is not an animal desire confined to life; a human slave is not a domesticated animal. And the selfhood from which the slave has shrunk in one form is in another form forced upon him. As the condition of slavery is pushed to extremity the animal fear, which has made the slave a slave, extends its range, deepens in agony, and thus changes in quality. The fear of this and that which the animal *has* turns into a fear which the human slave *is*, and it is a fear, no longer of this and that, but for his very being. Thus the being in which the slave has sought refuge from the risk of selfhood dissipates itself into nothingness, i.e., into the total and perpetual fear of death. He has "nothing to lose but his chains."*

He loses these chains through his labor. Initially, he *does* labor, chained to the nature belabored and the commanding master by the clinging to life which he *is*, but as the fear of death dissipates

---

* We refer, of course, to the famous phrase in Marx's *Communist Manifesto.*

his clinging to life the commanding master and the belabored nature both sink into inessentiality. He comes to *be* a labor no longer bound to another, i.e., a pure self-activity. He is free whether enthroned or enslaved in the external world—free because he *thinks* himself free, and capable of thinking himself free because he has *made* himself free. The Stoic, like all men, depends on nature, for he must eat, drink and die. But he does not fear death and is indifferent to eating and drinking. His selfhood is emancipated from nature. It is a *creatio* out of a nature become *nihil*. The Stoic is a free, self-made self.[17] *

Have we come close to the freedom which makes the times ripe for Hegelian "science," and to the thinking which is "science" it-

---

* In view of the influence of this famous section on Marx, it should particularly be stressed that it must be no more torn out of context than the section devoted to the prestige battle. Marx is correct in taking the *Phenomenology* as viewing the "self-creation of man as a process . . . [and hence] objective man . . . as the result of his own labor." (*Early Writings*, trans. T. B. Bottomore, [New York: McGraw-Hill, 1964], p.202.) But this can be made into the final significance only by means of a sharp left-wing turn, away from Hegel himself. (See ch. 4, sect. 3.) For Hegel himself, the meaning of "labor" shifts from context to context including, in addition to labor physically imposed by another and morally self-imposed labor, such forms of "labor" as religious cult and philosophical thought. Although he asserts that all nations have had to pass through a slavish discipline breaking the "self-centered will" in order to become free (*Enz.*, sect. 435.), he does not hold that individuals— or classes—within nations already free must, or indeed *can*, pass through that stage. In the light of twentieth-century realities one is doubtless unable to share Hegel's confidence that "if we assumed a [European] ruler who, following arbitrary whim, got the idea to make half his subjects slaves, we should know at once that this cannot be done, even with a maximum of force. Everyone knows that he cannot be a slave, that this is contrary to his essential being." (*Einl. Gesch. Phil.*, p.233.) Still—though far from bolstering optimism, this only deepens pessimism—it ought to be pointed out that Hitler could reduce non-Germans to slavery only after prior resort to an elaborate racial myth, the essential content of which was that non-Germans, and more especially non-Aryans, are not human. And he could enslave Germans themselves only after prior resort to the myth, so brilliantly expounded in George Orwell's *1984*, that "slavery is freedom." A more hopeful illustration of Hegel's belief in the power of the modern idea of freedom—and one wholly in line with his own thinking—is the fact that contemporary North America seems unable to resist the demand that a century-old promise to the American Negro be redeemed.

self?* We have come nowhere near either. Not one of the standpoints considered has taken itself as the self-making process, which
it is seen to be at the absolute standpoint. And the abyss between
these two standpoints is by no means bridged when we come to
Stoicism. The Stoic takes his thinking to be a fixed essence, and his
freedom from nature and from the human other as absolute. The
philosopher recognizes both as being the result of a self-liberating
process, and the liberation as one-sided and inadequate. The
Stoic's free thought is achieved, not by conquest of the natural
and human worlds, but rather by means of a flight from both. And
it has its nemesis, first, in a Skeptical thought which negates sensuous reality and yet cannot but recognize it, and finally, in a religious life which, while "unhappy" in a self-imposed servitude to a
distant God, is yet higher than a freedom which, confined to *mere*
thought, is incapable of either happiness or unhappiness. It is
higher because it is involved with sensuous reality—nature without and passions within. A thought which is *mere* thought, in
contrast, has merely fled from both.

3. *In Search of the Category of Spirit*

The account thus far given, even if vastly expanded either by
Hegel or on Hegel's behalf, would be in principle inadequate for
Hegel's phenomenological purposes: its *terms* are inadequate.**
*No dialectic of individual self-making could begin to touch either
the most primitive (but genuine) society or the most primitive (but*

* In pursuit of our question stated in sect. 1 we here break off even though
the *Phenomenology* itself sees a necessary development from Stoicism to
Skepticism and then to the Unhappy Consciousness of an individualistic,
medieval, other-worldly piety. We are in any case as yet unable to see a
necessary development which is visible only to a thought already at the absolute standpoint. (See sect. 5 and especially sect. 6, pp.69 ff.) It will be recalled
that we presently hover between the examining and the examined standpoints.

** This section is our first approach to "Spirit," the fourth major division of
the *Phenomenology*. (For our second approach, see sect. 5.) Hegel himself
is *necessarily led to* a more-than-finite Spirit. We on our part cannot yet so
take it, and hence can comprehend finite spirit only.

genuine) history, and, not touching either, it does not, and is not meant to do, full justice to the individual either. The category thus far used, were it meant to be final, would leave society indifferent or hostile to human selfhood, and it would either destroy all history or—which is the same thing—fragment it into as many histories as there are self-making selves. It is no wonder, then, that we have come nowhere near those nineteenth-century social and historical realities which, according to Hegel, have made the times ripe for "science."

In no society—primitive but genuine—do individuals achieve selfhood by the solitary risk of life, exercise of lordship, or slavish labor. Even the primitive family extends positive recognition to its members. As for the activities of self-making described, these occur in *social contexts*, which furnish *standards* of recognition. In such a context, the victor in a prestige battle becomes a permanent member of the society whose standards of membership he has satisfied; as for masters and slaves, these belong, respectively, to peer-groups of masters and classes of slaves. To deny the relevance of social standards for the self's selfhood would be to affirm the absurd doctrine that conflict and withdrawal can and do, but love and a sense of common purpose cannot and do not, enter into the self-making process, and also that, as regards the possibilities of human selfhood, history cannot and does not advance. The realities described in the preceding section, then, must be placed into a richer and truer context, and they can be taken as *being* realities in their own right only in times of social disintegration and chaos.[18]

How must such a placing be done? Social standards must be viewed as capable of *entering into* the self's selfhood, i.e., as capable of *being appropriated by* the process of individual self-making. If incapable of being so viewed, they would necessarily be external to the self-making process; the social whole sustained by them would be indistinguishable from the natural whole; and the self about to achieve or augment its selfhood would be forced to tear itself loose from both. But while Hegel admits that there are "bad" states and external history he insists that there are "true" states also, and that history can and does carry the possibilities of human selfhood beyond those primitive ones which exist in ages as yet barely historical. The terms needed for the philosophic grasp of the nature and genesis of social standards, then, cannot be wholly other than those used in the preceding section.

But neither can they be wholly the same. One cannot take social standards and the social wholes sustained by them as the product of mere sums of individual selves, initially owned wholly privately and only subsequently shared as if by an agreement or contract. For precisely this sharing must thus remain unintelligible. Social standards cannot function for individual selves unless they can enter into and be appropriated by them, but they cannot be either social or standards at all unless they have an objective validity beyond and apart from the appropriating process—if any subsequent sharing is destroyed by the private whim in their origin. In searching for adequate terms, then, we are faced with the problem that genuine social standards cannot be simply external to individual selves, nor be simply their individual or collective product.

This search produces the concept of a social whole somehow more than the individual selves which compose it, while yet acknowledging their selfhood, of a "substance"* which, while alive only in the acts of appropriating selves, yet *is* a substance because it is somehow already there prior to and apart from the acts of appropriating selves, with a law and structure of its own. The

---

* This term here applies to every relatively complete objective reality whether, like nature, it is what it is without reference to selfhood or, like the social whole presently considered, it requires reference to selfhood. Ultimately, only absolute—i.e., Spinozistic—Substance *is* Substance. And to understand it, like Spinoza, *as* Substance, and yet, unlike Spinoza, as neither divorced from nor destructive of selfhood—*all* forms of selfhood—is the ultimate goal of Hegel's philosophy. Hence he writes: "In my view, which can justify itself only in the presentation of the system itself, everything depends on this, that the True be comprehended and expressed not as Substance [only] but just as much as Subject." (*Phän.*, p.19 [*Phen.*, p.80].) See further the remainder of this chapter and also, especially, ch. 6, sect. 2(c).

social whole or substance or—as Hegel is not averse to putting it—
"organism"* is, however, sharply distinct from the natural whole.
This latter is less-than-self, a whole of mere parts which forces the
individual self to tear itself loose from it. The former must be
more than the individual self's self-activity and yet can be more
only if it allows selfhood full scope, i.e., if it includes or leaves
room for it.** This relation, therefore, cannot be one of whole and
mere parts. It is *between* what "in itself" already is, and acts of appropriating "for self" which come to be and are yet to be, and
whose scope is no less than *the whole* of what "in itself" already is.
The concept arrived at takes hold of an inner bond between "substance" and "self," in which each points to the other and both are
done justice. This is our *first glimpse of the most decisive of all
Hegelian concepts—that of "Spirit."* Hegel writes: "Qua Substance,
Spirit is unbending righteous self-sameness, self-identity; but qua
for itself, self-existent and self-determined, its continuity is resolved into discrete elements, it is the self-sacrificing soul of goodness, the benevolent essential nature in which each fulfils his own
special work, rends the continuum of the universal Substance and
takes his own share of it."[19]

But the passage just quoted, obscure in any case, asserts far
more than is warranted by the account thus far given. According
to it, Spirit can be and is complete or infinite, and this assertion is
thus far unjustified and indeed unintelligible. For it must thus far
on the contrary seem that Spirit can *be* a bond between substance
and self, if at all, only if it is eternally *fragmentary*.

* We try to avoid this biological term (although Hegel himself uses it
rather freely) because it is dangerously misleading, particularly since the
rise of vitalistic philosophies.
** The paragraphs immediately following explain this cautious formulation.
In Chapter 4 we will see that Hegelian "science" recognizes contingency even
as it rises above it, and it may here be mentioned that whereas Hegel's *Philosophy of Right* seeks to grasp the state as a larger whole it sharply opposes
doctrines which make the state an "organism" which does, may, and indeed
must dissipate the rights of the individual selves who are its members. See
further ch. 6, appendix 4.

True, the foregoing account asserts forms of selfhood which merely appropriate what is "already there," i.e., social wholes which are "ethical worlds" because they contain "ethical life already found . . . which yet at the same time is the deed and work of the subject finding it." [20] But there can be no warrant for confining the self to the appropriating of the already found. This would freeze into eternal permanence what we have every reason to take for a finite social substance, and to take it, moreover, as having dropped arbitrarily from heaven. Correspondingly, it would be to view acts of self-making asserted *against* "ethical life already found"—and such acts are surely possible and actual— as asserting themselves against the preexisting social whole precisely as against the natural whole, tearing themselves loose absolutely from both. In short, the nemesis of a *complete* spiritual unity of substance and self would be a complete war between these elements, destructive of the spirituality of both. *The spiritual bond between them must be a tension as well as a union.* The finite social substance *contains* the ethical life which the self can and does appropriate, but to leave room for acts of self-asserting *against* such life is part of its inner being, and this is why when such acts actually occur they *transform* its actuality. These acts on their part may assert themselves as absolute protests; in truth, however, they are only *relative* protests, which do not occur in a vacuum but rather in the context of the preexisting conditions against which they are asserted. The spiritual bond between substance and self, then, is a *fragmentary* reality, finite but with an infinite nisus, and its fragmentary reality is *history*. Here for the first time we are to consider that "science," if possible at all, might conceivably be rendered possible by the realities of *human history*.*

---

* That the assertions made in this paragraph have only preliminary truth will emerge in the remainder of the present chapter. That their preliminary truth is preserved in the higher Truth will be seen in ch. 4 and, in the most specific form, in ch. 5, sect. 9 and ch. 6, sects. 4–6.

But we cannot yet consider this possibility seriously. A history as thus far understood might produce nineteenth-century European spirit. It could not produce a spirit making the time ripe for "science." Itself finite, it could only produce—in times of harmony between substance and self as well as in times of discord—spiritual standpoints themselves confined to finitude, and philosophy, if possible at all, would share this finitude. Thus the reflective grasp of the nature and genesis of nineteenth-century European spirit would itself share the standpoint of that spirit; and the one as much as the other would be doomed to be superseded by subsequent spiritual developments. If spirit in life is confined to finitude, then no period in history is any riper than any other for the absolute standpoint of Hegelian thought, and whenever this latter comes on the scene, it comes shot from the pistol.[21]

But the definition of Spirit quoted earlier in this section already shows that the *Phenomenology* claims to grasp an *infinite* or *complete* Spirit manifest in historical life. Indeed—concerned as it is not to give science but rather what may be described as the shortest road to the standpoint of science[22]—it deals with infinite or complete Spirit *only*. The presence of such Spirit might have been glimpsed even in isolated selfhood—when it is driven beyond abstract but self-sufficient Stoic thought to the unhappy insufficiency of a search for God. And it becomes unmistakable in the section of Hegel's work explicitly devoted to Spirit. Thus the ethical world which precedes the conflict between substance and self is not seen as a simply-finite, purely-human reality but rather as one whose visible worldly actuality has an invisible trans-worldly counterpart and nemesis. The "belief in the fearful and unknown darkness" of Fate and the Eumenides of the spirit of the dead[23] disclose the finitude, respectively, of the ancient Greek social whole and the individual self living in it. An infinite, transcendent dimension remains as Roman and medieval "cultural" self-activity destroys the idyllic harmony of the Greek ethical world; it remains even though here society undertakes the task of subduing "harsh actuality" by its own labors. For the counterpart of this worldly "realm of culture" here created remains a "world of faith," a divine "Essence" which transcends, and is unaffected by, all cultural labor. And while this dichotomy ends when the medieval heaven descends to a modern earth this descent is by no means tantamount to a reduction of infinite Spirit to finitude.*

But even if the spiritual realities described by Hegel—and we have thus far barely listed some of them, and done nothing to show how Hegel arrives at them—are rightly described, a hurdle appears which at this point cannot be passed. The *Phenomenology* claims to see *one* Spirit whose "ethically" experienced or "culturally" produced worldly presence is complemented by a feared, or trusted, transworldly Divinity. For the standpoints seen, however, there are *two* realities, of which one is presently experienced or produced *by* finite spirit and the other, the transcendent divine object *of* finite spirit. Hegel himself insists that the Divine is here grasped as "absolute Essence" from the "standpoint of consciousness," i.e., the standpoint of a spirit which, limited by its object, remains finite.[24] Must the *Phenomenology*, then *bring* the category of complete or infinite Spirit to the spiritual realities it sees? If so, how can these realities make the time ripe for science—cr science fail to come shot from the pistol? No way is yet visible by which the gap between the standpoints of life phenomenologically observed and the standpoint of thought, which does the observing, might possibly be bridged.

---

* Even the most cursory comparison between Hegel's *Philosophy of History* and the section of the *Phenomenology* presently under discussion shows that, by Hegel's own standards, the account in the *Phenomenology* of the ancient, medieval, and modern worlds would indeed be most arbitrary were it intended to be an account of the self-movement of Spirit in history. It is, however, an account of the self-movement of phenomenological thought as it passes from standpoint to standpoint. As will be seen (*Infra*, sects. 5, 6 and especially pp. 69 ff.), this is why it passes from the dialectic of Reason, not to the earliest form of spiritual life in history, but straightway to that form of Spirit which is the truth of Reason, i.e., the ethical life of Greece.

4. Of Religion, or "Absolute Spirit Manifest"

We might hope that the bridge between these standpoints is found as philosophical thought turns to a complete or absolute Spirit manifest *in* human life and *for* humans conscious of the fact.* Such a manifestation, according to Hegel, occurs in the life of religious faith, and it is complete in the life of the Christian faith. As has just been noted, the Divine may be a mere distant object, for human subjects whose present individual and social world exists *beside* it, and as such it is merely for "the standpoint of consciousness." We now confront a divine *presence, in* and *for* human subjects, and hence *permeating* their individual and social worlds. Here we find, Hegel states, the "self-consciousness of Spirit."[25]

But it must at first sight seem that what is hopefully approached as the needed bridge on the contrary challenges most radically the entire phenomenological enterprise. Thus far we could hope that the gap between standpoints of life and the standpoint of absolute thought might somehow be bridged. Now that we have abruptly** come upon the bridge—or, at any rate, upon the reality without which, it will turn out, there can be no bridging—this seems to protest absolutely against *being* a mere bridge. The standpoint of religious faith bears witness to a human relation to nothing less than the Divine: surely it asserts that relation absolutely, i.e., so as

* This section is devoted to "Religion," the fifth major division of *Phenomenology* (*Phän.*, pp.473–548 [*Phen.*, pp.685–785].) Inasmuch as chs. 5 and 6 will be exclusively concerned with religion we shall here be as brief as possible. The *Phenomenology* is *necessarily turned* to religion, as to the "truth" of modern moral "certainty." (See sects. 5, 6, especially pp.69 ff.) In view of our commitments stated in sect. 1, we cannot—or at least not yet—follow this Hegelian turn. Furthermore, we must consider the religious truth before we can consider the moral certainty—if our purpose is to lead up to the conditions which, according to Hegel, have made his time ripe for "science."

** It will become clear that, whereas we have come upon religion abruptly, this is not true of the *Phenomenology* itself.

to rule out any higher standpoint from which it can be viewed. That different religions must make presumably irreconcilable claims is a grave enough challenge for a thought which must reconcile all irreconcilables. The challenge is total when they all unite in opposing a "science" which would grasp them in terms more ultimate than those in which they understand themselves.

We here come for the first time upon the issues which will be the central concern of our entire investigation.[26] They must for the present be dealt with briefly, and only in terms of the basic problem of the *Phenomenology*. In the preceding sections, we have followed Hegel's attempt to understand human selfhood—individual and social—as a self-constituting process. The religious faith or faiths now encountered may well seem flatly to assert that finite humanity is *not* such a process, at least not vis-à-vis the Divine; for the finite human is *receptively* related to the Divine, as its infinite Other: indeed this receptivity can be so total as to encompass the human self's very being. In a previous section, the Stoic "free" self was philosophically understood as a self-made *creatio ex nihilo*. Is such a philosophical understanding not in the most radical conflict with the Christian testimony to a God who is *Creator ex nihilo*—a testimony given by a self which acknowledges its own creatureliness? And does this not point to a total clash between religious (or Christian) faith and what since Fichte has been *the* basic doctrine of idealistic philosophy—that the human self is self-active insofar as it is truly human? Not accidentally Fichte had denied the Creator-God in the name of free selfhood and in turn was charged with atheism.[27]

But much has happened since the *Atheismusstreit*. Two interrelated developments, in principle complete in the *Phenomenology*, have at least mitigated the stark conflict between religious receptivity and idealistic self-activity.

First, Hegel has long ago assimilated the protests, made by

Schleiermacher and Schelling, against Fichte's one-sided exalta-
tion of moral self-activity, in behalf of spheres of life in which
the human self, being finite, is receptive as well as self-active.[28] To
go a giant step further, he has reached the view that this receptivity has ultimate reality, even when viewed from the absolute
standpoint to which (following the Schelling of 1801) he has
risen. By failing to do justice to this requirement Schelling had
dissipated all finite reality into a "night in which all cows are
black." But, as will gradually emerge, the entire philosophy of
Hegel's maturity may be viewed as one vast attempt to escape
this Schellingian fate.[29]

The other development is no less significant. Under Kantian
influence Fichte, Schleiermacher, Schelling, and indeed, the Hegel
of the *Early Theological Writings* had all been inclined to contrast
positive religions, taken as resting on little more than arbitrary
external authority, with an ideal religion of pure inwardness. Thus
they had very nearly ignored historical religious realities, in favor
of a true religion consisting, respectively, of rational hope, joyous
moral activity, pious religious passivity and the "revelation" of
art.[30] For the mature Hegel, a vital distinction still exists between
genuine religion and one of merely external belief or observance.
But it no longer coincides with the distinction between a merely
ideal religion and historical religious realities. This is due to a doctrine of the utmost consequence. In every genuine religion, the
human is both inwardly related to the Divine and remains *other
than the Divine; just as without the first a religion is not genuine
so without the second it is lacking in serious reality.* Hegel terms
the togetherness of, and strain between, these two aspects "religious representation," and holds that this has itself no serious
reality until it is *acted out.* But this acting out occurs, and has
occurred, in actual history. This is the reason why Hegel immerses
himself ever more deeply in the historical realities of religious
life and why—as will be seen—he alone, of all German idealistic

philosophers, achieves a genuine philosophical confrontation with the historical Christian faith.*

Can any religion thus understood—including the Christian— suffice to make the time ripe for Hegelian "science?" Our present, merely preliminary, account of Hegel's encounter with Christianity must remain wholly confined to this question.

In no genuine religion can the Divinity present be *simply* other than the human—both individual self and social whole—to which it is present. Above a nature other-than-self the self can rise, tearing itself loose from it. Above a Divinity other-than-self it cannot rise, for this is higher as well as other-than-self. Its presence, in stark otherness, would therefore simply destroy the self's selfhood. This, however, is no genuine religious possibility. It does not and cannot occur—even in that extreme case in which a radically infinite Divinity, incommensurate with all things finite, wholly dissolves the human self, disclosed as being radically finite. For the finite self recognizes what occurs, and without such recognition there would be no *religious* relationship at all. The self recognizes itself as dissolving in the very moment of being dissolved, and it recognizes the divine Infinity which does the dissolving. The world and all its finite works disintegrate, as does the self itself for which they disintegrate. But the self acknowledges the truth of this disintegrating, *in a free act of self-surrender*. It *is* this disintegrating and self-surrendering, and because it is the second as well as the first, it is a gaining-of-self even as it is a loss of it.

Hegel's identification of this religious possibility as an historical

* Like his immediate predecessors, the Hegel of the *Early Theological Writings* simply rejects authority in genuine religion. For the mature Hegel it has a necessary albeit subordinate role (See ch. 5, appendix 2.) because, whereas for the young Hegel in his brief romantic phase the human and the Divine all but merge in genuine religious experience, the mature Hegel holds that to be inwardly related to *and* divorced from the Divine is of the essence of any genuine religious human life which has not fled from human realities. Religious existence is representational—even Christian existence; for this preserves Good Friday even though Easter overreaches it. (For a full discussion of representational existence, see ch. 5, sects. 2 ff., and appendix 1; ch. 6, sect. 3.)

actuality is vague—deliberately so, it would appear.[31] It is a "religion of light" in which all finite realities disappear in an infinite but "empty depth." This could hardly be an *historical* actuality, however, if the finite realities simply disappeared. These latter, after all, do assert their historical existence, and they do so even in the moment of divine presence. The divine depth, then, is present in and for an "actual nation" acknowledging it, and this takes itself for, and is, the "nation of God." But here a radical strain manifests its presence. The infinite divine depth is "empty"; "the *actual* self" of the nation does not dissolve into emptiness but rather remains *not* empty—and finite. Hence the "nation of God" finds itself "rejected." Thus the divine-human incommensurability remains even as finite self and finite nation turn their being-dissolved into an act of surrender. The surrender cannot be made wholly real. On the contrary, the joy of the moment of union only accentuates the pain of actual separation which persists in real life.

Divine-human inwardness *already* exists in the religion of light. Divine-human otherness *still* exists in its extreme opposite, historically actual in the Greek "religion of art." At first sight this may seem to be a religion of pure inwardness. For the self and the nation here worship works of their own creating, which yet *can* be worshiped only because they are, and are known to be, not works of mere humanity but rather of a Divinity at work within it. In such worship, the self affirms itself even as it worships the Divine, and the gods, "friendly" to the worshiping nation and "recognizing its selfhood," recognize the actual historical life of the nation. And yet this recognition of the human by the Divine can only *seem* absolute and destined to last forever. A Divinity immanent in finite human acting and creating has lost its emptiness. It has done so, however, at the price of depth. And for all the commensurateness to the human acquired in its aesthetic immanence, the Divine retains transcendence, infinity, and incommensurability with all things human, and the religion of art, oblivious to trans-

cendence, is confined to idolatrous worship of finite gods. But as
the ignored or abandoned truth at length enters into consciousness
these gods, their worship, and the worshiping nation are all destroyed.[32] *

The Christian religion is the absolute religion because it contains, preserves and reconciles the depth of the "religion of light"
with the self or spirit of the religion of art. Here the Divine is the
depth of an Infinity incommensurable with all things finite and
human, and it has yet become absolutely commensurate with human selfhood, so radically as to enter into actual human finitude
and to suffer actual human death. As for the human worshiper,
he recognizes the divine depth, and in so doing dies the death of
his sinfulness, and he recognizes as well both the divine death
which has occurred on his behalf and the divine "death of death"—
the divine resurrection—which conquers all death. This recognizing, moreover, is, and is known to be, not a recognizing *of* the Divine *by* the human only but also the work of a Divinity other-
than-human *in* the human—the holy Spirit. Thus, Hegel asserts,
the divine-human relation which is actual in all genuine religion
finds its total consummation in a divine self-recognition in the
human—the "self-consciousness" of "absolute Spirit."[33]

So much, for the present, for the religious realities encountered
by philosophical thought, although even our brief account has
doubtless already moved beyond sheer encounter toward comprehension. Can Hegel's phenomenological thought move toward a
comprehension which will remove the religious protest against
the standpoint of absolute thought and, indeed, see religion as a
bridge to it? It can do so only if it can grasp the conflict between

---

* We here confine ourselves to the bare contrast between the religion of
light and the religion of art (succinctly stated in the presently expounded
passage), and to Christianity insofar as it resolves it. This is partly because,
as is by now abundantly clear, we cannot yet follow the *necessary* movement
undertaken by Hegel's phenomenological thought (See pp.69 ff.)—a movement which begins with the religion of light, passes through the Greek religion of art and arrives at the Christian revealed religion—partly because the
relation between Jewish, Greek and Christian religions will be dealt with at
length later, ch. 5, sect. 6; ch. 6, sects. 3 and 4.

the human self-activity already comprehended and the human receptivity to the Divine which is yet to be comprehended as being
a *relative* conflict only—one which vanishes when the two are comprehended as *aspects of a single whole*. Once again, then, a re-
structuring of previously comprehended realities is called for, in
terms of a category neither wholly other than the foregoing nor
wholly the same. *Finite spirit—individual and social—is seen as an
aspect of infinite or absolute Spirit; without suffering a loss of its
real finitude, it is a phase in the self-realization of divine Spirit.*

One must grasp fully the enormity of the step here to be taken.
In the preceding sections we have deliberately departed from
Hegel's own progression, and this in part precisely in order to
bring to light the enormity of the present step, and considered
only human—i.e., finite—realities, and the borrowed philosophical
category of self-activity was itself only finite. Within these limits
it remained wholly mysterious how any one time in human history
could ever become ripe for Hegelian "science," much more how
human history could move necessarily in that direction; the rise to
the standpoint of "science," if it was ever coming at all, was bound
to come "shot from the pistol." What has now emerged is that only
if history is not human but rather, as faith takes it to be, human-
divine can Hegelian "science" ever have an historically justified
beginning; Hegelian thought presupposes the prior existence of
religious (more precisely, Christian) life, and when it comes on
the scene it accepts, and must accept, the faith of that life as—
in some sense—true.[34]

This acceptance, however, does not exhaust the enormity of
the Hegelian step. It is more correct to say that it is only the necessary preliminary to that step. On Hegel's own admission and
insistence, religious faith does not grasp itself as the *Phenomenology* does and must grasp it. In its own self-understanding, it is
humanly receptive of a Divinity other-than-human, and remains
so even when what it receives is the Christian Grace which reconciles the human with the Divine; the self's self-activity—individual
or social—exists either beside or in the context of this receptivity,

and it remains finite and human. Understood in the light of the new philosophical category of infinite Spirit, however, religion becomes a divine self-activity in finite humanity; and in order so to grasp it *Hegelian thought must have done nothing less than rise above a self-active thought confined to human finitude in order to become a self-active thought which is infinite and divine.*[35]

But our question is, as it has been all along, how Hegelian thought can have reached this "scientific" standpoint. Does the presence of the Christian truth by itself suffice to make the time ripe for the rise to scientific thought? The answer is clearly in the negative. Indeed, a veritable gulf exists between the religious self which in its own self-understanding remains humanly receptive of the Divine, even when in possession of Christian Grace, and the philosophical self which, as has now emerged, must have become infinite and divine.

But this negative answer might, after all, have been expected. According to Hegel, the time has become ripe for science, not since Jesus of Nazareth in the first century, nor even since Luther in the sixteenth. It has become ripe for science only in his own time.

5. *Of "Spirit Certain-of-Itself"*

According to Hegel, this ripeness has been brought about by a post-Enlightenment, post-revolutionary "morality" which has come into existence in his own time.[36] Here Spirit—individual or social— is not merely self-active. It is, and knows itself to be, *infinitely* self-active. This is no longer the self-activity of a medieval culture, finite because Divinity remains a believed in, transcendent object. Divinity is, and is known to be, immanent in this self-activity. This morality is "Spirit certain-of-itself." We have observed Hegel accept the testimony of Christian faith. We shall now find him accept a contemporary moral testimony which has found philosophical articulation, fragmentarily in Kant, and more adequately in his own romantic contemporaries. It will emerge that for Hegel's phenomenological enterprise the one acceptance is as essential as the other.

This double acceptance raises three fundamental questions. Every standpoint thus far encountered by philosophic thought has been finite in its own self-understanding. This, obviously true of isolated individual selfhood and social realities as we have treated them, is equally true of religious faith even as it is in a divine presence; for the religious self takes itself to be receptively related to the present divine Infinity, and hence finite and human. But what is now to be encountered is a moral self-consciousness which claims infinity to be immanent in its own knowing and acting. This gives rise to three crucial questions. Can a philosopher in principle accept the claim which now makes its sudden appearance, or must he rather reject it as amounting to a claim to divinity made by finite humans, and hence to madness? Secondly, if the claim can and must be accepted, is it not in radical conflict with the religious claim already accepted? Can there be a greater conflict than between a religious faith which takes the human to be receptively related to a Divinity other-than-human (and hence itself finite) and a moral consciousness which asserts divinity as immanent in man's moral knowing and acting? The third question, raised at every stage in our inquiry, has now reached its final and climactic stage. Must the standpoint of a moral life in which "Spirit is certain-of-itself" not already *be* the absolute standpoint, thus rendering the standpoint of a still more ultimate "science" both superfluous and impossible?

To begin with, while our account has come suddenly upon a human claim to infinite self-consciousness, this is not true of the *Phenomenology* itself. We have thus far been compelled to depart from the internal progression of Hegel's work. It is now necessary to give some idea of what that progression is.

The very first section of the work[37]—thus far wholly ignored— watches the self-examination of consciousness, i.e., of a subject which takes itself to be wholly passively related to an object, taken as wholly independent; successively, the sense-certainty of a sheer here and now, the perception of sensuous things, and the scientific understanding of forces and laws by which they are governed. What is seen by the watching philosopher is the breakdown of any such subject-object relationship. Thus already the first of the six major sections of Hegel's work concludes that the truth of a consciousness externally limited by objects is an infinite self-consciousness not so limited—a conclusion which leaves one wondering why the vast and "complicated"[38] remainder of the work is still needed. It still *is* needed, Hegel tells us, because a truth already in principle reached by the observing philosopher is as yet far from reached by the subject observed by him. And unless this subject somehow *does* reach this truth, and indeed *has* done so, how can the philosopher *have* reached it?

In any case having reached this truth, the philosopher makes use of it as he turns from consciousness to self-consciousness. The self here observed asserts itself *against* its external other—nature and other selves—as objects of consciousness to be subdued by selfhood. The oberving philosopher already knows that this conflict with the external other is an internal conflict as well, and that therefore what seems sheer hostility is also mutual need.* Hence he will view the self's victories in a perspective different from that by which the observed self lives. What to the self is its final victory —a Stoic or Skeptical freedom of thought, bought at the price of withdrawal from or denial of nature and the human other—will be viewed as a one-sided victory, and the internally divided unhappy religious consciousness, as its nemesis. But the truth of self-consciousness pointed to by this nemesis is a selfhood which has at once internalized the other—natural and human—and itself lost individualistic isolation in the process. This truth is *Reason*.

Selfhood becomes "rational" when, rather than assert its individuality against the other, it asserts itself as a universality ideally

---

* The philosopher "already has the notion of Spirit" at this stage (*Phän.*, p.140 [*Phen.*, p.227].) This is not true of the self which he observes and criticizes.

inclusive of all otherness, and as in fact aiming at an actual inclusion in an infinite process of conquest. Reason finds theoretical expression in a natural science which, while it is "observing" because it takes nature as if it were a given other, yet *is* "reason" because it forever aims at the conquest of the merely given. And it finds practical expression in a moral life which, while arising from the conflict between what the self qua particular and real is, and what qua universal and ideal it ought to be, forever aims at the realization of the ideal. This Reason is a modern phenomenon, and Kant and Fichte are among its spokesmen. It is the "conscious certainty of being all reality."[39]

It must be noted that at this point the *Phenomenology* has already come upon a human selfhood which lays claim to an infinite dimension, and that this claim does not—at least not at this point—dissipate its finite humanity. The conquest of the real by the ideal is itself merely ideal, forever striven for but never wholly attained. The "certainty" of seeking does not become the "truth" of possession. Indeed, the self *is* this striving—a finite-infinite, real-ideal tension whose glorious and stern destiny is to be denied the peace of habitation at a fixed realm, and instead to be stretched, as it were, between the animals above which it is bound to rise and the angels whose blessedness it cannot reach.

If there is any one absolutely decisive step in the entire *Phenomenology*—one whose effects reverberate throughout the whole work—it is *the affirmation that Reason is not the final form of selfhood in life; that just as Reason is the "Truth" of self-consciousness so the Truth of Reason is Spirit.** We have already grasped Hegel's

---

* This affirmation is central to the argument with Fichte, who stops at the level of Reason. And it is central also to the internal argument of the *Phenomenology* itself. The four pages introducing the section on Spirit (*Phän.*, pp.312–16 [*Phen.*, pp.457–61].) are possibly the most important in the whole work. In any case, they divide what precedes from what follows them. For what here emerges is that all preceding forms of consciousness have been abstractions torn out of the context of Spirit. For this reason, the emphasis in the dialectic preceding these pages is negative whereas the emphasis in all that follows is affirmative.

Spirit as an inner bond between a social substance already there
and a self which is yet to come-to-be by its own self-activity. What
we thus far could only state but not grasp is that the Spirit singled
out in the *Phenomenology* is complete or infinite Spirit, i.e., the
inner bond between a substance which is more than a merely human whole and a self which transcends human finitude. The *Phenomenology* singles out such a Spirit because what it seeks and
finds is *the Truth of Reason.** The rational dichotomy between the
simply finite real and the merely ideal infinite is an abstraction
when frozen into fixity, and it is in fact unfrozen in the actual
spiritual life from which it is abstracted. In such a life, the substance which already is is itself shot through with ideality and
infinity, and the self which is yet to affirm its ideality and infinity,
is permeated in this affirmation with reality and finitude. What for
abstract Reason is a frozen opposition is in concrete spiritual life
the *self*-opposition arising from a prior unity, which for this reason
seeks self-reconciliation. But when at length the self consciously
appropriates this totality of spiritual life it transcends the stage
of a Reason merely certain of a reality forever *yet to be* appropriated. It has found itself in all reality. It has become "Spirit certain-
of-*itself*."

To appreciate the crucial importance of the step here taken we
do well to pause for an historical reminder. As will be shown in
the companion volume to the present work already repeatedly referred to, in 1801 Schelling had transcended the Fichtean "idealism
of the finite self." The Fichtean self had remained finite, for
it had to take infinity as a mere ideal, forever aimed at but never
reached. And, because selfhood cannot in philosophical thought
transcend the limits of selfhood in life, the standpoint of Fichtean
idealism had itself remained finite. To be sure, the Schellingian

* See *Phän.*, p.328 (*Phen.*, p.479): "What Reason has grasped merely as
object has [now] become Self-consciousness. . . . What observation knew
as something in which the self had no share is here ethical life already there—
an actuality which is at the same time the deed and work of him who finds
it already there."

thought of 1801 had risen to a standpoint of absolute selfhood; but in so doing it had produced a vast gulf between a thinking self risen to infinity and a living self remaining—even in art, according to Schelling its highest achievement—confined to finitude. It is just this gulf which Hegel's phenomenological introduction to "science" seeks to bridge, and the step presently under consideration is crucial for his entire enterprise. For if—as Fichte maintained—Reason is the highest stage of selfhood in life then philosophical thought too must remain confined to the standpoint of finite selfhood. It can rise to the Schellingian absolute selfhood only if selfhood in life can become, and has in fact become, "Spirit certain-of-itself."

How can the self in life find this certainty? It cannot so long as the self's oneness with complete or infinite Spirit is observed only by the philosopher, and is not grasped by the self observed. We have already noted that whereas the *Phenomenology* sees *one* infinite Spirit binding the harmonious Greek ethical world to the dark Fate which is its nemesis, those who live in that world experience *two* separate realities, of which one is immanent but finite, and the other, infinite but transcendent, and also that whereas the *Phenomenology* sees Roman and medieval cultural self-activity as the *self*-alienation of *one* infinite Spirit those engaged in that self-activity are left with *two* worlds, of which one is a present, lived in, earthly, human "cultural" product whereas the other is a divine world, believed in, eternally *un*produced and in heaven. It remains here to be added that cultural self-activity remains alienated—i.e., falls short of being Spirit certain-of-itself— even as it seeks to appropriate Substance, thus bringing down the medieval heaven to a modern earth. It is true that the Age of Enlightenment "turns against faith" and "transforms all being-in-itself (*Ansichsein*) into being-for-itself (*Fürsichsein*),"[40] and that the French revolution which acts out this transformation makes "absolute freedom" an earthly reality. But because here "objectivity is destroyed . . . substantiality [is] . . . lost"[41] rather than appropriated; the absolute self-certainty in question is a merely finite and human self-activity, idolatrously absolutized. This is evident even in the merely halfhearted and merely theoretical Spirit of the Enlightenment, which reduces all things to objects of a merely human use. The evidence is overwhelming in French revolutionary radicalism; having absolutized a merely human freedom, it becomes a "self-destructive actuality," which ends up in terror.[42] The certainty which Hegel seeks and needs, then, can be found only if Spirit has overcome this self-alienation, so as to appropriate *as* self *for* itself a Substance which *remains* Substance *in* itself. And this, he asserts, has at least in principle occurred in a post-Enlightenment, post-revolutionary "morality" existing in his own time. What is that morality?

It is—at least to begin with—once again the morality articulated by Kant but now considered, not as an imperative abstractly opposed by a legislating rational self to the world, but rather as a concrete spiritual life lived by the self *with* the world, and hence as a "moral view of the world" acted out *in* the world. In order for there to be such a view and such an acting-out there must be, in addition to the opposition between the ideal and the actual, a postulated harmony between them.

The first postulate . . . [is] the harmony of morality and objective nature; the other . . . the harmony of morality and will in its form of sensuous inclination, the final purpose of self-consciousness as such. The former is harmony in the form of being-in-itself, the second, in the form of being-for-itself or self-consciousness. But what connects these two final purposes and mediates between them is *the movement of overt acting itself.*[43]

But this overt acting discloses a "whole nest of contradictions." First, legislating Reason must be both purely universal and within me; yet the duties it legislates must be countless contingent duties which is why, to retain its purity, the Reason which is within me must also be represented as a "holy Legislator" apart from me. Secondly, the postulated harmony of morality and nature must be my task, and this latter must be absolute, i.e., incapable of completion. Yet the harmony must also "*be*, not *remain* a mere task"; hence what is my task must also be hoped for as a divine gift. These and other contradictions arise because in the "movement of overt acting" infinite ideality and finite actuality are both at war and united.[44]

What matters, however, is not that a philosopher can detect these contradictions. It is that the "movement of overt acting," being *one* movement, can itself rise above them, and has in fact done so in a post-Kantian moral life. The self of the moral view of the world remains internally divided into an abstractly universal and a contingently particular aspect. A post-Kantian conscience or conscientiousness[45] has boldly accepted itself as a unity, in which ideal universality and contingent particularity are inextricably intertwined. Moreover, it has accepted conscience or conscientiousness in others, and what for the moral view of the world is an abstract unity of mankind, constituted by an abstract universal duty, has given way to a community of conscientious persons, united through mutual recognition.[46]

Discord, however, inevitably persists. Hence conscience or conscientiousness must seek to purify itself of the "blemish of determinacy" and free itself of "every content of duty," thereby becoming "moral genius . . . [to which] its inner voice is the voice of God." Having thus fled from determinacy, its acting reduces itself to "the contemplation of its own divinity"; and this "solitary worship of the God within" is communal only in that there arises a community of "beautiful souls, . . . assuring each other of their conscientiousness, good intentions and purity of purpose."[47]

Conscience or conscientiousness thus flees from discord. It suffers an internal and external nemesis of this flight. "Living in dread of contaminating its inward radiance by action and existence" it suffers internally the loss of action and existence and dissolves into insubstantiality. It is externally challenged by the moral agent who has *not* fled from action and existence but on the contrary con-

sciously accepted its blemish and dirties his hands; indeed, this
latter hard-heartedly asserts his "egotistic purposes". For this,
to be sure, he is judged by the beautiful soul, and rightly so by
its pure standards. But this judgment in turn invites the accusa-
tion of hypocrisy. For the beautiful soul has remained beautiful
only at the price of not acting at all.[48]

But the final state of the final morality—for in Hegel's view this
morality is in idea unsurpassable, however inadequately realized
in fact—is not this "unforgiving" conflict. The beautiful soul lets go
of its beauty in recognizing its own unreality. The man of action
recognizes an ideality which calls his egotism into question. A
"word of reconciliation" is spoken, and a "mutual recognition" is
accomplished. This latter, however, could not be accomplished by
the unaided moral self-activity which lives in and between the two
extremes. The tension is transcended only because what the moral
self—in both its poles—produces, and forever is yet to produce,
already *is* as Substance; and because, in recognizing and accepting what already is, the *moral* self turns *religious*. The
"reconciling yea" which it recognizes and accepts is "the God
who appears."[49]

The questions asked at the beginning of the present section can
now be answered. More precisely, they have already answered
themselves. First, the modern moral self contemplates an inward
divinity; it does not rise above humanity and become divine. For
when it aspires to real divinity it dissolves into unreality, and
when it is action and existence it is tarnished by their blemish. In
modern moral self-activity, then, Spirit is *certain* of itself. But it
does not transcend human finitude and fragmentariness so as to
convert this certainty into *truth*.*

Secondly, this moral certainty points to a truth which is religious.
The certainty is moral because it is a knowing and doing of what

---

* This is why, whereas religion is a form of absolute Spirit, morality even
at its highest only points to absolute Spirit. See further ch. 6, sect. 5.

forever is *yet to be* accomplished. The truth pointed to is religious because it is a reality *already* accomplished. The infinite autonomy of modern moral selfhood, far from challenging religious truth, on the contrary refers to it, as *its* truth, and since it may be described as the highest and most concrete self-assertion of autonomous Reason in modern life, the Hegelian philosophy may be described as an attempt to reconcile a Reason which asserts itself *against* the reality which is with a religious truth which *already* is.*

Thirdly, Hegel holds this reconciliation to be already in principle actual in modern life. It is not, however, as yet *grasped* as actual. Moral self-activity points only either to further moral self-activity, thus remaining eternally fragmented, or else to an unfragmented religious truth which remains beyond its self-activity because it is *received* as already *being*. Religious faith, on its part, is in its own self-understanding not a self-activity at all; it does not self-actively produce reconciliation but rather receives it as the gift of divine Grace. The Christian truth, which is the essential "content" of "science," has been actual in human history for nearly two millennia. And self-activity has reached in modern moral life as ultimate a "form" as it can ever reach in life. But because it remains human in both its religious and its moral aspects, human life has not in either aspect risen, and could not have risen, to an infinite and self-complete self-activity. The time has become as ripe for "science" as life can ever make it. Only philosophical thought can be the self-activity which *produces* science.

6. *The Standpoint of Absolute Knowledge*

The last-named of these answers requires further explication. As viewed by the *Phenomenology*, the final moral self-activity and the final religion "fall to begin with apart." They are, nevertheless,

---

* This reconciliation is here given only within the limits of the phenomenological enterprise. For a fuller account, see ch. 6, sects. 5–6.

"already implicitly united"—in religion. For religion is the Truth of the moral certainty. What is religiously received as *already done* would not be final if what morally is *yet to be done* fell simply outside it. The workaday week of "action and existence" points to the Sunday of rest and reconciliation—a Sunday not divorced from the week but rather *of* the week.[50] What then is still needed? "The unification which is still missing," Hegel tells us, "is the simple unity of the Notion."[51] What is this Notion?

It *is* what it *does*, and it does what *remains* to be done. What is still missing is a spiritual acting, which (like moral "Spirit certain-of-itself") is, and knows itself to be, an infinite self-acting and which (like Christian faith) has transcended the fragmentariness of a certainty of what forever is yet to be done, and has come into complete possession of what already is. This self-activity is the explicit *knowledge* of the unity which implicitly already is.

To a degree, this self-activity is foreshadowed in the beautiful soul, for it is a "self-contemplating of the Divine."[52] This latter, however, is a divine self-contemplating in the human only, and for this reason can maintain itself in purity only at the price of flight from the blemish of finite humanity. It is, therefore, doubly contradicted by the human realities from which it has fled—by blemished but real "action and existence," and by a faith which, while receptive of a God other-than-human, itself remains fully and concretely human. In contrast, the divine self-activity which is the Notion does not flee from these realities but rather *unites* them, and it can do so only by *reenacting* them so as to *transfigure* them. This is done by complete or absolute Spirit, already actual in the final religion, but recreating itself in that ultimate form of self-activity which is already present in the final form of moral acting. It is the Self which, at long last, is *absolutely* free, i.e., no longer either in flight from, or limited by, any external reality. The human self which has risen to this selfhood has risen to the absolute standpoint. And what it is and does is in the final philosophical thinking—Hegelian "science."*

With this conclusion, both the nature of Hegel's phenomenological introduction to science and its relation to the Hegelian system as a whole have at least in principle established themselves. If the phenomenological road to science is "already scientific," it is because *it moves from beginning to end in the "circle"*[53] *of the free self-activity of the Notion.* Only thus can it view the variegated standpoints of life so differently from the way they view themselves, i.e., as forms of self-activity pointing beyond themselves, and ultimately to the absolute self-activity of the Notion itself. Only thus, too, can it move from standpoint to standpoint *by an internal necessity,* and view the self-examination which it sees in every standpoint as leading to the *necessary* abandonment of the examined standpoint.** Because the *Phenomenology* already moves within the circle of the Notion, it presupposes the "science"—Hegelian logic—which explicates that Notion. If nevertheless it is an introduction to science it is because, unlike science itself, it dwells on how each standpoint of life views itself before

---

* "The final shape of Spirit is absolute knowledge. It is Spirit which gives its complete and true content the form of selfhood, and thus realizes its Notion even as it remains within the Notion while realizing it . . . . Truth is here not merely implicitly identical with itself; it also has the shape of self-certainty . . . [This] is science." *Phän.*, p.556 (*Phen.*, p.747 ff.). Cf. also *Phän.*, p.554 (*Phen.*, p.795).

** This brings to light, at long last, the necessity without which Hegel's phenomenological road to "science" could not be "scientific." (*Phän.*, p.74 [*Phen.*, p.144].) What moves necessarily is not the reality observed but rather the phenomenological thinker who, reenacting each standpoint he observes in notional thought, is compelled to move from standpoint to standpoint. The observed standpoints themselves either do not move at all (e.g., when phenomenological thought abandons a standpoint because it represents an abstraction torn out of a larger context, i.e., in the case of each transition from one of the major divisions of the *Phenomenology* to the next), or else they move only conditionally—on condition that in fact they reach the extremities into which phenomenological thought pushes them. To be sure, they must have reached these extremities in *some* factual instances if the time is ever to have become ripe for "science." But at least not until Hegel comes upon

it criticizes it in the light of the Notion; and because, in doing both, it "hands the individual [the] ladder" to science.*

Does this answer the question which throughout this discourse we have been asking of the *Phenomenology?* Up to a point. The *Phenomenology* has not "instructed unscientific consciousness in science,"[54] and this holds true, as much as of any other such consciousness, of Christian faith and modern moral self-activity. What it has shown, however, is that not all individuals are equally remote from, or near to, "science." It is true that in "scientific" thinking "the individual walks on his head," whereas everywhere in life he walks on his feet. But the expectation that such a strange posture be adopted is not equally unprepared at all times. A moral self which already knows its being and acting to be "Spirit certain-of-itself" need but recognize and accept that the same Spirit which its own acting is forever yet to be already is in the divine-human relation manifest in the Christian faith—and he will have entered into the circle of the Notion. As for the *Phenomenology* itself, it may have moved within that circle from the beginning. It demonstrates at the end that the time in which this moving has been done has been made as ripe for it by life as life can ever make it.

Yet our question has been answered only up to a point. A radical gap, after all, remains between the standpoint of absolute thought

---

the crucial reality of Spirit (See p.61 n.) is there even any suggestion that this movement, a necessary condition for "science," is necessary in any other than this conditional sense. Dialectical necessity in the *Phenomenology*, then, is quite different from dialectical necessity in the *Philosophy of History* (which is in possession of the category of Spirit from the start). It also differs from dialectical necessity in the *Philosophy of Religion.* (See ch. 6, sect. 4.) Dialectical necessity in the *Philosophy of History* is a subject transcending the scope of the present work.

* This is the extent to which we can deal with the expository problem concerning the relation between the *Phenomenology* and the Hegelian system, stated in the appendix to this chapter. It suffices here to have shown that there is at least in principle no reason why the *Phenomenology* might not be both an introduction to "science" and a part of "science." The question left unanswered is whether it is *part* of science *only*, of rather *all* of science, in *one* of several possible forms, see ch. 4, p.85 n.

and even those standpoints of life which are closest to it. Why—this might be asked not only by Fichteans but also, *mutatis mutandis*, by Marxists—should the standpoint of moral self-activity grasp the ladder to the scientific standpoint when, having done so, it finds its certainty of what is forever yet to be done point to a Truth which already is done? Why—and this is in fact asked by Kierkegaardians and Barthians—should a faith humanly receptive to the Divine grasp this ladder when this requires no less a presumption than the rise in thought to divine Selfhood? Rather than ascend the Hegelian ladder, will not both standpoints protest against the Hegelian expectation, even at the price of radical conflict with each other? And will not this protest be enough to call the absoluteness of the standpoint of Hegelian science into question? Moreover, even if they are *willing* to ascend the Hegelian ladder, is either standpoint *able* to do so? As thus far considered, Hegelian philosophic science springs suddenly from nonphilosophic life—and it is a "circle."

These questions demand a far closer examination than we have thus far given them, and it will have to concentrate on the relation between Christian life and Hegelian philosophic thought. Hegel flatly asserts that the Christian religion is *the* presupposition in life of his philosophic thought, and that it already contains—in principle—in nonphilosophic form its essential content: yet our account of that religion has hitherto been most cursory.[55] He asserts, too, that his philosophy arises from, and consummates, not only history but also the history of philosophy. However, we have thus far not said a word about the relation between Hegel's philosophy and the history of philosophy; indeed, Hegel himself fully explicates that relation only many years after writing the *Phenomenology*.[56]

Another question, however, calls for more immediate attention: it will be dealt with in the chapter immediately following. The *Phenomenology* is a road to "science." It passes from standpoint to standpoint, and it would be quite justified in doing so along the straightest and quickest path. As for the superseded standpoints, these may and must be simply left behind. Yet these continue to assert their persisting reality, even when higher standpoints have become historical realities. Thus even if the Christian faith and the post-Kantian moral self-activity accepted by Hegel are in fact living realities in Hegel's own time—which of course might itself be seriously questioned[57]—countless other forms of human life indisputably exist beside them. This fact can be ignored by the *Phenomenology*, concerned as it is merely to hand the ladder to the absolute standpoint, to individuals at varying degrees of nearness to it. It cannot be ignored by Hegelian "science" proper. In producing a simple union, can the Notion ignore or deny the contingent realities of human existence which are shot through with finitude, conflict, and nonunion? But then surely any single protest made anywhere in finite life must suffice to shatter the pretensions of the Notion. Or can the unifying Notion recognize all nonunion? But then surely this recognition must reduce it to a mere form of finite thought. Unless Hegelian science can cope with this dilemma the introduction to "science" furnished by the *Phenomenology* will turn out to have been lost labor.[58]

This dilemma is not lost sight of even during the course of the *Phenomenology* itself. In pursuit of its goal, the work ought to move toward the absolute standpoint as speedily and elegantly as possible. Yet its actual movement is tortuous, and is arrested time and again as if Hegel were haunted by the fear that encountered standpoints of life, disposed of too quickly or glibly by a thought which is Notion, will arise to accuse the Notion of lifelessness. When finally the Notion appears on the scene in its own right, it does not expand its scope explicitly over the whole vast panorama of life previously viewed. It is merely tersely asserted—as a staggering demand. Hegel has not forgotten that the time which he sees as ripe for "science" is also (like all time)—one of conflict, chance, and brute fact, and that he—the self rising to absolute thought—is also a contingent self in the midst of time. Many years after the composition of the *Phenomenology* Hegel wrote: "I raise myself in thought to the Absolute . . . thus being infinite consciousness; yet at the same time I am finite consciousness . . . Both aspects seek each other and flee each other . . . I am the struggle between them."[59] This struggle—and the struggle to resolve the struggle—is in the end the sole theme of the *Phenomenology* and, indeed, of the whole Hegelian philosophy.

Appendix

The Place of the *Phenomenology* in the Hegelian System

(*See p.36.*)

The *Phenomenology* has been the subject of scholarly controversy for well over a century, and this has concerned not only its details but also its overall significance and place within the Hegelian system. Hegel's own statements on this latter question are not wholly consistent, or at any rate, clear; the main inconsistency—or apparent inconsistency—being that what is offered in 1807 as an introduction to (and first part of) "science" appears—or seems to appear—in the *Encyclopedia* (1st ed., 1817) as part of the scientific system, i.e., as a subsection of subjective spirit. (The main passages on this question are *Phän.*, pp.24 ff., 561 ff. (*Phen.*, pp.86 ff., 804 ff.); *Logik*, I, pp.5 ff., 29 ff., 51 ff. (*Logic*, I, pp.35 ff., 59 ff., 79 ff.); *Enz.*, sects. 413–39.)

Systematically, the central question is the relation between the *Phenomenology* and the system. For scholars despairing of a systematic answer, the question has been whether the later Hegel must be regarded as having abandoned his whole earlier phenomenological enterprise, in which case the question is whether the serious or significant Hegel is the author of the *Phenomenology* or that of the *Logic* and the *Encyclopedia*. More recently scholars have questioned whether the *Phenomenology* is a unity even internally, or rather a patchwork composed, as it was in its later sections, over an incredibly short period of time. (A prominent advocate of the patchwork theory is Theodor

Haering, *Hegel: Sein Wollen und Werk*, 2 vols. [Leipzig and Berlin: Teubner, 1929, 1938]. For an excellent account of the history of *Phenomenology* interpretations, see Otto Pöggeler, "Zur Deutung der Phänomenologie des Geistes," *Hegel-Studien* [Bonn: Bouvier, 1961], I, pp.255–94.)

We obviously cannot here enter in detail into these scholarly controversies. We confine ourselves to these comments:

(i) The hypothesis of an evolution of major significance in Hegel's thought from *Phenomenology* to system is rendered unlikely, if indeed not ruled out, by the facts (a) that Hegel gave an early version of the later system in his Jena lectures, prior to composing the *Phenomenology* (See *Jenenser Logik, Metaphysik und Naturphilosophie*, ed. Georg Lasson [Leipzig: Meiner, 1923], and *Jenenser Realphilosophie*, ed. Johannes Hoffmeister, 2 vols. [Leipzig: Meiner, 1931–32]); (b) that he began preparing a second edition of the *Phenomenology* just prior to his death—an unlikely eventuality if he had considered the work superseded by his later thought. It must be added, however, that to doubt or even reject the genetic hypothesis is not to have established that the problem of the systematic relation between the *Phenomenology* and the system can find a wholly satisfactory solution. (For my own tentative stand on this issue, see sect. 6 and especially p.70 n. of this chapter.)

(ii) The patchwork hypothesis has external evidence in its support, and it could be genuinely refuted only by a thorough systematic interpretation of the entire *Phenomenology*—a task of such proportions that it has never been attempted. Even so, any close, philosophically-minded student of the work must be suspicious of the patchwork hypothesis, if only because he finds time and again systematic order where there had seemed to be sheer chaos. This account of the *Phenomenology* is a systematic interpretation of selected aspects relevant to our purpose only, considered in the perspective expounded in sect. 1 of this chapter.

CHAPTER FOUR

The Hegelian Middle:
On the *Encyclopedia*
of Philosophical Sciences

It is the cowardice of abstract thought to shun
sensuous presence in monkish fashion.
Werke, XII, p.309 (*Phil. Rel.*, III, p.101).*

1. *The Central Problem of the Hegelian System*

An anticipating remark in the *Phenomenology*—Hegel's "appearing science"—outlines the task of the *Encyclopedia of Philosophical
Sciences*—Hegel's definitive statement of "science" proper.

If consciousness [already] knew Reason to be the essence of both things
and itself; and if it knew that Reason can be present in the stage peculiar
to itself only in consciousness itself: then it would descend into its own
depths and seek Reason there rather than in things. Having discovered
it there, it would then find itself directed once more to the actual world.
And it would behold in that world Reason's sensuous expression, but it
would take that expression at the same time as being essentially Notion.[1]

This statement neatly sums up the program of the Hegelian
system: its first movement, the *Logic*; its double second movement
which, directed on Nature and Spirit into which "the actual world"
divides itself, is itself divided into *Philosophy of Nature* and *Philosophy of Spirit*; and its third movement, already *in* the second
movement because it is a *double* movement, by virtue of which

* Abbreviations are listed on pp.245 ff.

the system, rather than fall into three separate parts, is a single "overreaching"[2] whole.

But the cited passage also indicates the central problem, not to say scandal, of the Hegelian system; it is the enigma which was to divide his followers into right- and left-wing schools, and is the rock on which countless interpreters have foundered. Is Reason the "essence of both things and consciousness?" If so how can philosophy, identified with Reason, recognize any actual world besides itself, toward which it is directed? Or does philosophy recognize such a world, namely, the contingent and fragmented world of human experience? How then can it take that world "as being essentially Notion"? From the outset and throughout, the Hegelian system seems faced with the choice between saving the claims of an absolute and therefore all-comprehensive philosophic thought, but at the price of loss of any actual world besides it, and saving the contingent world of human experience at the price of reducing philosophic thought itself to finiteness. However, the central claim of Hegelian thought is to repudiate the need for choice between these right- and left-wing alternatives;* to unite a pluralistic openness as hospitable to the varieties of contingent experience as any empiricism with a monistic completeness more

---

* As used in this chapter, the terms "right-wing" and "left-wing interpretation" refer exclusively to the horns of this dilemma. This latter, and its Hegelian solution, might be presented—to mention but a few possibilities—in terms of the relation between the Understanding as manifest in natural science and a philosophic Reason superseding it, or of a time which lends reality to history and an eternity which encompasses it. Here attention is focused on the contingency which permeates human life and the necessity achieved in philosophic thought because our final objective is to display the relation between the God-man relation manifest in religious life and the all-encompassing, self-developing and necessary Idea manifest in philosophic thought.

Right- and left-wing interpretations are often more profound and exciting than mediocre attempts at impartial exposition. Of recent examples, we may mention, respectively, Iwan Iljin, *Die Philosophie Hegels als Kontemplative Gotteslehre* (Bern, Switz.: Francke, 1946), and Alexandre Kojève, *Introduction À La Lecture de Hegel* (Paris: Gallimard, 1947). We are much indebted to these two works.

radical in its claims to comprehensiveness than any other speculative rationalism. Hegel's thought dwells in the middle between
these extremes, and how it can dwell there is its innermost secret.

2. *The Right-Wing Interpretation*

No doubt it is difficult to grasp this Hegelian middle. But to
understand Hegel's system without it is impossible. Such an understanding has often been attempted by means of a move from the
Hegelian middle to either of the extremes, but the most important
insights to be gained from such attempts are gained by watching
their collapse.

We consider, first, the right-wing interpretation. Here Hegel appears as a "transcendent metaphysician"[3] whose *Logic*—which he
himself call metaphysics[4]—describes an ontologically self-sufficient,
transcendent realm. In this, it might be supposed, Nature and
Spirit—Hegel's actual world—somehow participate as do Platonic
appearances in Platonic forms, and Hegel's *Philosophy of Nature*
and *Philosophy of Spirit*—which he himself calls "applied logic"[5]—
understand them as such participations.

To this we must say at once that the *Logic*, if it is a transcendent
metaphysics, must include far more than Platonic forms. Since
Schelling, indeed since Kant, metaphysics can no longer recognize
two worlds, of which one is its proper object. If possible at all,
metaphysics rises above all standpoints for which there are two
worlds, to an absolute standpoint for which there is *one* world,
and that is not an object. For Hegel, as for Schelling before him,
it is clear from the start that metaphysical dualisms of every kind
are mere symptoms of partial or total philosophical failure.[6] Moreover, that the *Logic* is in some sense all-comprehensive in scope
is disclosed by its very contents. It includes "mechanism," "chem-
ism," "teleology," and "life." Even chance or contingency makes
an appearance if only—so it seems—in order as such to vanish.

But if the *Logic* is an all-comprehensive transcendent realm what reality remains for an actual world outside that realm? And what functions for philosophies concerned with it?* It cannot be the case that whereas the *Logic* describes reality from the absolute standpoint, the other two parts of the system describe appearance from a finite standpoint. To be philosophies at all, these parts, as much as the *Logic*, must adopt the adsolute standpoint. Yet if the *Logic* already comprehends all reality at the absolute standpoint no function is left for its applications. It is thus with good reason that one interpreter, courageous enough to carry the transcendent-metaphysical interpretation to its logical extreme, is forced to write: "Is there in the world anything at all outside the *Logic?* According to Hegel one would, strictly speaking, have to answer this question resolutely in the negative."[7]

The right-wing interpretation has without doubt some considerable plausibility. And in forms less extreme but also less enlightening than that just stated it has always found adherents. Doubtless the other two parts of Hegel's system depend on the *Logic*, though this by itself means little until the precise nature of the dependence is specified, and this is exactly the problem. To this systematic one may add an historical consideration. The *Logic* seems, quite by itself, to correspond to Schelling's *My System* of 1801, as regards program, as well as to correct the faults Hegel finds with that work as regards execution. Both works grasp Totality, by means of a Reason identical with it. But while Schelling's Totality and Reason collapse into a sheer and hence empty union their counterparts in Hegel's *Logic* emerge as a self-differentiating Whole which encompasses nonunion as well as union. Must one say, then, that Hegel's entire and complete response to the night of Schelling's Indifference is to be found in that self-differentiating

---

* G. R. G. Mure writes:

If logic is not the whole of philosophy, but has in the philosophies of Nature and Concrete Spirit its essential complement, then surely in them there must be some integral element beside a blurred or distorted repetition of the categories, beside a mere attentuated simulacrum which could add nothing to the original. (*IH*, p.112)

Totality which is aimed at throughout the *Logic* and finally reached in the Absolute Idea?[8]

Nevertheless, the transcendent-metaphysical interpretation is utterly untenable. (And it is no small achievement of its radical version to disclose that fact.) It is contrary to Hegel's essential and life-long philosophical objectives. It requires the elimination of no less than two parts of a tripartite system, and unless we are mistaken, it renders unintelligible the internal progression of the *Logic* itself.*

First, Hegel's life-long endeavour was to find the Absolute not beyond but present *in* the world, the world in which men suffer and labor, despair and hope, destroy and create, die and believe. To be sure, this Absolute, when present as such, heals the fragmentation of the actual world *in which* it is present, for those *to whom* it is present, which is why its presence in and for thought may be called a mysticism of Reason.[9] But unlike so many mysticisms, this mysticism is no flight from the actual world, which takes that world as mere sham and illusion. According to Hegel, it is much rather such a flight which is a sham, compared to which

---

* Mure rightly asserts that only

a very careless reading of Hegel's Logic . . . [could] leave the impression that, because Hegel regards thought as self-developing, therefore the whole series of categories ought to flow with such strict necessity that any one who clearly grasped the first could deduce all the rest by mechanical application of a rule and *without reference to empirical thinking.* (*IH,* p.120, also p.74, italics added.)

But, it does not automatically follow that Hegel is wrong "to conceive the purity of pure thought as a complete freedom from any taint of the empirical" (*Study,* p.365.); and that

for all his perseverance in grasping the way of learning as a moment in spirit's activity, [the philosopher] . . . cannot wholly escape lapse to a lower level where it *appears* as a finite thinking, the exposition of which has to be *complemented* with an equally abstract exposition of spirit as absolute thought merely innocent of finitude. (*Study,* p. 44.)

As will be shown, Hegel's goal is a middle in which infinite Thought, although rising above finitude, yet saves this latter by overreaching it; and if Mure's conclusion is correct then his philosophy is *by its own standards* a partial if not a total failure.

steadfast existence in the actual world, even if taken as ultimately fragmented, has substance and reality. The Absolute, if accessible to thought at all, is accessible only to a thought which *remains with* the world of sense, not to a thought which shuns it in "monkish fashion."

This general conviction specifies itself in the presence, within the Hegelian system, of a *Philosophy of Nature* and a *Philosophy of Spirit*. In the transcendent-metaphysical interpretation these either vanish altogether or else figure awkwardly as a priori speculations on empirical fact. As such, they have always been widely criticized. But the critics might have noticed that their attacks on Hegel are paralleled by Hegel's attacks on his romantic contemporaries. Hegel viewed romantic speculation about nature as a fraud because he considered it an illegitimate substitute for empirical investigation.[10] Of Görres' philosophy of history he wrote: "The author apparently fails to realize that historical facts can be established only by means of critical examination of historical sources."[11] In contrast with such efforts, Hegel's own philosophies of nature and history do not replace but on the contrary presuppose not only empirical science and history but the whole reality of sensuous life as their necessary basis, even though, to be sure, the secret which *makes* them philosophies lies in their power to rise above that basis.[12]

These characteristics of Hegel's applied logic have far-reaching implications for the *Logic* itself. Hegel rejects from the outset all ultimate dualisms, such as between Reason and the actual world. And it has now emerged that his actual world—Nature and Spirit—does not reduce itself to a transcendent logical realm. Taken together, these two assertions imply that the logical realm is incomplete without the actual world, and that if it is taken by itself, it is done by virtue of an abstraction achieved by logical thought. Of that abstraction, Hegel does not hesitate to say that it is a "decision, which may also be called an arbitrary act."[13] The logical realm, then, apart from Hegel's actual world, is far indeed from being all-encompassing Reality. It is a "realm of shadows."[14]

3. *The Left-Wing Interpretation*

The collapse of the transcendent-metaphysical interpretation moves us on to its opposite—an "immanentism" which would confine the scope of Hegel's thought to the experienced world, or, more precisely, to the world as it is *humanly* experienced. Here, as before, it is the radical version which sheds most light. For it discloses that whereas the immanentist interpretation can make the most of precisely those elements in Hegel's thought which its opposite is forced to ignore or deny it pays the high price of abandoning, in principle, the fundamental goal of Hegel's entire philosophical enterprise.

In the immanentist interpretation, the world of human experience *exhausts* Reality, and it consists of the countless (though not chaotic) ways in which Nature and Spirit are related. These relations include natural science, which is the observation of natural objects by the spirit which is scientific subject, and historiography, which is the reenactment in the spirit of the historian of the spirit expressed in historical action—an action which involves Nature as well as Spirit. But the relations between Nature and Spirit are by no means exhausted by such theoretical kinds. They include also labor, which is the appropriating transformation of natural fragments by finite spirits, and the lives of states, which are spiritually constituted social wholes arising from, requiring, and partially subduing a natural base. Even religion belongs among the relations between Nature and Spirit. For it is a relation between finite spirits, limited by Nature, and an infinite Spirit which—in one form or another, depending on the religion—is Nature's source. "The experienced world," in short, has the widest possible connotation, including, in addition to the object-worlds of theoretical knowledge, what present-day continental philosophers would call the *Lebenswelt*, or what their Anglo-Saxon contemporaries might conceivably be induced to call the world of ordinary language.

All aspects of that world of experience have, *as humanly experi-*

enced, one thing in common: they are shot through with contingency, externality, factual givenness. This is true not only of natural science, which cannot eliminate the empirically given, and of historiography which, in addition, must be arbitrarily selective. It is true also of the highest and most comprehensive forms of spiritual life. Even the best of states remains dependent on the fortuitous conditions of Nature and on the fortuitous behaviour of other states.[15] Indeed, contingency would appear to remain even in the religious relationship. Thus in the highest religion—Protestant Christianity—sin appears as a groundless and hence fortuitous fall, and the Grace which redeems it, as a groundless and hence fortuitous gift.

In insisting on the reality of the humanly experienced world, the "immanentist" interpretation saves the crucial Hegelian claim that there is nonunion as well as union, and that the former, as well as the latter, is real *in the form in which it is humanly experienced.* For it would by no means satisfy Hegel's purpose to grant nonunion as a phase in a *logical* movement only, which passed through that phase only in order as such to abolish it. In the actual world nonunion persists *as* nonunion, and simply to deny it as such would be to dissipate the actual world into a realm which, while possibly beautiful, would nevertheless consist of mere shadows.*

But can *philosophic thought* remain limited by the bounds of contingent human experience? If so, it can be no more than

---

* In a passage exalting that "activity of separating . . . [which is] the Understanding, that most astonishing and greatest, or rather absolute power," Hegel writes:

Death . . . is of all things the most fearful, and to hold fast to the dead is what demands the greatest force. *Forceless beauty hates the Understanding, because it demands of it what it cannot do.* But the life of Spirit is not the kind which, shunning death, keeps itself pure from destruction. It is a life which endures death, and in death maintains its own being. It wins its truth only by finding itself in a state of absolute self-disruption. (*Phän.*, pp.29 ff. [*Phen.*, p.93], italics added.)

The passage is directed against romantic flights from reality.

finite thought, i.e., reflection on finite experience, undertaken at the standpoint of finite experience. Understood as such, the Hegelian applied logic could at best only state and justify the categories in which Nature and Spirit are experienced, thus reducing itself to a Kantian-type critique or to second-order discourse, modern style. As for the *Logic*, it would remain confined to the same task, presumably at a higher level of abstraction.

But the Hegelian philosophy has far more exalted aims than these. It incorporates reflective *restatements* of the categories of finite experience. But rising to the absolute standpoint, it *reenacts* these categories, in a thought which *alters* them in the process of reenactment.[16] Hence the *Philosophy of Nature* and the *Philosophy of Spirit* begin with empirically supplied truths, but they move at each step toward raising these truths to a higher Truth of their own. And the *Logic* is what gives them this raising power. This is because logical abstractions are not abstractions of an ordinary sort. They permeate the actual world from which logical thought has abstracted them.[17] Hence philosophic thought can extend its scope beyond logic; it need not and cannot remain in logical abstractness. It *need not* remain so because philosophical thought can confront the contingencies of the actual world and, by raising them, move to their conquest. It *cannot* remain so because not until this conquest is achieved is philosophic thought complete. Hegel has described the logical realm, taken by itself, as a "realm of shadows." He does not hesitate to refer to it, as well—in seemingly stark contradition—as "God as He was in His eternal Essence, before the creation of Nature and finite spirit."[18]

4. *The Hegelian Middle*

The immanentist interpretation of Hegel's thought, then, is as untenable as its transcendent-metaphysical opposite.[19] As a result of this double collapse, the task of entering into the authentic Hegelian middle is inescapable.

In this context, we can attempt no more than to grasp the principle of the Hegelian middle, abstaining from all efforts to enter into its details. And we shall seek to grasp it by interpreting Hegel's thought as a threefold mediation, of which each phase involves the other two. Elements of all three phases are found scattered throughout Hegel's works. But he would appear to have given a complete and systematic statement of what we shall call its logical phase only, in his *Encyclopedia of Philosophic Sciences*. That phase, if taken as exclusive of the other two, has always encouraged, though never justified, fatal misunderstandings, of which panlogism is the best-known. It will appear that these misunderstandings—or a good many of them—vanish, once due attention is given to the realistic and idealistic, as well as the logical, phases of Hegel's thought.

One Hegelian passage states the principle of the threefold mediation clearly, tersely, and completely—so much so that the whole remainder of this chapter may be devoted to its interpretation. Hegel writes:

Everything rational shows itself to be a threefold union or syllogism, in that each of the members takes the place both of one of the extremes and the mediating middle. This is especially the case with the three members of philosophical science, i.e., the logical Idea, Nature and Spirit. Here, first, Nature is the mediating member. Nature, that immediate Totality, unfolds itself into two extremes, the logical Idea and Spirit. But Spirit *is* Spirit only insofar as it is mediated by Nature. Secondly, Spirit—known by us as individual and active—is the middle, and Nature and the logical Idea are the extremes. For it is Spirit which recognizes the Idea in Nature and raises Nature to its Essence. Thirdly, the logical Idea is itself the middle. It is the absolute Substance of both Spirit and Nature, that which is universal and all-penetrating. These are the three links of the absolute syllogism or union.*

---

* *Enz.*, sect. 187 *Zus.* (*Werke*, VI, pp. 353 ff.). Additional supporting passages will be given in their proper places below, although we may here list these enlightening, but admittedly by themselves inconclusive, passages: *Enz.*, sects. 17 and 24 *Zus.* 2 (*Werke*, VI, pp. 87 ff.); *Logik*, I, pp. 55 ff. (*Logic*, I, pp. 83 ff.)

5. *The Realistic Mediation*

First, Nature mediates. This is Nature *itself*. It is by no means either a transcendent Idea of Nature or a subjective experience we may have of it. Nature, as such, may be "immediate," i.e., subject to both logical and spiritual mediation. It is, however, an "immediate *Totality*," i.e., a self-existent Whole in its own right, and it persists in such self-existence throughout all mediation. For in order to be a middle between logical Idea and Spirit, Nature, while "unfolding itself" into these "extremes," must at the same time remain distinct from them, unless these extremes are to collapse into an empty identity. "It is my body," Hegel writes, "which constitutes the middle through which I find contact with the external world."* That body, it will become evident, is essential not

---

All quotations throughout this chapter to which no references are given will refer back to this passage (*Enz.*, sect. 187 *Zus.*), which will be treated as the key passage in this chapter.

So far as I know, the interpretation along the lines of the remainder of this chapter has never been attempted, although the suggestion that something like it should be undertaken was made long ago by Karl Rosenkranz (*Hegels Leben*, pp.xix ff.), and then again by Georg Lasson, in prefaces to his editions of *Logik*, I (pp.xxvi ff.) and *Rechtsphil.* (pp.xii ff.). I hesitate to rest my exposition, following Lasson's suggestion, on the important but obscure last three sections (575–77) of *Enzyklopädie* and am confirmed by James Doull of Dalhousie University in my hesitation. Also, while agreed with Lasson that *Enzyklopädie* represents what I shall call the logical phase of the threefold mediation, I am by no means certain that the *Phenomenology* and the *Philosophy of Religion* represent fragments of the other two. For a criticism of such a role ascribed to the *Phenomenology*, see Otto Pöggeler, *Hegel-Studien* (Bonn: Bouvier, 1961), I, p.291.

* *Enz.*, sect. 410 *Zus.* (*Werke*, VII 2, pp.236 ff.) This passage deserves to be quoted in full.

One must declare as wholly empty the idea of those who think that ideally man ought to have no body at all, since it forces him to attend to his physical needs, distracts him from a purely spiritual life, and renders him unable to become truly free. Even the naively religious person is far from this hollow view. For he considers the satisfaction of his bodily needs a worthy object of prayers addressed to God, the eternal Spirit. As for philosophy, it must recognize that Spirit can be for-itself only by opposing to itself the natural, partly

only for a primitive self, barely risen above Nature; it remains indispensable even for the highest knowledge and the highest form
of selfhood, which are nothing but philosophic thought itself.

How then does Nature mediate? *Finite* spirit, at any rate, "is
spirit only insofar as it is mediated by Nature." This much is clear
from our preceding chapter, in which finite selfhood—individual
and social—was seen to be a self-making process, dependent on
Nature.[20] This dependence is total in the case of primitive selfhood
which, being a self-asserting negation of Nature, requires a persisting Nature to negate. But the dependence continues, as well,
in all higher forms of finite selfhood, even though the essential
focus here is on the relation between selves. For while all Spirit
mediates Nature no finite spirit can mediate it wholly. It is, as
finite spirit, a dialectical tension between immersion in immediate
Nature and a transcending mediation of it. But except for a
persisting immediate Nature neither of these aspects would have
substance and reality.

---

in the form of his own corporeality, partly as the external world as a whole,
and by then leading what has thus been distinguished back to union with itself, mediated through opposition and its sublation. By nature, there is a
still more intimate connection between spirit and its own body than between
it and the rest of the external world. Because of this, the immediate activity of
my soul upon my body is not finite or simply negative. I must in the first
instance maintain myself in the immediate harmony of soul and body . . . ,
must give to my body its due, look after it and keep it strong and healthy, not
treat it with contempt and hostility. It is just through neglect or even mal-
treatment that I would bring myself into a relation of dependence and of
external necessity. For I would thus make it negative and hostile toward me,
its identity with me notwithstanding, and force it into hostility and the taking
of revenge. If I follow the laws of my physical organism my soul is free
within it.

Yet the soul cannot remain with this *immediate* identity with its body.
The form of immediacy of such harmony contradicts the notion of the soul—
to be self-related ideality. To become adequate to its notion, . . . the soul
must transform its identity with its body into a mediated one, one *posited* by
spirit; it must, that is, *appropriate* its body by making it an *obedient* and *fit
instrument* for its activity, so transform it as to enable the soul to become self-
related. Thus the body becomes an accident in harmony with the substance of
the soul, which is freedom. The body constitutes the *middle* through which I
find contact with the external world as a whole . . . .

By itself, however, this relation between Nature and Spirit does not make Nature a middle, which is between *two* extremes. One of these—the logical Idea—emerges only because Hegel asserts far more than a doctrine of selfhood, understood as a self-constituting process. He asserts an idealistic doctrine of Nature. That doctrine, moreover, is not a Fichtean "idealism of the finite self," for which Nature is nonself conquerable, in infinity, by self. It is a Schellingian "idealism of the infinite self," for which Nature is the finite self's pre-self, taken by that self as other-than-self only because it is finite.[21] Unlike Fichte, Schelling requires a rise in philosophic thought to infinite selfhood. How otherwise could thought recognize Nature as pre-self, instead of taking it, as on its own terms all finite selfhood must, as other-than-self?

But this position, first approached by Schelling in 1800, gives rise to a dilemma glaringly obvious in Schelling's *My System* of 1801. Either the struggles, victories, and failures of the finite self have the meaning and reality which the finite self takes them to have, at least at one or some of the points which it is capable of reaching. But then Nature must ultimately *be* other-than-self, just as the finite self takes it to be, and the philosophic project of understanding it as pre-self is a mere wayward fancy: philosophical idealism is at most a Fichtean "idealism of the finite self," if it can be even as much. Or else philosophic thought succeeds in displaying Nature as pre-self; but then this display reduces to mere appearance Nature-as-other-than-self, and along with it all finite selfhood, which takes that appearance for reality. In Schelling's *My System* of 1801 the many-colored processes of finite realization were indeed *meant* to be preserved in the one white light of an infinite Reality. Yet in Hegel's view the Schellingian system could not live up to its intentions. The glare of its absolute light is indistinguishable from an absolute darkness—a night in which all cows are black.

In what may thus be said to amount to a conflict between Fichte and Schelling, Hegel fully and unequivocally subscribes to the

Schellingian program. His sympathies with Fichte are manifest in his dissent with the Schellingian execution. Absolute idealism must *recognize* the reality of the finite self, and hence that of the whole actual world, even while itself rising to a standpoint of infinite selfhood. And this means nothing less than that, even in recognizing Nature as pre-self, it must recognize it as other-than-self as well.

If Schelling's *My System* of 1801 could not supply this double recognition it was, in Hegel's view, because of an error not in program but execution. Schelling did not err in seeking to descend into Nature in order to reproduce it as pre-self in philosophic thought. He erred in *identifying* Nature-as-reproduced-in-thought with Nature *itself*.[22] But Nature mocks at this identification, for it is shot through with contingency, and to be so is part of its essence.

Nature thus resists an idealism which *denies* natural contingency, but it does not, according to Hegel, resist an idealism which *abstracts* from contingency. Such an idealism reproduces in thought, not Nature, but only the *structure* by which Nature is maintained. For Nature, though contingent, is not *sheer* contingency. It is a *Totality*, made so by a *structure*. That structure, moreover, can be reenacted by thought without leaving a residue. For it is internally fragmentary, and it integrates itself, as a subordinate element, into the structure of finite selfhood, which is less fragmentary, but both these structures integrate themselves into an ultimate and all-comprehensive structure which is no longer fragmentary—the structure of nothing other than the reenacting thought itself. The thought which does this reenacting accomplishes at once two ends. It recognizes Nature as other-than-self, for it abstracts from its contingency. And it displays Nature as pre-self, for it reenacts the structure by which Nature is maintained, so as to integrate it, as a subordinate element, into the structure of finite selfhood and finally its own. Such is the double task of the Hegelian *Logic*.[23]

The *Logic* accomplishes the second aspect of this task because, while reenacting categories already *manifest* in the actual world, it *alters* them in the process of reenactment, so as to remove their appearance of independence and mutual externality. As a result, the final category of the *Logic*—the absolute Idea—is not one category *besides* others, such as those manifest in the actual world; it has so altered all others as to incorporate them. And logical thought which thinks this Idea is not *besides* or over against Nature and finite selfhood; it is—in a sense—the absolute Self, which has made the whole actual world its pre-self.

However, this is true in a sense only. For if logical thought is capable of any altering appropriation of the actual world, it is only at the price of abstraction, and what it abstracts from is a contingency essential to both Nature and finite spirit. Logical thought, therefore, is forced to recognize Nature as other-than-self in the very act which displays it as pre-self; in so doing it recognizes, as well, the reality of finite selfhood, which takes Nature as other-than-self. Consequently, if the absolute logical Self supersedes existing finite selfhood, it is only at the price of an abstraction which leaves finite selfhood a persisting reality: a reality, moreover, of which logical thought itself stands in persisting need. For the abstracting and altering reenactment of the structure of the actual world (which is logical thought) is not the permanent result of a process accomplished and done with. It is the perpetually reenacted process itself. Thus logical thought displays itself as being, not a pure dwelling in a sheer infinity, related at most only accidentally to the actual world. It is a *rise to* Infinity which requires the reality of the finite in order to *be* that rise. It is not by some accident that logical thought has a human embodiment, in a self endowed with a body immersed in Nature. That body is essential for logical thought.[24]

Thus it may be said, in sum, that the dilemma with which Schelling's program of 1801 confronts Hegel is resolved if Nature itself, as it were, comes to the rescue. On the one hand, Nature "unfolds itself into two extremes" of which the one—Spirit as logical thought—reenacts the other—the logical Idea, by fragments of which Nature and finite spirit are maintained. Yet on the other hand Nature also persists *as* Nature, and *between* these extremes, by virtue of a contingency which is of its essence. Nature does not dissolve into these extremes, thus causing their collapse into an empty identity. It is the persisting middle between them. But what lives between the extremes is the full and unabridged reality of the whole actual world.

After Hegel's death, Schelling reappeared on the philosophical scene, to assail Hegel's logical realm as a mere intellectual figment.[25] Had Hegel been alive, he might simply have replied that Schelling's own philosophical descent into Nature had already revealed the logical realm. This, to be sure, Schelling had never admitted. For, first, his absolute idealism had not recognized the distinction between Nature itself and Nature as reproduced in philosophic thought, and this had led him to deny the reality of the contingent but actual world. And, second, his subsequent positive philosophy, which recognized the contingent but actual world, despaired of the whole program of absolute idealism. In Hegel's view, however, the denial of the contingent but actual world had been a mere error on Schelling's part, in no way essential to absolute idealism; hence Schelling's subsequent despair of absolute idealism was wholly unnecessary. Were Hegel alive today, he might give this exact response to Schelling's present-day existentialist heirs and successors.[26]

6. *The Idealistic Mediation*

So much, for the present, for Hegel's first mediation, which may be called realistic because its middle is a self-existent Nature. It will be seen that the realistic mediation remains indispensable. For the present, however, we must note that by itself it is fragmentary, if indeed not unintelligible, thus pointing to a larger whole to which it belongs.*

To recognize its fragmentariness one need but inquire into the relation between contingent Nature and the logical realm by which it is maintained. Either Nature after all reduces itself to the logical realm, in which case there is no mediation: logical Idea and the Spirit which reenacts it in thought collapse into an empty identity. Or else contingent Nature remains simply distinct from the logical realm, in which case the realistic mediation remains fragmentary. A dualism remains, then, between the actual world of Nature and finite spirit, and the logical realm which maintains both. Spirit, if capable at all of philosophical knowledge of the logical realm, can achieve such knowledge only by virture of a *leap*, which leaves the actual world, unmeditated, behind. Such leaps, to be sure, have been tolerated throughout the history of Western philosophy, at least from Plato on. But it is Hegel's profound conviction that for precisely that reason all such thought, until his own time, has remained in principle incomplete.[27]

But it now emerges that such consequences follow only from a dogmatic realism which, failing to distinguish between immediate Nature and Nature-as-mediated, mistakes Nature for a fixed and simply given object, known by an equally fixed *and wholly passive* subject. They vanish by virtue of an idealistic unfreezing of all such fixities. This takes hold of the decisive truth that Spirit is "individual and active," and that its activity vis-à-vis Nature is to mediate its immediacy. The total, and wholly self-conscious, grasp of that decisive truth is the life of Hegel's second, idealistic mediation.[28]

---

* As will be seen in sects. 6 and 7, the realistic mediation is complete but can be so only because Nature, while "presupposed by Spirit as independent . . . , [is also] posited" by it (*Enz.*, sect. 384), and because, while external, it is *the Idea* self-externalized (*Enz.*, sect. 274).

First and foremost, that mediation has long been in progress before philosophic thought appears on the scene, although this latter is necessary both for its completion and its full comprehension. For it is *all* Spirit, by no means Spirit in the form of philosophic thought only, which is individual and active, and it is therefore the work of all human life, as well as of infinite Thought, to mediate Nature's immediacy. In consequence, Nature, for man, is many things: one for primitive man, for whom it is both source of and threat to precarious survival; another for laboring man, for whom it is instrument of human use; yet a third for social man who subdues it to the needs of a communal whole; still a fourth for scientific man, for whom it is a system of objects observed by a subject. Wrong-headed philosophers hold that only this last-named relation is *knowledge*, on the grounds that whereas in all other relations Spirit transforms Nature, in this alone it passively apprehends it. But the privileges of scientific objectivity do not consist either of the sheer passivity of a knowing subject or of the sheer givenness of a natural object. For Spirit is individual and active in *all*—including its scientific—manifestations, and to have risen above animal existence is to have mediated Nature's immediacy. Indeed, not even the animals are wholly excluded from this idealistic wisdom, which is denied by no one except wrong-headed philosophers. For, on being confronted by natural things in their claim to immediate independence, they simply devour them.[29]

A doctrine of this kind may seem to dissipate Nature into a system of subjective experiences. Nothing is further from Hegel's thought, which is, much more than Heidegger's after him, naively realistic enough to assert a primordial openness of experience to the external world. In his view, such a wrong-headed idealism is the mere counterpart of a wrong-headed realism. The latter divorces what Nature *is* from the richly varied ways in which it is humanly *experienced*. The former, which holds fast to these experiences, must abandon a self-existent Nature only because it accepts that divorce. Both errors are undercut by a philosophy which accepts a wisdom by which nonphilosophic men live anyhow:* that human selfhood is primordially open to Nature and that, this being an *active* openness, it everywhere mediates Nature's immediacy.

This doctrine answers at least one question concerning the relation between Nature and the logical realm which maintains it. This is not a relation between two *objects*, apprehended by a passive philosophical *subject*: for there is no such subject. Logical thought may *see* Nature as maintained by the logical realm; but it is an *acting* as well as a seeing. And what is grasped by it is not a transcendent *object*, divorced from another object which depends on it. The logical realm becomes divorced from Nature, only in and for the logical thought which *abstracts* it from Nature, and even then it is no mere object. Logical thought *reenacts* what it sees enacted, and because it is pure and infinite this reenacting is not a mere reduplication of the enacted. It *alters* the fragmented structure of Nature so as to integrate it into its own unfragmented life, and in so doing it transfigures its own *reenacting seeing* into a pure activity.[30]

By itself, however, this does not cure the fatal dualism. Indeed, it but causes a shift, from an age-old and time-honored *ontological* dualism, between two worlds passively apprehended, to what may be called an *existential* dualism, between two relations of Spirit to Nature. The one remains an *immersion* in actual, i.e., contingent Nature, of a Spirit which is itself but finite and contingent. The other is a *transcendence* of Nature, by a Spirit which, while infinite, remains confined to the form of abstract logical thought. Moreover, since these two relations must be manifestations of *one* Spirit, the relation between them is an inner conflict

---

* See the passage quoted on pp.85 ff. and *Enz.*, sect. 7: "The principle of experience carries with it the infinitely important condition that in order to accept and believe any content, man must himself be present with it; more precisely, that he must find this content united with the certainty of his own self."

between finite and infinite aspects which threatens to be wholly destructive.[31]

This threat is not removed by the decisive idealistic truth that *all* Spirit actively mediates Nature, that, consequently, while infinite logical thought mediates all Nature (albeit in abstraction from its contingency) even the humblest form of finite spiritual life mediates actual, i.e., contingent Nature (albeit never more than natural fragments). Because of this truth, to be sure, the internal conflict between finite existing self and infinite thinking Self need not remain in frozen arrest. It is capable of *historical development*, and it may be said—with qualifications—that history *is* that development.* Even so, the conflict between the finite and infinite poles of selfhood seems to remain in principle unresolved, and if it remains so the idealistic remains as fragmentary as the realistic mediation, whose fragmentariness it was meant to cure.

In Hegel's view, such a cure is possible only on two conditions: *that nonphilosophical human existence is not everywhere confined to simple finiteness*, and *that philosophical thought is not doomed to remain in logical abstractness*. We have already taken note of religion, which is one manifestation of the first of these conditions, and further examination will show this to be the decisive manifestation.[32] Here we must take note of another, namely, natural science. This is necessary for an explication, however brief, of the relation between natural science and philosophy of Nature.

Natural science deals with actual Nature, inclusive of contingency. What is more, the contingent *remains* contingent, i.e., empirically given to a thought receptive of it. This thought, therefore, is a form of finite spirit, but it is not *simply* finite. For natural science deals with Nature *as a whole*, and it acquires the power of

---

* The decisive qualification is that infinite Spirit is not confined to philosophical—let alone logical—thought. We cannot here inquire into the implications of the present chapter for Hegel's philosophy of history, except simply to assert that its central problem concerns the relation between finite and infinite Spirit, complicated by the fact that the latter, though essentially transhistorical, is by no means simply indifferent to history.

so dealing with it by radically abstracting from practical interest. Natural science "lets [natural things] be," thus making Nature as a whole an observed *object*, while itself becoming an observing *subject*, i.e., theoretical thought.

Wrong-headed philosophies regard the natural object as simply given, and the theoretical subject as simply passive. In truth, however, the scientific subject-object dichotomy is an *achievement*, by a Spirit which is "self-effacing stemming of desire." And the Spirit which achieves it partakes of both finiteness and infinity. It partakes of finiteness because the Nature which *is* let be remains shot through with contingency and givenness. It partakes of infinity because what it lets be are not fragments of Nature but is Nature as a whole. Natural science, then, is not a simply finite and passive apprehension of a simply given Nature. It is an *arrested mediation*.

This truth displays itself in a double contradiction, one between scientific theory and the total spiritual existence from which it is abstracted, the other within scientific theory itself. As for the first, the theoretical letting be of natural things is contradicted by the whole of nontheoretical life which does *not* let them be, but rather "directly refutes the one-sided assumption . . . that natural things are persistent and impenetrable to us." The Nature which is object of scientific thought, and the natural fragments which are part of our *Lebenswelt* are *both* one-sided abstractions from *one* Nature, i.e., partial mediations of its immediacy.

This conclusion is reinforced by natural science, taken by itself. Qua theoretical it lets natural things be, as "beyond and alien" to itself. But qua thought it aims at their comprehension, which is a denial that they are beyond and alien. Natural science is a movement which begins with the letting be of things only to transcend this beginning and yet forever to return to it. "In thinking things we make them into universals. But the things themselves are singular. And the 'lion as such' does not exist."[33]

Nonphilosophic human life, then, is not in all its forms confined to simple finiteness. Is it the case, as well, that philosophic thought need not remain in logical abstractness? Can such thought, rather than flee in "monkish fashion" from the contingencies of the actual world, confront and conquer them? That it can do so is the deepest conviction of Hegel's philosophy, and it is systematically expressed in it insofar as it is not *Logic* only, but rather a whole composed of a *Philosophy of Nature* and a *Philosophy of Spirit* as well as of *Logic*. The *Logic*, taken by itself, *abstracts* from contingency. The total philosophy of which the *Logic* is but one phase is the *conquest* of contingency: applied logic is just that conquest.*

The two disciplines of which the applied logic is composed, then, presuppose the totality of empirical knowledge, of which natural science is an indispensable part. But they do not remain bound by the limits of their presuppositions. For, by virtue of the *Logic* of which they are applications, they *alter* the empirical material supplied to them, so as to raise it above contingency and givenness, thereby completing in philosophic thought a mediation already in part achieved throughout the length and breadth of nonphilosophic life. All human experience, and hence natural science, is a partial mediation of Nature. The *Philosophy of Nature* comes on the scene both to complete that mediation and to recognize its ultimate Truth. It accomplishes both ends by "recognizing the Idea in Nature . . . [and in this recognition] raising Nature to its Essence." The *Philosophy of Spirit* accomplishes the same end for finite spirit, raising it above finiteness by recognizing the Idea in it.**

But how can philosophic thought raise Nature to an Essence which is yet its own? Either Nature ultimately *is* contingent; but then it must escape at least in part all spiritual raising, thus reducing the raising Spirit itself to finiteness. Or else the Essence in question is Nature's own, but then natural contingency was all along a mere sham, and so was the finite spirit which took it for

---

* See appendix 1 to this chapter, pp.112 ff.
** See appendix 2 to this chapter, pp.114 ff.

reality. Nature either cannot or need not be raised to an Essence above contingency, and the idealistic mediation either remains fragmentary or else collapses into a vacuous infinity. In short, the old, nagging dilemma seems still unresolved, and on reflection this can hardly come as a surprise.

Nor can its resolution be surprising. The realistic mediation requires that Nature itself should come to the rescue. The idealistic mediation requires that Spirit itself do likewise. There is, however, a difference between these two rescue activities. The realistic mediation, if divorced from all else, remains fragmentary; by itself Nature cannot *both* remain distinct from, *and* yet unfold itself without remainder into, the two extremes of logical Idea and Spirit. The idealistic mediation, in contrast, achieves completeness, and lends the realistic mediation completeness as well. This is because *Spirit at once requires Nature, as its presupposition, and yet is required by Nature, as its presupposition.**

This fundamental assertion gives the first clue as to how the basic dilemma of the Hegelian middle will find its Hegelian resolution. Only if Spirit presupposes Nature can Nature be other-than-self, and the finite spirit which takes it as such, a reality.** Only if Nature presupposes Spirit can Spirit rise to absoluteness,

---

* *Enz.*, sects. 382, 384. As has already been asserted (p.91 n.) and will forthwith be shown, it is more correct to say that whereas the realistic mediation achieves completeness only because Nature is doubly overreached, the idealistic mediation achieves completeness because Spirit overreaches Nature: Spirit has "as it were, the sovereign ingratitude to sublate and mediate that through which it appears itself mediated [i.e., Nature], to reduce it to something persisting only through *it*, thereby making itself wholly autonomous." (*Enz.*, sect. 381 *Zus.* [*Werke*, VII 2, p.23].)

** Hegel writes:

Awakening spirit does not yet recognize its unity with the implicit spirit concealed in Nature, hence is related to Nature externally . . . Self-consciousness and consciousness here still fall apart, and Spirit, its self-containedness notwithstanding, is still with another independent of it, immediately at hand, and only presupposed by Spirit, not posited by it . . . . (*Enz.*, sect. 384 *Zus.* [*Werke*, VII 2, pp.30 ff.].)

Such manifestations of finite spirit must be preserved by the idealistic mediation *without loss*.

i.e., to the philosophic recognition of Nature as pre-self. Only if both conditions prevail at once can there be a complete mediation of any kind—realistic or idealistic—which at once saves without loss the contingent and finite world, and yet raises it to a Truth above contingency and finiteness.

But how *can* both these conditions prevail at once? Only by virtue of a seemingly unmitigated paradox. Nature must remain other-than-Spirit, so radically so as to reduce Spirit itself to the ultimate in finiteness, which is death, and yet it must be so wholly included in Spirit as to manifest the supremacy of spiritual power in the very death of Spirit. Hegel writes: "The life of Spirit is not the kind which, shunning death, keeps itself pure from destruction. It is a life which endures death, and in death maintains its own being. It wins its truth only by finding itself in a state of absolute self-disruption."[34]

Hegel calls this double power, ascribed to Spirit, the power of overreaching.[35] * "Overreaching" is perhaps Hegel's most important term, and the presence of overreaching power in Spirit may be called without exaggeration *the* decisive condition of the possibility of the complete philosophic thought. For just as Spirit must overreach Nature unless it is either to reduce itself to concrete but finite spirit or to dissipate itself into an infinite but empty Spirit, so the complete philosophic thought—which is the culminating form of Spirit—must overreach all reality, unless it is either to reduce itself to merely finite thought limited by the actual world or else to dissipate itself into an infinite Thought which, while imagining itself as encompassing the actual world, is a mere flight from it. To *conquer* the actual world, philosophic thought must, first, recognize its reality, and it can do so only by itself assuming a finite, i.e., human, embodiment. It must, secondly, rise above that embodiment, so as to raise to infinity both the human thinker

* The present abstract assertion of overreaching power will emerge as a concrete reality in life in ch. 5, sects. 8 and 9, and as a philosophical comprehension of that reality in ch. 6, sects. 4 and 5.

and his actual world. And it must, finally, in this very act of raising affirm and reconstitute the persistent reality of both the unraised actual world and the humanity of the thinker. Hegel rejects, as mere escapism, all attempts to deny the struggle between the finite and infinite poles of selfhood: both the escape into an empty mysticism of a simply infinite Thought, and the escape into a simply finite thought supposedly devoid of all transcendence. If nevertheless he does not remain with a self-destructive struggle, it is because the infinite overreaches the finite pole. The concrete philosophic thought is the perpetually reenacted raising of the finite to the infinite which, while raising the finite without remainder, must yet in so doing affirm its persistence *as* finite, lest its own activity of raising reduce itself to a mere lifeless transcendence. According to Hegel, philosophy is the Sunday of life.[36] * But there can be no Sunday unless, first, the workaday week is a reality; and unless secondly, instead of there being a meaningless alternation between work and rest, Sunday is the meaning and truth of the whole.

7. *The Logical Mediation*

But in order for the idealistic mediation itself to be possible there is need for yet a third, logical mediation, in which "the logical Idea is itself the middle . . . , the absolute Substance of both Spirit and Nature, that which is universal and all-penetrating." As has been said, this mediation alone Hegel gives in systematic completeness, in the *Encyclopedia of Philosophic Sciences.* Our pres-

---

* It is significant that Hegel also writes—with obvious approval—that "all peoples knew . . . that religion is the source of their dignity and the Sunday of their lives (*Werke*, XI, p.5 [*Phil. Rel.*, I, p.3].); and also that philosophy "unites these two aspects: the Sunday of life, on which man humbly renounces himself, and the workaday week, during which man stands on his own feet, is master and acts according to his interests." (*JE*, XVII, pp.125 ff., *HL*, p.2301; also *Einl. Gesch. Phil.*, p.220.) The last-cited of these passages appears to be most important, and to express most admirably Hegel's ultimate intentions, and we shall return to it for fuller treatment. (Ch. 6, sect. 1.)

ent purpose cannot be to reproduce it completely, or even in general outline, but merely to understand the logical mediation in its relation to the other two. That purpose is best accomplished by showing that it is already implicit in these two, as the condition of their togetherness.

We begin with a review of the main tensions between the realistic and idealistic mediations. First, Spirit must presuppose Nature, if finite spirit is to have reality, but Nature must also presuppose Spirit, if Spirit is to be able to rise to absolute philosophic thought. Secondly, the logical realm must *be*, independently at any rate of *our* thought, if the Nature which is maintained by it is to have self-existence; yet it cannot be a transcendent object, over against a passive thinking subject. Thirdly, contingent Nature must remain contingent, unless Idea and Spirit, rather than linked by it, are to collapse into an empty identity; yet philosophic thought must be able to raise it to an Essence above contingency, unless such thought is either to be finite or else a flight from reality. It has emerged that the Hegelian middle *requires* all these antithetical realities, but also that it will break asunder if these *remain* antithetical. As thus far understood, the Hegelian middle depends entirely on the claim that Spirit has overreaching power—a power which in turn makes possible the overreaching power of philosophic thought.

But a closer look now reveals that this claim on behalf of Spirit requires a corresponding claim on behalf of the Idea. Spirit and Idea must *both* have overreaching power, and the ultimate question to be asked of the Hegelian system will concern the relation between these two powers.

Consider, first and in isolation, the logical realm. If Nature, which is maintained by that realm, is to have self-existence apart from Spirit, that realm must *be*, apart from logical thought, which merely *sees* it. Logical movement, therefore, is not a movement of thinking only, which moves mere ideas which are inert apart from it. The Idea *itself* must move, while logical thought, as it were, simply looks on. This much the realistic mediation requires. The idealistic mediation requires that there be no passive subject, apprehending an external and transcendent object, but rather a self-activity so pure as to allow nothing external to it, and hence no object. How then can logical thought be at once a pure realistic surrender to the movement of the Idea, and a pure idealistic self-activity? This is possible, we now learn, only *if the surrender of our thought to the movement of the Idea is the self-movement of the Idea in us: if our logical thought is that self-movement.*[37] *

The Idea, then, must have at least *some* overreaching power: it must have the power to overreach that Spirit which is logical thought. Because the logical realm, in isolation, can overreach logical thought only, which latter is abstracted from the actual world, it is itself abstract, a "realm of shadows." But because it is the Idea which moves logical thought, not logical thought which moves it, it is at the same time "God . . . before the creation of Nature and finite spirit."[38]

Consider, next, the relation between the actual world and the Spirit which, being the *complete* philosophic thought, is to be its *conquest*. The actual world must remain as contingent if, as both the realistic and the idealistic mediations require, Spirit presupposes Nature. But it must also be raised above contingency if, as the idealistic mediation requires, Spirit is to overreach Nature, and indeed, the complete spiritual overreaching of the whole actual world *is* the complete philosophic thought. But how can philosophic thought *both* recognize *and* conquer the actual world? It may well seem that such thought must either reduce itself to finite thought or to an empty infinity: that the complete philosophic thought aimed at by Hegel is impossible.

The question may also be put as follows. As philosophic thought

* Hegel writes of logical thought that "it should no longer be called consciousness. For that includes opposition between Ego and its object, which is not present in that original activity" (*Logik*, I, p.45 [*Logic*, I, p.74].), and he criticizes the Kantian-Fichtean philosophy for remaining limited to the standpoint of consciousness. (*Enz.*, sect. 415.)

turns from the logical realm to Nature it must, to achieve *applicability*, take a *leap*, from infinite self-activity to finite acceptance of the given. But if it is to be applied *logic*, this leap cannot *remain* a leap. If no leap is made, all philosophic thought is logic; and if the leap remains a leap, philosophic thought becomes natural science after having made it. In either case the philosophic conquest of Nature which is philosophy of nature is impossible. It *is* possible, according to Hegel, only if the Idea overreaches far more than the logical thought which reenacts it: if it overreaches nothing less than Nature *itself*.

For Hegel's purpose, it would not be enough, as for some philosophers it might, if Nature were a tension *between* the Idea and its radical Other—an externality which is the ultimate source of all contingency everywhere.* This, to be sure, would go considerably beyond a dualism between Nature and the logical realm which maintains it, making Nature a system of stages with increasing logical penetration, and yet qua Nature bound to the limits of its external pole. But it would allow the external pole at once too much scope and too little. If Nature were a tension between two mutually external poles how, in the realistic mediation, could it *wholly* unfold itself into Idea and Spirit? How, in the idealistic mediation, could it be raised to its Essence *without remainder*? To

---

* From Hegel's point of view, one might thus characterize A. N. Whitehead's *Process and Reality*. Doubtless Hegel would consider Whitehead's modern Platonism as both anachronistic and inferior to the original Platonism. If Platonism remains with dualism, it is because it safeguards the infinity of the Idea, as well as that of the speculative thought which rises to it. (See ch. 6, sect. 2[a].) Whitehead overcomes dualism only at the price of destroying the infinity of both the Idea and speculative thought. For if "physical" and "mental" poles belong to any and every process, and are mutually both dependent and irreducible, then (i) the Divine reduces itself to finitude—according to Hegel, an anachronism since the rise of Christianity; and (ii) speculative thought, like all other mental activity, remains limited by a physical pole—a condition destructive of its speculative aspirations. To be sure, Whitehead explicitly defines speculative thought as a mere expansion of scientific—i.e., finite—thought. But Hegel would charge any such definition with incoherence, and indeed would criticize it at his extreme as radically as positivists criticize it at the opposite extreme.

make both these mediations possible the Idea, first, must be the "Substance'" which wholly "penetrates" Nature; secondly, it must so penetrate it as to preserve the externality without which Nature would not *be* Nature; and thirdly, it must—because it *is* that penetration, not a Substance which *is* independently of what it *does*—itself assume the form of externality. In religious or quasi-religious language, this is expressed in the contradictory terms that Nature is at once a divine creation and yet constituted by a fall.[39] In the language of a purely philosophic thought, one must say that Nature is "the Idea in the form of externality,"[40] the form into which the Idea "freely releases itself."[41] *

Here, at last, is the missing condition, long looked for, of both a complete realistic and a complete idealistic mediation. Only if Nature is external and yet *the Idea* externalized can it at once keep apart Idea and Spirit and yet wholly unfold itself into them. Only then, too, can it at once *require* being raised to its Essence and be *capable* of being raised, without remainder. Such raising, fragmentarily and haphazardly accomplished by all Spirit everywhere, is accomplished wholly by the Spirit which is philosophy of Nature. For whereas *Nature* is the externalized Idea, *philosophy* of Nature is the *recognition* of Nature as the externalized Idea; but while Nature is external the recognition of its Truth is not. Hegel asserts that Spirit, as such, is the Truth to which Nature itself points. The *complete* Truth of Nature is the Spirit which recognizes the Idea in it.**

---

* These are, of course, among the most famous, or notorious, Hegelian statements. Utterly unintelligible to both right- and left-wing interpretations, they become intelligible only if one enters into the Hegelian middle and understands the Hegelian system as a threefold mediation.

** Hegel asserts that "Nature turns into its Truth, . . . Spirit." (*Enz.*, sect. 376.) He also asserts that

philosophy of Nature *teaches us* how Nature sublates its externality by degrees [i.e., turns into its Truth]; how already matter through gravity refutes the independence of isolated multiplicities; and how this refutation, begun in gravity and even more in light (which is inseparable and simple) is com-

Such recognition is possible, however, only on the decisive additional condition that the Idea overreaches Spirit as well as Nature,
i.e., *all* Spirit, by no means the Spirit which is philosophical
thought alone. For if finite spirit were *our* spirit *only*, then Nature
might well be the Idea externalized; we on our part should be in
principle incapable of recognizing it as such. Our finite spiritual
existence would mediate actual Nature, but fragments only, of a
Nature which as a whole would remain external and other-than-
self. And our infinite philosophic Thought would remain confined
to logic, recognizing the Idea in logical abstractness; it could not
recognize its concrete embodiment *in* Nature. Such a recognition
is possible only if the Idea overreaches *all* Spirit, as well as all
Nature: if it is the "Substance" which "penetrates" both.

But if Nature and Spirit are both to remain what they are, these
two penetrations must differ in kind. Nature is externality. Even
the humblest form of finite spirit to a degree transcends natural
externality. Hence in order to preserve finite Spirit in overreaching
it the Idea must, as it were, move finite spirit in the same direction
in which finite spirit moves itself, even though it supersedes its
finite goals. Finite spirit takes itself as a fragmentary conquest of
a Nature which, qua unconquered, remains simply external and
other-than-self. It is in truth a phase in the Idea's return-to-self,
from a Nature which is its self-externalization.*

---

pleted in animal life . . . . (*Enz.*, sect. 389 *Zus.* [*Werke*, VII 2, pp.51 ff.];
italics added.)

As the remainder of this section seeks to show, it is crucially important to distinguish between Nature *itself*, which persists in its untruth even while turning into its Truth, and *philosophy* of Nature which, being the Spirit into which
Nature ultimately has turned as its Truth, is the total conquest of natural
untruth.

* For the notion of Spirit, as this having-returned, see *Enz.*, sect. 381.
However,

immediately, Spirit has not yet comprehended its Notion. While *being*
rational knowledge, it does not yet *recognize* itself as such . . . . To reach such
recognition, Spirit must free the object, in itself rational, of the form of contingency, isolation, and externality which in the first instance attaches to it,

This truth remains hidden from finite spirit because it is finite. It does not remain hidden from all Spirit because, in philosophic thought, Spirit rises to infinity. The Spirit which recognizes the overreaching power of the Idea must itself be overreached by it. But because it recognizes itself as thus overreached, it is no mere phase in the return of the Idea from otherness. It is the *complete having-returned*. Such a recognition is not *of* the Idea *by* thought. *It is the self-recognition of the Idea in thought.*[42] We saw above that logical thought, taken by itself, is the self-movement of the Idea, in a thought abstracted from the actual world. It has now emerged that the *complete* philosophical thought, which includes philosophy of Nature and philosophy of Spirit as well as logic, is a total conquest of the actual world—its transfiguration into an infinite spiritual life. And it can be this conquest only because it is the return-to-self of the Idea, from self-externalization in Nature.

That conquest is not a final dissipation of the actual world. Hegel writes: "Nature is too impotent to exhibit . . . the logical forms in their clarity."[43] This impotence, which is of a strange sort, is the dynamic union of two powers. One is the natural power to point, as to its Truth, to Spirit and in the end to philosophical Spirit, and this permits the rise to an all-transfiguring philosophic thought. The other is the power to *persist as* Nature, i.e., in natural untruth, and this lends persistent reality to the whole actual world. Only because these two powers combine their forces can philosophical thought be an actual conquest of the actual world, not a pseudo-conquest, which is a mere flight from it. For the spiritual life which

---

and in this way make itself free in relation to what is other than it. The *finiteness of spirit* belongs into this road toward liberation . . . . But the finiteness of spirit must not be regarded as being absolutely fixed, but rather as a form of spirit which, despite this form, is infinite in essence. Herein lies that finite spirit is an immediate contradiction, an untruth, as well as the process of overcoming this untruth. This struggle with finitude and the overcoming of limitation is the manifestation of Divinity in the human spirit. It is a necessary stage of eternal Spirit. (*Enz.*, sect. 441 *Zus.* [*Werke*, VII 2, pp.292 ff.].)

is philosophic thought is not a sheer infinity unsullied by finiteness. It is a laboring *rise to* infinity and a having-risen which, in order itself to have substance and reality, requires the reality of the world which is the object of its labor. In the complete philosophic thought the Idea manifests itself as a divine play. But this play has reality only because it *includes* the whole pain and labor of human life. The philosophical Sunday is no other-worldly joy, indifferent to the grief of this world, against which indifference the unredeemed world would rise as an unconquered witness and accuser. It is a this-worldly joy, which can *be* joy only because its very life is the conquest of the world's grief.

8. *The Hegelian Middle and Its Crucial Assumption*

This completes our account of the three phases of Hegel's threefold mediation. It remains for us to display it as a middle which, as we put it above, combines a pluralistic openness as hospitable to the varieties of contingent experience as any empiricism with a monistic comprehensiveness more radical in its claims than any other speculative rationalism. It also remains for us to identify one indispensable assumption of that middle, as well as to ask whether —and if so, why and how—Hegel's thought, by its own terms, is entitled to that assumption. This will turn out to be *the* decisive question to be asked of the whole Hegelian philosophy.

First, if understood as one threefold mediation Hegel's thought maintains itself against all threats from the right. If taken in isolation, the logical mediation may seem to involve an initial sheer leap into a pure and infinite logical realm, which loses all contact with the finite thinker and his finite but actual world, and as thought turns from pure into applied logic it may seem to indulge in a priori deductions which never regain the contact initially lost. This interpretation, anyhow made implausible by the texts, is wholly ruled out once the logical mediation is placed into the context of a three-phased whole. For within that whole Nature

persists in its natural immediacy even while unfolding itself into
Idea and Spirit, and Spirit persists as fragmented by Nature into
finitude even while raising Nature to its Essence and itself to
infinity. Within such a whole, human thought cannot reach pure
logical infinity by means of a leap which simply *denies* the reality
of the finite and contingent, as well as its own humanity. It can
only *rise to* infinity, recognizing the reality of the finite in the very
act of rising, and it can only *achieve* purity, recognizing the reality
of the contingent in the very act of abstraction which achieves
such purity. Again, if pure is to become applied logic it must
become capable of having applications, and it can become so only
by reencountering the contingent from which logical thought has
abstracted, and by reimmersion in the finite above which logical
thought has risen. This encounter and immersion, to be sure, result
not in a surrender to the contingent and the finite but rather in
their conquest. But if this is to be an actual conquest it requires
the persistent reality of what is conquered by it. For this conquest
is a "result" which is nothing but the perpetually reenacted "process" of conquering. The Hegelian middle, then, is far indeed from
the right-wing extreme of a speculative pantheism which would
deny the reality of the finite and contingent. It not only recognizes
that reality, *besides* the life of speculative thought. Possibly alone
among all speculative philosophies, the Hegelian requires the
finite and contingent as an essential element in the life of speculative thought itself.*

The Hegelian middle equally maintains itself against all threats
from the left. No doubt it is possible to reduce the Hegelian Idea
to mere human ideas, and to alter Hegel's thought in the light of
this reduction. But it is not possible to do so in a manner which
would reject the logical phase in Hegel's threefold mediation and

* Henrich's article, cited in appendix 2 to this chapter (p.115), makes
the not unrelated point that Hegel, far from denying the reality of contingency, attempts, alone among speculative philosophers, to demonstrate its
necessity.

retain the others unimpaired. For in Hegel's threefold mediation Nature unfolds itself into Idea and Spirit even while persisting in natural immediacy, and Spirit raises both Nature and itself to infinity even while persisting as fragmented into finitude. But if the Hegelian Idea reduces itself to mere human ideas then neither Nature nor Spirit can continue to perform such functions. To reject one phase of Hegel's threefold mediation is thus to shatter all into fragments. But against such a fragmentation the Hegelian middle maintains itself as both internally complete and all-comprehensive: hence as radically immune to external assault.

But this self-maintenance against both extremes rests on one fundamental assumption, which, already stated, must now come under explicit scrutiny. *Nature, and hence the whole contingent but actual world, is* doubly *overreached, by Spirit and Idea.* Spirit overreaches the actual world by raising Nature above naturalness and Spirit above finiteness. The Idea overreaches it by self-externalization in Nature and return-to-self through finite spirit. Only *if* the actual world is thus doubly overreached can there be that middle which is philosophic thought. For such thought is, in the final analysis, the *identity of Idea and Spirit*, and yet it is not a *sheer* identity which simply *excludes* nonidentity. It is a *having-grown-into identity*, of an Idea which can be a having-returned-to-self only after self-externalization in Nature and after the process-of-return-to-self in finite spirit, and a Spirit which can be infinite Thought only after the conquest of that finiteness which is real not only in Nature but also in Spirit insofar as it is *not* infinite Thought.[44] Nor is this having-grown-into identity a result which, achieved once and for all, renders unreal the process which has led to it. The result *is* the process—its perpetual reenactment. And the human thinker who qua thinker participates in it must remain human to be capable of such participation. The thought which transfigures his human life requires the persisting and untransfigured reality of that life if it is itself to be a life, not the end of *all* life.

But how can Hegel assert *that* the actual world is doubly overreached by Idea and Spirit, and that philosophical thought is their having-grown-into identity? As thus far expounded, this appears as a mere *assumption*, which, unless it can be philosophically *demonstrated*, allows and indeed invites rejection. We have called this the decisive question to be asked of the whole Hegelian philosophy.

But one must be sure not to misstate the question. Without doubt Hegel's overreaching Spirit and his overreaching Idea stand in a relation of mutual confirmation. The assertion that the actual world is overreached by Spirit rests on the assumption that it is overreached by the Idea; and the assertion that it is overreached by the Idea rests on the assumption that the Spirit which recognizes this truth is not a finite spirit external to and limited by the actual world but itself infinite Spirit overreaching it. Positivistic critics will be quick to point out that this makes Hegelian thought a self-enclosed system, which can afford to be radically open to all empirical facts and all contingent experience only because, while they are allowed to confirm the system, they are systematically forbidden to refute it.* In the minds of positivistic critics, to point out this circularity is in itself enough to reject the whole Hegelian

---

* Hegel writes: "The impotence of Nature sets limits to philosophy." (*Enz.*, sect. 250.) What are these limits? Not that philosophy, to remain infinite Thought, must remain indifferent to natural fact (and for that reason empirically both unconfirmable and irrefutable); nor that, limited by Nature as its external other, it is reduced to finite thought (hence empirically both confirmable and refutable). It has become amply evident that both these limitations are ruled out by Hegel's conceptions of Nature, natural impotence and philosophy. The true limitation admitted and indeed insisted on by Hegel is that philosophical thought cannot at once *both raise* Nature to its Essence *and still confront* Nature in its unraised condition. This latter confronting, to be sure, is part of the process of raising Nature (of which process natural science is possibly the most notable, but by no means the sole, manifestation); however, it *remains* a confronting only so long as the process is *arrested*, and it is a confronting no longer in the *complete* result of the process which is its Truth. This result is *philosophy* of Nature, and its relation to the empirical is that it finds selective confirmation in it but that the empirical, when it fails to confirm it, constitutes, not a refutation of philosophy but rather a manifestation of natural impotence. If the exposition just given is correct, then Hegelian philosophy is unable to fulfill Herr Krug's famous request to deduce his writing pen (*Werke*, XVI, pp.50 ff.; *Enz.*, sect. 250.), and yet is in no way confounded by this inability.

enterprise, as in principle unacceptable and indeed a gigantic blunder.

But this is to judge the Hegelian philosophy in the light of external standards which, moreover, it explicitly repudiates. In Hegel's view, *scientific* thought—the Understanding—requires external empirical confirmation and allows external empirical refutation, for it is finite. In contrast, *philosophical* thought is infinite, and the *complete* philosophical thought has internalized all external verification and is incapable of external refutation. Positivistic criticism makes no effort to come to grips with the Hegelian position. It merely rejects it. Here as elsewhere positivism ignores a philosophy which might well challenge it, indulging instead in the solitary airing of its own dogmas.

The question to be asked of the Hegelian system is not whether it satisfies external standards. It is whether it satisfies its own. Is it entitled to the assumptions, mutually confirming, of an overreaching Idea and an overreaching Spirit, growing into identity in philosophic thought? Only if it can convert these assumptions into a demonstration. Such a demonstration, however, cannot be given by a thought which stands *over against* the total reality which is *not* thought and in this stance merely *asserts* its overreaching power. Against such an assertion life would protest too loudly, and the protest would fall outside the asserting thought. Falling outside, it would reduce the philosophic claim to a mere dogma, which, while irrefutable, is also indemonstrable. Protests of this kind were to be made by the varieties of existential philosophy, and unlike positivist criticism, these are not external and irrelevant to the Hegelian philosophy.[45]

Such protests can be met only if the dualism between nonphilosophic life and philosophic thought is the last of all the false dualisms; that is, if the having-grown-into-identity of an overreaching Spirit and an overreaching Idea is not a philosophic assertion over against a nonphilosophic life, itself wholly devoid of such identity, but rather a reality already *present in life* before philosophy comes

upon the scene to *convert it into thought*. And philosophy will be
a *demonstration* of its central claim only if, on the one hand, this
conversion comprehends wholly and without loss the reality of
nonphilosophical life and if, on the other, it shows itself to be a
conversion which life itself requires.

Such is in fact Hegel's position. In his view philosophy in the
ancient world was bound to a crucial limit. It could grasp the
Necessary and the Infinite. But it could only ignore the contingent
and the finite. This was because the ancient world was pagan. The
modern world, however, has long been Christian. Here the Infinite
and Divine has manifested itself in the finite and human, so as at
once to preserve its finite humanity and yet to raise it above it.
This modern world, then, *already is* doubly overreached, by a creating, preserving, and redeeming God and by a Spirit which,
manifest in man, accepts itself as created, preserved, and redeemed, and in the Christian world, there already is a divine-
human identity in the midst of persisting discord. This is the decisive condition without which modern philosophy could not break
through the limits of ancient philosophy, in order to overreach in
thought the contingencies of the actual world already overreached
in life.*

The problem of the Hegelian middle thus turns into the problem
of the relation between religious life and philosophic thought. In
a previous chapter devoted to the *Phenomenology*, we saw that
Hegel must adopt the standpoint of absolute thought in order to

---

* For the contrast between pagan and Christian philosophy, see perhaps
most succinctly, *Werke*, XIII, pp.118–27 (*Hist. Phil.*, I, pp.101–110). See
also, e.g., *Enz.*, sect. 384:

The word Spirit and its representation have been discovered in an early age.
It is the content of the Christian religion to make God known as Spirit. To
grasp what is here *given* to representation, and what is *in itself* the Essence,
in its own element, namely, the Notion—that is the task of philosophy. And
philosophy has not completed its task truly and immanently so long as the
Notion and Freedom are not its object and its soul.

The contrast between pagan and Christian philosophy is dealt with more
fully below, ch. 6, sect. 2.

hand the individual the "ladder" to it. In the present chapter, devoted to the *Encyclopedia*, we have seen that Hegelian thought can be a middle overreaching the actual world only on the assumption that it has overreaching power. Hegel's "appearing science" and his "science proper" must both fail to *demonstrate* their crucial assumption unless the final dualism can be disposed of: between the totality of nonphilosophic life and the philosophic thought which is to comprehend it. Hegel asserts, with unwavering insistence, that Christianity is the absolutely true content, and that his philosophy both can and must give that content its absolutely true form. Our sole remaining task is to examine that assertion.[46]

Appendix 1

Natural Science and Philosophy of Nature

(See p.96.)

In this book we cannot expound in detail Hegel's view concerning the relation between philosophy of Nature and natural science. The subject is of great complexity, and only a brief outline can here be given. Schelling wavers between three alternative doctrines, of which only one would grant empirical science a status in principle independent of philosophy of Nature. (This subject will be dealt with in "The God Within.") Hegel agrees that philosophy of nature supersedes natural science but unequivocally grants this latter independent status. (At least in his mature thought, any wavering on this point is against his better judgment.) Natural science has autonomous methods and purposes, even though philosophy "raises" both natural science and Nature itself. As this whole chapter seeks to show, this doctrine is essential to Hegel's entire philosophy, and it is certainly the crucial difference between the Hegelian and Schellingian philosophies of Nature.

How then do the two disciplines differ? Not as perception and thought, for both are forms of thought. (*Werke*, VII 1, p.6.) The difference is between finite and infinite Thought. The possibility of, and need for, both types of thought is grounded in Nature itself, by which Spirit "is attracted because sensing itself in it, and yet repelled as by something alien in which it does not find itself" (*Ibid.*, p.7) —and which yet is a reality "raised" by Spirit to a transnatural Truth.

The finite thought of natural science consists of universal hypotheses that are subject to empirical confirmation, and that are valid—since this thought is finite and hence the empirical is a datum for it—only if they explain all relevant data. In contrast, the infinite Thought of philosophy of Nature moves toward the dissipation of fixed givenness, by means of the discovery of *stages* in Nature, a discovery which in the end leads this thought beyond Nature as a whole. In this dissolving movement some data, no longer *mere* data, confirm the movement, while others, failing to confirm it, are left aside. Far from refuting philosophy of Nature, these latter data illustrate the need for it, being instances of that "impotence of Nature" which imposes on philosophy the task of raising Nature to its Essence. "Philosophy has no cause to be uneasy if it fails to explain all phenomena." (*Enz.*, sect. 270 *Zus.* [*Werke*, VII 1, p.124]. On the above doctrines, cf. also e.g., *Enz.*, sect. 246 and *Zus.*, 247 *Zus.*, 254 *Zus.*, 286 *Zus.*, 326 *Zus.* [*Werke*, VII 1, pp.11 ff., 24 ff., 45 ff., 172, 364].)

The Hegelian *distinction* between natural science and philosophy of Nature is thus fairly clear. The main difficulties concern their *relation*, both in principle and in detail. For, on the one hand, philosophy of Nature is not bound by the conclusions of natural science; yet on the other hand it is required to make selective use of them. Regardless of the state of science at a given time, it can "raise Nature to its Essence." Yet the use of scientific conclusions is part of the raising process. Among the many problems this raises is whether Hegel can steer between the Scylla of illegitimate philosophic interference in intra-scientific disputes, and the Charybdis of philosophic eternalization of purely temporary, and soon-to-be-outmoded, scientific conclusions. There is an obvious danger of the first, and the danger is the greater the higher the stages of Nature in question. (Hegel is able to say flatly that "life can only be grasped speculatively," *Enz.*, sect. 337 *Zus.* [*Werke*, VII 1, p.425].) Yet it would appear—and this is ironical, in view of positivistic criticisms heaped on Hegel—that he falls prey far more frequently to the second danger, especially in his treatment of the lower stages of Nature.

The whole question—concerning both Hegel's principles and his practice—can be adequately treated only in a far more thorough and de-
tailed study of the subject than has ever been attempted.

Hegel's understanding of his own doctrine in historical terms may be
summed up as follows. Modern is superior to ancient philosophy in that
it extends full recognition to empirical fact, thus emancipating natural
science from philosophy. (On Aristotle, see *Werke*, XIV, pp.441 ff.
[*Hist. Phil.*, II, pp.296 ff.]; on Bacon, see *Werke*, XV, pp.258 ff.
[*Hist. Phil.*, III, pp.175 ff.]; see also below, ch. 6, sects. 2[a] and [c].)
But it is the task of the final modern philosophy (i.e., Hegel's own) to
reunite philosophy and natural science in an overreaching union which
yet is not reactionary but rather does justice to, and preserves, modern—
i.e., emancipated—natural science.

Appendix 2

Contingency

(See p.96.)

Although the subject of contingency runs through this entire chapter,
a few brief remarks specifically on that subject should here be made.

First and above all, the contingent, defined as the externally related
"whose presence or absence does not produce disturbance or alteration in other things" (*Werke*, XII, p.468 [*Phil. Rel.*, III, p.271].) is
real in both Nature and Spirit—at any rate, in *finite* spirit. It is real in
Nature where, e.g., "the species of animals are subject to chance."
(*Enz.*, sect. 370 *Zus.* [*Werke*, VII 1, pp.653 ff.].) It is real in finite
spirit which is shot through with irrationality and license (See Iljin,
p.246, for a good summary.), and this includes not only individual men
but also history as a whole. (*Werke*, IX, pp.45 ff. [*Phil. Hist.*, pp.36 ff.].)
In all these cases, contingency or chance is real, not mere appearance,
if by appearance is meant "a mere subjective idea which must be removed in order that we may get at the truth." (*Enz.*, sect. 145 *Zus.*
[*Werke*, VI, pp.290 ff.]—a good summary of Hegel's entire doctrine of
contingency.) One must go so far as to say that were it not for the fact
that contingency receives its due there would be, for Hegel, no actual
world at all.

Second (and this is already obvious), rather than deny contingency by means of fanciful constructions, philosophy must recognize its reality. What is not immediately obvious is that, on the one hand, such recognition is intrinsic to philosophic thought, and that, on the other hand, far from reducing philosophic to a form of finite thought, it leads philosophy on toward both the vindication of its own infinity and the conquest of contingency. That the togetherness of this recognition and this conquest is not impossible may be seen at least in the relation between a truly free will and a merely contingent will (*Willkür*). (i) The free differs from the contingent will; (ii) it contains within itself, as conquered, the contingent will; and (iii), since it *is* that conquest, it requires the reality of the contingent will if it is itself to be real. (*Enz.*, sect. 145 *Zus.* [*Werke*, VI, p.289].)

But, third, more than random illustrations or analogies are needed if philosophic thought is both to stand in *inherent* need of recognizing the contingent and yet—regardless of the manifestations of the contingent— to be capable of its conquest. What is needed is provided in the *Logic*, which furnishes the *category* of contingency, as itself *necessary*. The implications of Hegel's logical doctrine of contingency are admirably stated by Dieter Henrich, "Hegels Theorie über den Zufall," *Kant-Studien*, 50 (1958–59), p.135:

Necessity posits its own conditions, but it posits them as contingent. An actuality proves itself to be necessary just in this, that it emerges from any and every set of conditions. Hence the conditions posited for itself by such a necessity are random and arbitrary . . . . Necessity can be indifferent to what particular things perish in it precisely because it is certain before they are posited that they cannot resist it . . . . Only if there is something absolutely contingent is necessity thinkable. What does the conditioning and determining is, in relation to the necessary, absolutely contingent precisely because contingency is necessary for it. It is by no means the case that everything contingent disappears in a necessary process in which nothing, not even the most insignificant, can be other than it is. According to Hegel's theory contingency itself is necessary without qualifications. On account of the necessity of the Notion there must be contingency in the world.

CHAPTER FIVE

The Religious Basis
of the Absolute Philosophy

Religion . . . contains essentially the
relation of man to God.

Werke, XII, p.507 (*Phil. Rel.*, III, p.317).*

Faith already has the true content.
What is still lacking in it is the form of thought.

Werke, XII, p.353 (*Phil. Rel.*, III, p.148).

Religion can exist without philosophy.
But philosophy cannot exist without religion.
For it encompasses religion.

Enz., second preface (*Werke*, VI, pp.xxi ff.).

1. *Introduction*

Hegel writes: "Religion can exist without philosophy. But philosophy cannot exist without religion. For it encompasses religion."[1] The present chapter will examine the first of these assertions; the one to follow, the second. More specifically, we will first describe the Christian religion as, according to Hegel, it "exists without philosophy," for Hegel asserts that it is presupposed by his own philosophy with which, indeed, it is said to be identical in essential** content. And then we shall examine how Hegel's philosophy, while presupposing Christianity, yet turns against it *as* presup-

---

* Abbreviations are listed on pp.245 ff.
** The Hegelian philosophy as a whole—as distinct from the *Philosophy of Religion*—reconciles the content of the true religious faith with the remainder of man's *Weltanschauung*, see ch 6, sect. 6.

position by so transfiguring its form as to encompass its content.

Such a two-phased account, suggested in any case by the passages just quoted and the doctrine just indicated, is vital as well to our overall purpose. In the preceding chapters, we have argued that neither the *Phenomenology of Spirit* nor the *Encyclopedia of Philosophical Sciences* can reach their respective goals unless religion (or more precisely the Christian or "absolute" religion) emerges as an infinite Life to mediate between finite life (and the finite thought which is part of it) and infinite Thought: not the one because finite standpoints of life falling outside the standpoint of infinite Thought would destroy its claims to absoluteness; not the other because infinite Thought would either dissipate the reality of the actual world (thus becoming a "night in which all cows are black"), or else recognize the actual world at the price of its own reduction to finitude. But whether or not religion (or the Christian religion) can in fact *be* the necessary bridge requires two separate investigations, of which the first inquires how it "exists without philosophy," i.e., *in the religious self-understanding*, while the second tries to discover what occurs when religious life is transfigured into philosophic thought.

But as has already been stated,[2] the proposed two-phased treatment is faced with a grave methodological problem. The Hegelian texts treat religious and Christian realities extensively. They never give an account of them which is severely confined to the standpoint of religious self-understanding. The Hegelian "standpoint of thought . . . [claims to] comprehend both religion . . . and itself," while in contrast the religious "standpoint of representation" is said to understand itself in representational terms only, and philosophy not at all.[3] Hegel's own central writings on the subject—the *Phenomenology*, the *Encyclopedia* and the *Philosophy of Religion*—all treat religion *as it is already reenacted and transfigured by philosophic thought: they give no sustained description of religion from the representational—i.e., philosophically unreenacted and untransfigured—standpoint of religion itself.* Here lies the problem. Our description in this chapter of religion as, according to Hegel, it exists without philosophy, must be based on texts which themselves do not give such a description; it must reconstruct what Hegel would, or might, or must say but in fact does not say. Such a reconstruction poses obvious methodological problems to which there can be no total or wholly safe solution.**

However, the task must be undertaken. In the preceding two chapters, it has become clear that the central problem of Hegel's philosophy is not so much philosophical comprehension as the relation between such comprehension and the realities comprehended; and already we can see that this problem has its critical dimension in the relation between philosophical comprehension and *religious* realities. In examining this last-named relation we must first of all make every effort to describe the philosophically *un*comprehended religious realities presupposed by the Hegelian comprehension. Not until we have grasped Hegel's view of Christian realities in their own self-understanding—i.e., in "representational" form—can we hope to understand the claim of the Hegelian

---

* This is because the *Encyclopedia* and the *Philosophy of Religion* both already are "science," and because the *Phenomenology* can be a "road to science" only by virtue of being already "scientific." More specifically, on this latter road religion is viewed as the Truth of "Spirit Certain-of-Itself," see above, ch. 3, sects. 4–6.

** The problem is neither the idea nor the general method of such a reconstruction. The idea has its warrant in the Hegelian doctrine that philosophy presupposes religion and that in comprehending religion it transfigures it. The method must elicit from the Hegelian texts (which have already speculatively transfigured religion) the representational form in which these texts take religion to exist apart from and prior to its speculative transfiguration. (The major difficulty here concerns a precise grasp of what is meant by "religious representation" [*Vorstellung*], a subject dealt with implicitly throughout this chapter [See especially appendix 1, pp.154 ff.], and explicitly in ch. 6, sects. 1, 3, and 4.) The method *does* become problematic, however, in its actual employment. For here one must face the fact that while there is explicit textual support in some cases, it is inevitably lacking in others. Particularly controversial reconstructions will be given an explicit defense. (See appendices 3, pp.157 ff, and 4, pp.158 ff.)

philosophy to comprehend, transfigure, and "make peace" with Christianity.

Christian theologians have never taken the *Philosophy of Religion* seriously.[4] Falling into the virtually universal error of mistaking Hegel's speculative transfiguration of Christianity for an attempt to describe it, they have dismissed it as a mere piece of armchair speculation with no serious resemblance to their historical faith. But this chapter will show that the Christianity presupposed and transfigured by the *Philosophy of Religion* is astonishingly close to the Christianity of history. The chapter to follow will show that, whatever may ultimately be said of the Hegelian speculative transfiguration of Christianity, it is at any rate of the most serious import. Far from a mere armchair enterprise, it is one which Hegel sees forced upon thought—*both* theological and philosophical thought—by the situation of the Christian faith in the modern world. And Hegel's modern world is in large measure still ours.

2. *Provisional Description of Religion-in-General*

We have thus far deliberately failed to discriminate between religion and the Christian religion. To discriminate between them is to confront a difficulty which threatens Hegel's enterprise from the start. Like the romantics before him, he rejects the natural or rational religion-in-general of the Enlightenment, as a mere lifeless construction. There exists, not religion, but only religions, and each has a life of its own. But if this is true, must there not be a sheer plurality of religious claims to truth, and no possibility of rising above their conflict? Nor does it seem that philosophic thought (if it requires a basis in religious life) can settle this conflict. Surely it must remain bound to the limitations of its specific religious basis, and contradicted by alternative philosophies with alternative religious bases!

But all religions have a unity in their very plurality. This doctrine, too, Hegel shares with the romantics. However, whereas these latter naively view it as solving the difficulty, Hegel is well aware of the fact that, by itself, it merely evades it. This section will give a description of what religions have in common, but it will turn out to be merely provisional.

To begin with, this provisional description may distinguish genuine from spurious and decadent religion. Magic is pseudoreligious (as well as prereligious). An attempt at human control of the Divine, it places the Divine below the human rather than above it. But a religion for which the Divine is not above the human—which is not *worship*—is no religion at all.[5] *

If magical pseudoreligion is prereligious, certain forms of modern religious decadence may be called postreligious. Thus Deism reduces God to a mere object of thought, and man to a mere observer without subjective involvement. Its opposite—romantic subjectivism—possesses such subjective involvement. But it possesses nothing else, for it is cut off from an objective Divinity, and hence is feeling for feeling's sake, i.e., the idolatry of the human heart.[6]

From these strictures upon false religion emerge decisive characteristics of genuine religion. Genuine religion is a relation of the human to a Divinity *other* than human and *higher* than human, and it is a relation in which *man's very being is involved.*

What is this involvement? It is, at least to begin with, *feeling.*

---

* While Hegel contrasts magic with religion he also calls it "the first form of religion": the first for the reason we have given; the second because the belief in magical control of nature is higher than animal fear of nature, and because it expresses the truth (which, however, does not *become* a truth *for* magical consciousness) that Spirit is higher than nature. The magical possibility recurs at a higher level in Roman religion (See below, sect. 6, ch. 6, sect. 4.) when the gods are reduced to instruments of human use. According to Hegel, this—or any other—destruction of the Divine by the human is self-destructive of the human: "When man is posited as the highest it follows that he does not respect himself. Only with the consciousness of a higher Being does man reach a standpoint at which he can respect himself truly." (*Werke*, IX, p.117 [*Phil. Hist.*, p.95].)

For to feel is to be geared to the felt, not in abstraction from one's singularity but rather *in* one's singularity: my feeling is mine *essentially*, and in total concreteness. Romantic subjectivism shows that genuine religion requires more than feeling; Deistic detachment, that it cannot be without it. Even the most exalted God is a *mere* concept unless He is *my* God; indeed, one may say that a God-*concept* is not a *God*-concept at all.[7] *

But by themselves feelings are no religion. For they provide no criteria for distinction, nor does mere intensity or sincerity furnish them. A religion of mere feeling would lack all distinctions, not only between good and evil or noble and base, but even between religious and nonreligious. Indeed, feeling by itself is what man shares with the animals; these too are capable of total involvement and, in fact, of nothing else. A religion of pure feeling would have to be, at any rate, one of *religious* feeling, as was recognized in Schleiermacher's definition of the feeling as radical dependence. But, in the absence of an objective reality which the dependence is *on*, can the feeling of dependence be identified as religious, or even distinguished from animal feeling? Not according to a famous Hegelian remark to the effect that, if Schleiermacher's definition were correct, a dog would be the best Christian.[8]

The quality of feeling depends on the object to which it is geared.[9] Religious feeling, first, must *have* an object; it cannot remain in self-enclosed subjectivity. Secondly, the object must have content; it cannot be an empty mystery. And thirdly, by virtue

---

* On Hegel's criticism of "observation," see especially *Werke*, XI, pp.167 ff. (*Phil. Rel.*, I, pp. 172 ff.). Hegel writes: "To observe is to be related to something external which is to remain external . . . . Piety is only for the pious, i.e., for him who *is* what he observes." It will follow that if philosophical thought is to comprehend religion, i.e., "to find the ground of religion, it must abandon the relation of observing. . . . [for] if observation seeks to observe the Infinite in its true nature, it must itself be infinite, i.e., no longer observation of the matter at hand (*die Sache*) but rather that matter itself." (*Werke*, XI, pp.197 ff. [*Phil. Rel.* I, pp.203 ff.].) On this subject, see further ch. 6, sect. 4. We shall then see that the Hegelian Notion of religion has nothing in common with God-concepts, in the sense in which this latter term is presently employed.

of this content the object must be higher than human, and thus is capable of being worshiped. Indeed, it must, as it were, be absolutely high, i.e., universal and infinite rather than particular and finite. (For Hegel holds that no genuine religion is *simply* idolatrous). All these characteristics are contained and united in religious *representation*.*

The term "object" in the context of religious representation must not be misunderstood. As is already clear from the repudiation of religious subjectivism, it does mean that the Divinity represented is other than the subjective act of representing. It does *not* mean that it is an object of either empirical observation or detached thought: not the one because (as is implied in the rejection of simple idolatry) the Divine is not a finite empirical object, not the other because (as is implied in the strictures upon Deism) even the nonempirical object of thought cannot be the God of religious worship—not, at any rate, if the thought remains in a state of detachment. *Just as feeling must be inwardly bound up with representation to be religious, so representation must be bound up with feeling to be religious.*

The required aspects of religious representation all unite in the religious *symbol*. The represented must be other than the representing, and indeed in its divine Infinity *radically* other than the representing in his human finiteness; otherwise the relation would not be genuinely religious. And it yet cannot be so *wholly* other as to be an inaccessible Beyond; in that case there would be no relation at all. The relation requires a symbol which *points to the divine Infinity while being itself finite*. It thus mediates between the Divine and the human, at once relating them and keeping them apart.[10]

But while in inward mutual relation, feeling and representation form no complete whole of religious life. Still lacking is what may be called the element of existential seriousness. Religious feeling is an at-oneness of finite human singularity with divine Infinity.

* See appendix 1 to this chapter, pp. 154 ff.

Religious representation preserves the mutual apartness in the relation between the Divinity represented and the act of representing. There is a tension between the aspects of feeling and representation which are yet united, but unless something *happens* or *is done to* this tension it loses its seriousness, and the aspects united fall apart. Feeling, no longer religious, either dissolves its particularity and thus into an empty infinity, or else withdraws from that infinity into the vanity of finite self-conceit. Representation, losing the power to relate what it yet must keep apart, is fragmented into a mere object incapable of generating religious involvement and into a subject who is mere detached observer. The relation *between* the Divine and the human must preserve its tension even while it does its relating, and it can do so only by *acting it out*, in a labor which so thoroughly permeates the whole length and breadth of existence as to cause it, not merely to *feel* transformed but actually to *be* transformed. This labor is *religious cult*.

Without cult, religious feeling remains a pious "fog"; for man's actual existence remains outside the religious relationship. Religious representation, on its part, remains without cult a mere idea. It represents a divine Infinity which destroys all attempts of finite existence to remain indifferent. The represented Divinity is idea only so long as finite existence remains in fact indifferent. It is in cultic labor that the *actual* self is at work, no longer its mere feeling, and it is in cult that what in representation remains mere possibility becomes actuality. The life of cult acts out the clash and apartness of the Divine and the human in the divine-human relationship in all its undiminished reality, and it *transfigures* that relation so as *actually* to unite them.[11]

But just as feeling and cult remain fragmented without cult, so cult remains fragmented without feeling and representation. Feeling without cult is unreal inwardness. Cult without feeling is a merely external observance. The represented God remains without cult mere idea. Without this represented God, cult is a meaningless reality and a purposeless labor. *Every genuine religion, then, is a totality of existence in which the inwardness of pure feeling is united with outward action and overt occurrence, through a represented meaning which permeates both.* *

This total existence may also be called *faith*. Faith is not a merely theoretical affirmation which asserts a mere object. Nor is it mere feeling, an inward life divorced from the outward, and hence lacking in reality. Faith is the total inward-outward life of finite man in his relation to the divine Infinity. Such a life can only accidentally be initiated (not essentially produced) by external authorities, such as miracles, divine threats or promises, or the letter of a Holy Writ, for these fail to touch and transform inwardness. What produces the life of faith exists *within* the divine-human relation rather than outside it. "The true ground of faith is Spirit."[12]

3. The Status of the Preceding Account

The account thus far given is mainly based on the first part of the *Philosophy of Religion*, "The Notion of Religion." It has not, however, reproduced the Hegelian Notion. This latter is grasped only by a thought which "encompasses religion in its own being," whereas our purpose has been to describe religion as it "exists without philosophy." What then is the status of the preceding account?[13]

It is not that of a detached observer, for whom what the believer takes as an actual divine-human relation is the mere empirical fact of human *belief* in such a relation. Such a standpoint, if amounting to a dogmatic atheistic reductionism, is utterly un-Hegelian. And it is equally so if it amounts to the nondogmatic view of an observer who abstracts from the divine side in the believer's divine-

---

* This formulation is meant to convey that "representation" refers *both* to the thinking aspect of religious existence *and* to the form of religious existence as a whole.

human relation and yet hopes adequately to comprehend the empirical phenomena which remain on the human side; in Hegel's view, a comprehension of this sort is in principle impossible. Moreover, it could not, were it possible, describe the religious basis of the Hegelian philosophy. For this is by no means the mere *human belief* in a divine-human relationship. It is an *actual* relationship of this sort.

Our preceding account must therefore before all else be amplified in one decisive respect. Religious feeling is not the *mere* feeling of being geared to the Divine; it is an actual *being*-geared which is *in* the feeling. The act of representing is not a merely human act, and the represented God, a mere human projection; a divine Reality is present in the representation, and the act of representing which takes itself as both other than that Reality and yet related to it is in fact both other and yet related. Cult is not a solitary human acting; it is a divine-human interacting. Finally faith—and the Spirit which is its ground—are not the product of the human heart; they are actual in the heart only as it stands actually related to a God beyond it. Such, at any rate, is Hegel's doctrine. And, as will be seen, such it must be if religion is to be the basis of his philosophy.[14]

But from what standpoint may this religious basis be described, insofar as it exists without philosophy? Not from that of infinite or philosophical thought, for this will "encompass religion in its own being."[15] Nor from that of finite or "observing" thought, for this has proved to be in principle incapable of grasping the divine-human relation. Can one doubt that a Hegelian description of the religious basis of philosophy would have to be in terms of religious self-understanding?* Yet this is hardly what our preceding account

---

* Hegel does not fail to consider the possibility of a finite thought which detaches itself from, and reflects upon, religious self-understanding, only in order to recognize what it has lost in this process. (See ch. 6, sect. 1.) It would appear, however, that he fails to consider one possibility: that thought might be forced to become radically uncommitted, objective and universal and that yet, rather than destroy or supersede the religious God-man relation-

has given. According to Hegel, there exists no religion but only
religions. Can any one of these possess criteria adequate even to
recognize other religions as genuine, and hence distinct from
spurious? Can it possibly go far enough to admit them to be actual
relations between man and Divinity? Our above account of
religion-in-general, then, is provisional, and its status is problematic.

Our difficulties in describing the religious basis of Hegel's philosophic thought point to a dilemma arising for his own enterprise,
one already referred to but now requiring explicit statement.
Either Hegel's philosophy remains bound up with the religious
basis it is said to require: but then (since there is no religion
but only religions) must it not be confined to the limitations of one
religion, thus losing its claims to absoluteness? Or else it preserves
its absoluteness, and renders each religion what may be its due:
but is it not then cut off from its religious foundation, which is one
specific religion? In either case religious life fails to furnish the
bridge between finite life and infinite philosophical Thought. Yet
it is this bridge which we have found to be indispensable for the
entire Hegelian philosophy.

The dilemma, of course, is not a new one. It is already contained
in romantic religious pluralism which grants each religious standpoint ultimate truth and which yet, to do such granting, must itself
transcend all religious standpoints and deny their ultimacy—a
nineteenth century posture which, incidentally, is reenacted by
those twentieth century pluralists who, in comparing religions to
players in a symphony orchestra, unconsciously assume the role
of conductor.

---

ship in this stance, it might be compelled to *point* to it, as an "immediacy
after reflection" demanded *by* reflection; or (otherwise put), that it might be
compelled to point to a leap *into* existence demanded by the *idea* of existence.
On this possibility centers both the negative philosophy of Schelling's last
period and the existential dialectic of Kierkegaard.

Schleiermacher's "religion of religions" is little more than an ad hoc escape from this dilemma, shot through with Christian apologetics.[16] Hegel's *Philosophy of Religion* confronts the dilemma head-on, and indeed may be said in its entirety to be its explicit repudiation. On the one hand, it seeks to do a "justice" to all religions which no religion, (the Christian included) can mete out to them. On the other hand, it discovers one religion which both enables philosophy to do such justice and yet survives the philosophical activity of doing it. The relation between philosophy and *this* religion, barely touched on by Schleiermacher, becomes an explicit, and indeed the central, problem. As for this religion itself (which in Hegel's as in Schleiermacher's case is Christianity), this is for Hegel the actual Christianity of history. At least for the Schleiermacher of *On Religion*,[17] this had been virtually replaced by "Intuition."

This Christianity of history must supply a decisive condition if the *Philosophy of Religion* is to rise above the romantic dilemma. While *confronting and opposing* other religions, it must also somehow *absorb* them and, moreover, *recognize* itself as doing so. The *revealed* religion must be the *comprehensive* religion: indeed, it will emerge that *"comprehensive" is what "revealed" means*.

In the light of these considerations, our description of religious self-understanding must make a new start. The previous terms—"feeling," "representation," "cult," "faith," "Spirit"—must be given their specifically Christian meaning. And in the light of that meaning Christian self-understanding must be seen as absorbing as well as opposing non-Christian religious self-understanding. Moreover, the claim to comprehensiveness which emerges from this confrontation must be strong enough to assert itself against future possible as well as against past actual religions. For nothing less will enable the Hegelian philosophy (which will "encompass in its own being" Christian religious life) to rise to absoluteness of thought.

4. *Provisional Characterization of the*
Christianity of History

There are many Christianities in history, and they oppose each other as Christian opposes non-Christian religions. Hegel cannot simply bow to the contingencies of external history. What is the *genuine* Christianity of history?

This question is answered in part by the strictures previously described upon spurious and decadent religion. A merely magical use of Christian relics is a pseudoreligious remnant in medieval Christianity. Modern forms of Christian decadence include romantic subjectivism which, having lost faith in the present God, has withdrawn on the merely human feeling of divine presence. They also include a Deism recognizing a merely transcendent divine thought-object, and a humanism exhausted in the search for the historical Jesus. All these are marked by the common failure to accept an actual incursion of the divine Transcendence into human flesh.[18]

From these strictures it emerges that Hegel's genuine Christianity of history is an *orthodox* Christianity, if by such orthodoxy is meant an actual relation between man and a trinitarian God who, though infinite and transcendent, has yet become flesh in Jesus Christ to redeem the flesh by His death and resurrection.* But *what* Christian orthodoxy? Not one based on external authority, whether the letter of Scripture, the power of a church or—despite Hegel's Lutheran inspiration—the words of Luther. The *Philosophy of Religion*, unlike the *Early Theological Writings*, no longer rejects external authority in genuine religion. Even so, such authority can have only a subordinate role.** Our provisional account of

---

* Hegel himself refers to "what have always been regarded as the basic truths of Christianity," and adds: "Nowadays it is not philosophy alone, but philosophy above all, which is essentially orthodox." (*Werke*, XII, p.207 [*Phil. Rel.*, II, p.345].)

** See appendix 2 to this chapter, pp.156 ff.

genuine religion has removed all doubt that the true authority of Hegel's genuine orthodox Christianity must be internal rather than external. It is Spirit.*

But a more precise definition of Hegel's orthodox Christian cannot at this stage be given. To this latter, Greek-Roman paganism is as indispensable for the advent of Christ as Old Testament Judaism. His Christian truth is only initiated by the events reported in the New Testament, and completed in the cultic life and speculative thought of the Christian church. And while he is by no means simply anti-Catholic this Christian is in the end Protestant and more precisely Lutheran. All these characteristics may well seem to make this Christianity very partisan in its orthodox claims or even—notably in the case of the first-named characteristic—cast its orthodoxy into serious doubt. It is therefore necessary not to hold on too tightly to preconceived notions of orthodoxy, and instead to discover what the Christianity of Hegel's Christian is.

5. *Creation and Fall, or the Christian Understanding of the Human Condition*

Hegel's Christian** knows himself to exist in a divinely created

---

* The Christian religion will emerge as "the religion of Truth and Freedom. For Truth consists of not being related to the objective as something alien. Freedom expresses the same as Truth, with a determination of negation. . . . Here the negation of the distinction of otherness is stressed, hence Freedom appears in the form of reconciliation." (*Werke*, XII, pp.207 ff. [*Phil. Rel.*, II, p.346].)

** Hegel writes: "The Idea was first in the element of thought; this is the foundation and we have begun with it. In philosophical science the universal and more abstract must come first . . . *In fact, however, it is later in existence.*" (*Werke*, XII, p.247 [*Phil. Rel.*, III, pp.33 ff]; italics added.) This passage clearly indicates that Christian existence and self-understanding begin with what for their Hegelian speculative reenactment will turn out to be the "Kingdom of the Son." (See sects. 5–7 of this chapter and ch. 6, sect. 4.) We can also say with certainty that Christian existence and self-understanding move into the "Kingdom of the Spirit." (See sect. 8 of this chapter, and ch. 6, sect. 4.) Whether Christian existence and self-understanding can rise to the Hegelian "Kingdom of the Father" (which is "in the element of thought!") is a more

world: in a *world* because it is a whole independent in its own right; in a *created* world because it nevertheless wholly depends on a God beyond it. Christian faith thus contrasts equally with that of mystics who dissipate the world into Divinity, and with that of such mythological religions as take the world, or any part of it, as itself divine. The world actually exists side by side with the Divine: this idea is expressed in the distinction between an initial *creatio ex nihilo* and a subsequent divine activity of mere preserving, as if the world, once created, stands only accidentally in need of divine support. Yet the world is in its very being dependent on God: this dependency is expressed in the belief that the creation *is ex nihilo* and that, were God ever to cease to maintain it, it would vanish into nothingness; in that the distinction between creation and preservation, though necessarily made, is made only in order to be abolished. Thus the making and the abolishing of the distinction are both part of Christian representation. Compared to its represented dialectical truth, there is only a one-sided error to an abstract metaphysical thought which either simply makes or simply denies the distinction. Debates as to whether God created the world eternally or in time are empty.

The created world has its correlate in divine Goodness and divine Wisdom. Abstract metaphysical thought treats these as attributes, external not only to each other, but also to the God possessing them, as well as to a world which manifests them as characteristics superadded to its being. But a *divine* and therefore infinite Goodness and Wisdom must be internally related to each other as well as to Divinity itself, and their manifestation in a *finite* created world must penetrate the whole length and breadth of that

---

complex issue. In the end it involves the question of the relation between a theology which is *part* of Christian existence, and a final theology which reenacts and transfigures Christianity as a whole into speculative thought. This final theology may be regarded, with reservations (See ch. 6, sect. 6.), as identical with the Hegelian philosophy. See below, sect. 9 and appendix 4 to this chapter, and ch. 6, especially sects. 2(b), 3–6, and appendices 1 and 3.

world's being. To manifest both the independence granted by divine Goodness and the dependence flowing from the Power of divine Wisdom *is* the being of the created world.[19]

Christian faith affirms this truth, not from the standpoint of an observer but from that of a participant. Man himself is a creature, and only as he recognizes himself as such does he recognize either the created world or the Creator. His being, too, is creaturely—a togetherness of independence granted by divine Goodness and dependence flowing from divine Wisdom.

But while the creation is a single whole it divides, nevertheless, into nature and finite spirit. Nature and man are both divinely created. Only man can *know* of this truth concerning either. Nature is a divine revelation, but only for man and not for itself.

For this reason, human creatureliness, as distinct from the natural, is *doubly* dialectical: man is created in the divine image. Qua created, his being is a togetherness of divinely granted independence and divinely imposed dependence. But qua created in the divine image, he manifests, as well, an independence which must be a human achievement rather than a divine gift. For the knowledge of God—and this *is* the divine image—is God-given only as potentiality; its actualization is a task handed over to man. Not until the knowledge of God is actual is the image of God itself actual, and its actualization completes that independence which is the gift of divine Goodness, and hence completes the creation itself.

Yet the act which actualizes the creation at the same time runs counter to the creation, thus being a *fall*. The act which completes God-given independence is also a defiance of God-imposed dependence. And the dependence is of a finite creature on an infinite God!

Christian faith thus sees man as in a paradoxical condition. He is by nature good. For he is created in the image of God apart from his own doing, and his knowledge of being so created (which is the original human act) is for that reason also the original anti-divine act. But he is also, and at the same time, by nature evil, for the divine image remains potential until he himself rises to the knowledge which actualizes it. Hence animal innocence is an imaginary past always already lost, and the guilt which is man's self-willed condition is also his God-willed destiny. It is not by accident that the primary meaning of "to be guilty" is "to be responsible."[20]

Such, in brief, is the human condition. The faith which faces up to it becomes conscious of a need for redemption. No merely human acting can heal the breach between the human and the Divine, for it is the original human acting which has produced it. Nor can a divine acting heal it if it is simply alien to human acting and destructive of its significance. For the human acting which makes man stand in need of redemption is also what makes him worthy of it. Hegel's Christian clearly is not the liberal kind for whom the fall is simply a fall upwards; nor the orthodox kind for whom it is a simply contingent event which should not and need not have occurred. And therefore it may be expected that this Christian can find redemption neither in the liberal Jesus who is merely human teacher nor in an orthodox divine incarnation which, *absolutely* contingent, cannot be expected before its occurrence: which must be blindly accepted after it has taken place.

Like all symbolic philosophical interpretations of Genesis, the above is doubtless controversial. Unlike most others, however, the Hegelian interpretation regards the symbolic form as essential to the content and, moreover, as recognized by the religious consciousness for what it is. Thus in Christian consciousness itself—not merely in a philosophical reinterpretation of it—each man is Adam, created innocent, falling by his own will, and yet forever already fallen. Without the first, all responsibility would be divine rather than human; without the second, it would be another man's; and without the third, it would not be a universal and necessary human condition. This is why sin, though each man's responsibility, must yet be represented as hereditary.

There is equal need for the Biblical representation of the fall as a contingent event contrary to the divine will—one which need not and should not have occurred. How otherwise could the human creature be represented as owing its all to the Creator, while an act which is a human achievement is represented as anti-divine? And yet—so Hegel insists—the Biblical narrative itself is dialectical; dialectic is not a philosophical import into it. For according to the Bible the free human act which opposes God results in a human godlikeness which knows good and evil. These, it may be objected, are the words of the tempter. But, Hegel rejoins, "the serpent does not lie. God Himself confirms its words."[21] *

6. *The Meeting of Jewish East and Greek-Roman West, or the Ripeness of Time for Christ*

The faith of Hegel's Christian is deeply immersed in the opening chapters of the Old Testament. It virtually passes over its entire remainder. Or rather, whereas creation and fall are integral parts of his Christian truth, Old Testament Judaism as a whole is a mere fragmentary anticipation, and one which, moreover, is not less but also not more significant than another fragmentary anticipation of Christianity—the pagan, Greek-Roman world. The confrontation of Hegel's Christianity with both Jewish East and Greek-Roman West will shed much light on what that Christianity is.* *

---

* The account of creation and fall given above may seem to bear no resemblance to what is generally known of Hegelian doctrine: that creation is a divine self-othering in nature and finite spirit, and that the fall symbolizes the truth that man "must make himself into what he is" (*Werke*, XII, p.267 [*Phil. Rel.*, III, pp.55 ff.].), i.e., that he must become for himself what to begin with he is only in himself. But we are presently concerned with what creation and fall are in Christian self-understanding, not yet with what they become through transfiguration into philosophy. A close reading of the texts referred to in nn. 19, 20, and 21, together with the distinction made in sect. 1 of this chapter, will, we think, bear out our interpretation presented above.

** See appendix 3 to this chapter, pp.157 ff.

A clue to the attitude toward Judaism lies in the remarkable assertion—which must be taken as attributable to Christianity, not as a Hegelian judgment upon Judaism only—that the doctrines of creation and fall "had no influence on the subsequent development of Judaism . . . [but remained a mere] prophecy, the universal element in which did not become a truth for the people of Israel."[22] The flaw here asserted is not, or not primarily, that the God who to begin with is universal confines His subsequent effective relation to one particular people. On the contrary, this exclusiveness is for Hegel's Christian (and for Hegel himself) part of the grandeur of Judaism, inevitably bound up with its essential truth. This truth—and it is one which Hegel's Christian recognizes—is the relation between a God who having smashed all idols is One, Infinite, and therefore Holy, and a man who remains in the fulness of his human finitude. The Jewish God is infinite and transcendent: this distinguishes Him from all pagan deities, those of Greece and Rome included. The Jewish man is related to Him in all his human finiteness: this distinguishes Judaism from every mystical or philosophical flight from the world. But it is this truth which forces the Jew into a twofold stubbornness: resistance to a pagan world worshiping pagan gods, and persistence in his national particularity. For it is in this particularity that he must be faithful to a God who is universal.[23]

But in Christian perspective the truth of Judaism is only fragmentary. Its God is one and infinite; He is one and infinite *only*, and hence remains in the utter transcendence of sheer Lordship. The man who worships the Lord remains simply human, hence in utter servitude. Such servitude remains fragmentary because it cannot reach what it seeks, thus remaining in the fear of radical distance. But while the fear of the Lord is the beginning of all religious wisdom it is no more than that.[24]

Judaism survives so long as it remains ignorant of this fragmentariness; so long as the failure to reach oneness with God is viewed as the mere "failure to observe this or that commandment,"[25] and correspondingly, righteousness remains a goal pursued by merely human effort despite all previous failures. But while unable to transcend its fragmentariness Judaism comes at length to recognize it, and thus to point beyond itself. As the effort to do the will of the Lord becomes radical the contradictoriness of the divine-human relation is recognized as itself radical, i.e., of the human essence. And when this occurs Jewish existence is filled with absolute pain. "Pain exists only in contradiction against something affirmative which ought to be."[26] Such pain is absolute when what ought to be is the union of finite man with the infinite God. Jewish existence, then, throughout its development *manifests* that dialectical condition which finds expression in the doctrines of creation, the divine image and the fall. It is only as it approaches its end that it comes to *recognize* that condition, and thereby to long for a redemption beyond its reach. The time has become ripe for the advent of Christ.[27]

Such ripeness requires, however, an unhappiness in the Greek-Roman West corresponding to the pain in the Jewish East. Indeed, as he confronts the pagan religious world which culminates in this unhappiness, Hegel's Christian accepts it as matching the Jewish in Christian significance, despite its idolatrous worship of finite gods.*

Hegel's Christian accepts every genuine religion as expressing at least the true human need to worship the higher-than-human. But pagan worship cannot match the Jewish in Christian significance when it remains ignorant both of the true infinite object of worship and of the true subject who partakes of infinity in the act of worship. (Such ignorance characterizes nature religions in which finite nature is worshiped in place of its infinite Creator, and which exalt the worshiped nature above its human worshiper.)** Pagan worship can match the Jewish only if it rises

---

* This will become only partly intelligible in this chapter and wholly so only in ch. 6, especially sect. 2(a) and (b).

** Philosophical thought, however, recognizes that even nature religions have a degree of truth, see below, ch. 6, sects. 3 and 4.

above such ignorance and if its development is such as to reach an historic point at which, like Judaism, it points to the higher Truth which redeems the world.

Greek religion matches the Jewish in Christian significance. The Jew knows the infinite Creator, not *as* Creator but only as transcendent Lord; hence he knows himself as simply finite only, not as created in the divine image. As for the Greek, he knows of no Creator either (for his gods are finite); yet he has a knowledge of sorts of the divine image which is in him. For he worships, not a nature which is below the human, but rather a Beauty which is above him and which is yet immanent in the human whose creative vision perceives it. To be sure, because the Beauty is immanent in the human *only*, this worship is idolatrous, and the finite gods worshiped are mere human projections. Even so the Greek religion is a true celebration of human worth, which is beyond the ken of Judaism: a divination of the human as worth saving. Indeed, while it lasts, the beautiful flower which is ancient Greece is nothing less than a pagan anticipation of Christian Grace.[28] Hegel has justly been charged with prejudice against Judaism, (although in our view the charge must primarily be leveled *against Hegel's Christian*). This prejudice is seen in perspective only if seen together with the prejudice of Hegel's Christian (and that of the Hegelian philosophy itself), for ancient Greece and all its works.[29]

But few Hegelian doctrines are ever simply the result of mere prejudice. Greek religion could hardly match the Jewish in Christian significance unless, like Judaism, if suffered the nemesis of its limitations. As the ancient world runs its course Greek religion is doubly demythologized and thus destroyed: by Greek philosophy in the realm of thought and by the Roman state-religion in the actual world.[30]

If Greek religion is the "religion of humanity . . . [in which] confidence in the gods is at the same time human self-confidence,"[31] then Rome is that universalization and radicalization in which the self-confidence in the end destroys the confidence, and thus the religion. As Rome expands into a universal empire it assembles all gods in a pantheon. And as it radicalizes human self-confidence, it reduces the gods to mere instruments of human use. In the pantheon, the gods are all assembled and all destroyed.

This radicalization is a radical human self-liberation, but in Christian perspective the radical human self-enslavement to which it has in fact led is inevitable. Man in the Christian view becomes fully human only when worshiping the higher-than-human and must, when denying the Divine, exalt the merely human to pseudo-divinity. The Roman world ends with unhappy emperor worship, and this end discloses the truth of wordly pagan existence as a whole. To the Christian—not to the Roman himself—it discloses the truth that finite man is not, and cannot be, "satisfied" in a godless world.[32]

The Christian shares this knowledge, however, with some ancient pagan philosophers if not with nonphilosophical pagans, and unless this were the case paganism could not equal Judaism in Christian significance, and even less (as will be seen) be superior to Judaism in its significance for the Hegelian philosophy. As the Roman world sinks into unhappy self-enslavement, philosophers escape into a worldless thought. And the last among them—the Alexandrinian Neoplatonists—achieve access to nothing less than what will be seen to be the preworldly trinitarian God of Christian faith.[33] Without this climactic achievement, the Roman unhappiness, which remains unconscious of its need for redemption, could not wholly match the Christian significance of the Jewish pain, which is conscious of that need. Paganism matches Judaism by virtue of its philosophy. This achieves an actual oneness with the true God which is beyond both pagan worldiness and Jewish faith.

And yet for Christian faith (if not for its Hegelian reenactment), the Jewish anticipation of the Christian redemption remains as vital as that of pagan philosophy. To find access to the true God, the pagan philosopher must resort to flight from a godless world. The Jew serves Him *in* the world, and his pain reveals that He cannot and yet must be found in it. Jewish painful service of the infinite God in the finite world; philosophical flight from this godless world to a worldless God; Roman unhappy self-enslavement in a godless world: these are all needed if the world is to become ripe for the Christian redemption.[34] For this redemption is the all-comprehensive reconciliation of the Divine in the extremity of its transcendent infinity with the human in the total concreteness of his worldly and human finitude.

7. The Incarnation

We have thus far described the Christian understanding of the human condition in abstraction from the Incarnation. Much encourages the conjecture that Hegel's Christian can have such an understanding only after the Incarnation, and on the basis of faith in its actual occurrence. Thus in the view of Hegel's Christian, the Jew has but an inadequate knowledge of the creation and the fall, and the pagan (whether Greek, Roman, or philosopher) has no knowledge of it at all. But if this knowledge arises only after the Christian consciousness has transfigured both the Jewish and the pagan how can it exist except after the redemptive event which has produced that transfiguration?

Yet despite such doubts we must finally opt for the alternative interpretation. To be sure, for Hegel's Christian the Incarnation is a contingent event and indeed—because it is the incursion of the Divine in the extreme of its infinity into the human in the extreme of its finitude—the most radical possible case of contingency. It is, however, not *simply* contingent because it is *expected*, and it is expected because it is recognized as *needed*. Without this prior expectation and recognition the redemptive event would not be recognized as redemptive when in fact it occurs. In short, as Jewish East intermingles with Greek-Roman West there arises what may be called a proto-Christian consciousness which develops a criterion of the needed redemption. That criterion is *comprehensiveness*.*

The belief in Creation has accepted an infinite God and an actually finite world—the latter is actually finite because it exists separately from the infinite God and yet, because it is finite and God infinite, it is wholly dependent on Him. As for the belief in the divine image in man and the fall of man, it has accepted a unique place for man within the creation; a divinely-willed destiny himself to actualize the potentiality to know God, which is also antidivine because it is done by man. Redemption, in order to *be* redemption, must be all-comprehensive. That is, it must *preserve* without loss the extremes in the divine-human relation, of which one is the Creator in His infinity and the other the human creature in his finitude. It must *reconcile* these extremes in their very extremity. And the comprehensiveness of this reconciliation must be so total as to encompass not only all aspects of the past worlds of Jewish East and Greek-Roman West, but also what may appear on the scene as future post-Christian worlds. (It will be seen that, were it not for this *all*-comprehensiveness it finds in Christian religious life, the Hegelian philosophy—which claims to encompass this life in its own being—could not venture to rise to all-comprehensiveness in the realm of thought.)

What, then, is the redemption expected by the proto-Christian consciousness? Not a self-redemptive acting of man; it would only accentuate the unredeemedness already manifest in extreme form in Jewish pain and Roman unhappiness. Nor is it a divine acting which remains trans-worldly: this, inaccessible to existing man in

---

* The Hegelian text moves from creation and fall, through the need for Christ manifested in the meeting of Jewish East and Greek-Roman West, to the Incarnation. (*Werke*, XII, pp.249 ff., 270 ff., 277 ff. [*Phil. Rel.*, III, 35 ff., 59 ff., 66 ff.].) Despite this fact it gives no wholly conclusive support to the interpretation for which we have opted. For it must be remembered that the text gives the Christian truth as reenacted by philosophical thought, whereas we are presently engaged in presenting that truth as it exists for Christian self-understanding.

the world, is already accessible to a philosophical thought which flees from the world, but it leaves the world unredeemed.[35] To redeem the human, the Divine must *enter into* the human world, and yet it must preserve both the humanity of the human and its own divinity. It cannot destroy the human: for it is precisely *as* human that the human is, so to speak, worth saving. It cannot (if such were possible) destroy its own divinity; a god who *simply* died in the human world would be but an additional member in the Roman pantheon of dead gods.

The divine redemptive act, then, must unite the Jewish transcendent Lord with the immanence and humanity of the gods of Greece. To bring about this union, He cannot, like the Greek gods, be merely *represented* as human. To Christian consciousness, these represented gods had been mere human projections, and they were destroyed, by philosophy because they were mere finite projections and by Roman worldliness because they reigned not over the actual world but only over an idealized world of Beauty. In the Christian view the Greek gods were not too anthropomorphic but rather not anthropomorphic enough;[36] and yet the needed extreme anthropomorphic manifestation must be the act not of man but of the transcendent God. This act, then, is a divine assumption of *actual* human existence, not an idealized image of human existence. And it is manifest not to a sense of beauty only, which is a mere aspect of actual human existence, but rather to human existence in full empirical concreteness. Such is the central redemptive event of the Christian faith. It is a "tremendous composition" of the Divine and the human.[37]

In accepting the actual occurrence of this event, the Christian consciousness, already dialectical in its understanding of the divine-human relation, explodes into paradox. Holding together in representation what undialectical thought cannot hold together— the creatureliness which makes man wholly depend on the divine Infinity and yet have independence, and the *human* creatureliness

which makes the achievement of its human destiny both a fall and
a divinely willed destiny—it now encounters a composition which
it cannot hold together and must, therefore, at least to begin with,
accept as a sheer fact. The proto-Christian consciousness can expect redemption but cannot predict or anticipate it, and it is not
therefore in its proto-Christian state already Christian. It is as it
accepts what is no anticipated necessity but contingent and paradoxical fact that it becomes Christian: the act of acceptance transfigures it.*

How can what, at least in the first instance, Christian consciousness cannot hold together yet *be* held together? Only by divine
action. This cannot be the life of Christ, taken by itself: Hegel rejects a liberal Christianity which, confined to the life of Christ,
finds divinity at most in his teachings. These latter cannot by themselves compose the Divine and the human, nor can obedience to
them redeem man from his fallen condition. Indeed, Hegel goes
so far as to say that the life of Jesus, could it be taken by itself,
would differ little in significance from that of Socrates.[38] **

The redemptive event is not the life but rather the death of
Christ. This exhausts human finiteness in all its extremity, both
the natural (death itself), which all men suffer, and the spiritual

---

* The event of the Incarnation thus remains tremendous for Christian consciousness even in the interpretation for which we have opted—that the
Christian is preceded by a proto-Christian consciousness. Hence whether, and
if so how, Hegel can come to "see the necessity" (*Werke*, XII, p.286 [*Phil.
Rel.*, III, p.77].) of the Incarnation, and what is meant by such a necessity
and such a seeing, remains a major problem (if not *the* main problem) for
an understanding of his speculative transfiguration of Christian faith. (See
ch. 6, sects. 3–5.) On *no* tenable interpretation of the texts may it be held
that Hegel arrives at his *terminal* speculative necessity by means of an arbitrary *initial* denial of radical contingency, i.e., of the contingency of the Incarnation which is accepted by Christian faith and self-understanding.

** Hegel pours scorn on the half-heartedness of enlightenment theologians for whom Christianity is reduced to a teaching, and Christ to "a divine
teacher, a teacher like Socrates, only more perfect since he was without sin.
Either Christ was a mere man or 'the Son of Man.'" (*Werke*, XII, p.349
[*Phil. Rel.*, III, p.144].)

(sin), which makes Christ suffer death on all men's behalf. Yet this very extremity is the supreme test of faithfulness—the faithfulness of both God to man and man to God.[39] *

The divine Infinity is "pure Life." Death is most alien to it and of all possibilities the "most fearful." Yet if the Divine remained alien to death It would remain alien to humanity also, and Its love, a play of divine self-love. The most fearful possibility becomes actual as the Divine, because of love for the human, is penetrated by death. Yet this very penetration by death is the conquest of death, for, unlike finite pagan deities, the true infinite God is not *penetrated* by death as an unwilling victim. He *freely submits* to death, and the love which causes this submission conquers death. The death of God carries in train the "death of death"—the divine resurrection. In this death of death, man is at once recognized in his humanity and redeemed from his self-alienation from God. He is given his "highest confirmation."[40] *The reader will recall that in an earlier chapter we saw the activity of overreaching, as decisive for the whole of Hegel's thought.[41] We have now come upon that activity, as according to Hegel it is already manifest apart from all philosophy—for Christian faith in the religious life.*

Can the divine confirmation of the human become a reality *for* the human? Not for the detached spectator. For him, the dying as well as the living Christ must remain human only, a part of human—not human-divine—history. The human is confirmed by the Divine only when he accepts himself as confirmed: the divine death of death is a reality only for Christian faith.[42] **

---

* Initially, God's faithfulness to man consists in His death on man's behalf; that of man to God, in remaining true to the redeeming God even though He has died and the external world has remained unchanged. But this is only the beginning of the two activities which will become—or rather turn out to have been all along—*one double* activity, and which will become eventually —in the final philosophical thought—*one single* activity.

** This reality is as yet incomplete, since the "basis" of faith—Spirit—has not yet explicitly come into view. See above, nn. 7 and 12.

But faith by itself—the pristine faith of the New Testament—only begins the confirmation. The believer who first hears the good news of the transfigured world exists in a world still untransfigured. Therefore, to begin with, he can only be in this world and not of it, negating it like Stoics and Skeptics. But the quality of his negation differs from theirs. He does not flee from the world, abandoning it to the control of untransfigured worldliness. Rather, he must dispute that control, and indeed, radically "invert" the world with all its untransfigured values. Only when this inversion has become wholly actual will the divine confirmation of the human have penetrated the whole of the human being.[43]

A previous part of this chapter (sect. 4) which characterized the Christianity of Hegel's Christian as generally orthodox was forced to postpone a more precise characterization. This latter is now beginning to emerge. Hegel's Christianity will be not New Testament Christianity, but rather the life of a church only initiated by New Testament faith. This life will be—though this is a more complex matter than is generally recognized—of the modern Protestant rather than of the medieval Catholic church. Even the life of Protestant faith will be fragmentary unless it is in creative inter-relation with secular life. These implications, though still far from obvious, have already begun to emerge; for the life, death, and resurrection of Christ has initiated a process which seeks completeness once it is explicitly initiated. And it will not have reached completeness until an infinite, transcendent heaven has descended to a finite, transfigured earth.*

8. Christian Cult and the Holy Spirit

The Incarnation objectively confirms the human. How does it become actual for the human subject who is to be confirmed? As thus far described, the Divine has entered into the human, but into

---

* The meaning, possibility, and actuality of such a final descent will be treated as the climactic issue of the entire Hegelian philosophy in ch. 6, sect. 5.

one particular human other than the human worshiper. If there were no more to describe, then the saving event would be objective only, external to the subject who accepts it, and this subject, external to the saving event, would remain untransfigured in his human finitude. And he would accept the death of death, not as a present reality but as a mere past historical fact.

Hegel here comes upon a question raised by Lessing. There are "necessary truths of reason" and "contingent truths of history." No one would "risk anything of great, permanent worth" for the latter; for they are external to him and accepted on external authority, and yet Christian faith stakes all on one of these! "That," so Lessing had summed up his difficulty, "is the ugly, broad ditch which I cannot get across, however often and however earnestly I have tried to make the leap. If anyone can help me over it, let him do it...."[44]

The Hegelian help consists, not of constructing a philosophical bridge between the eternal and the historical which would otherwise remain unbridged, but it consists of showing *that the bridge already exists* apart from all philosophical activity. It exists in the cult which is the life of the Christian church.*

The general truth that religious representation and feeling remain fragmentary without cult here begins to assume its specifically Christian meaning. Christian representation composes the infinite eternal God and one finite man in the historical past. The good news from the past remains of the past only and does not become present reality if the composition represented remains a mere object, external to an activity of representing which remains merely finite subject. For this latter, taken by itself, the Father of the historical Christ would flee into the transcendence of mere

---

* This is not to deny that the Hegelian philosophy, too, is a bridge between the eternal and the historical, and indeed one which must take itself as superior to that of Christian faith. But, as will emerge, it can take itself for such a bridge only by encompassing a bridge already existing in Christianity. This conclusion has important implications for Hegel's philosophy of history which cannot, however, be investigated in the present volume.

lordship, while his Son would be "sent back two thousand years into Palestine."[45] The good news of the divine presence in the human would not become present reality for the human.

A presence of sorts, to be sure, is possessed in Christian *feeling*. But by itself this must lose the divine-human composition. It must either dissipate its own finiteness into a divine Infinity devoid of all finiteness, or else cut itself loose from the divine Infinity and make itself pseudodivine. Humanity is either lost or deified. It is not transfigured and redeemed.[46]

Genuine Christianity resists all these possibilities, as mere perversions. For in it (as in every genuine religion) feeling permeates representation, and representation, feeling. Because of the one, the Christ who is historical and past is also sought in the present, and it is essential to Christian representation to "waver" between these two poles.[47] Because of the other, a mysticism which would flee the human condition is arrested by the God who has entered into that condition, and a romanticism which would deify human feeling is stopped short by the manner of His entrance: into an actual past man other than the present worshiper so as first to suffer the agony of human death before achieving the victory of the resurrection.

But the mutual interpenetration of representation and feeling produces a tension, resolved only in Christian *cult*. This cult alone encompasses both the undiminished reality of the human in its finite concreteness and the Divine in its serene Infinity; suffers the whole agony of their conflict, and yet by its labor can transfigure this agony into total reconciliation.

How can Christian cult reach this goal? It cannot if its labor remains a merely human labor, albeit that of a pious community imbued with a present representation of a divine incursion into the human past. The past divine incursion becomes present reality only if it *lives in* the present community, as well as being the past object of its present representation. The redemptive event of Christian faith, then, is only begun by its occurrence in the historical past. It completes itself in its perpetual recurrence in the community which lives by its believing acceptance. *Christian worworship is not of Christ only. It is in Christ as well.* As for Christian cult, this is not the single activity of a merely human labor, appropriating the divine gift. The gift here given is a Grace operative in the human, not one external to the human. This Grace, to be sure, leaves room for a human freedom to receive or not to receive it, which is why it is not a single divine activity destructive of the human aspect of the cultic labor. However, no fixed line can be drawn between the giving work of God and the human work of receptive appropriation, and to draw such a line is to lose the reality of both. *Christian cult, then, is one double activity, uniting the Divine and the human, and the antimony which lives in this uniting is of the Christian essence. The redemption begun in the Christ is completed in the Holy Spirit.*[48]

This double activity permeates every aspect of Christian cult. Baptism is a sacrament (not a man-made ceremony), an objective event by which the individual, already naturally born, is reborn in Spirit. It is, however, not objective *only* and to take it as such is to reduce it to an external observance. Baptism has an objective-subjective life in the consciousness of the community into which the reborn individual is received. The life is objective-subjective because the holy Spirit lives in the community, perpetually reenacting that death of death *in* the communal cult which, *for* Christian representation, is already objectively complete.[49]

This objective-subjective life, however, is only begun in baptism, for two reasons. The baptized individual is accepted into the church; the acceptance does not become real for him until he himself accepts it. His second birth supersedes the first, yet this latter continues to assert its unredeemed power, and the moral struggle with sin, in one sense already over and done with, is in another not even begun.* Moreover—and this is decisive—the

* *Werke,* XII, p.336 (*Phil. Rel.,* III, pp.129 ff.). Hegel here contrasts Christian consciousness for which "the struggle is over" with Kantian

church into which he is received cannot itself perpetually repeat the divine death of death unless it "expressly" repeats it, i.e., *in consciousness. The core and climactic event of Christian cult is the sacrament of Holy Communion.* Here at length the "tremendous composition" of the Divine and the human—already objectively actual in the historical past and for Christian representation—becomes present objective-subjective reality *in* as well as *for* the life of faith. On the one hand the host is an objective presence of physical immediacy, "offered to the individual for immediate [that is, psychosomatic] enjoyment." On the other hand, it does not remain an "outward, material, unspiritual thing." (This thing would become—in another perversion—"actually present God" only through an external act of consecration and would leave the individual in a state of merely empirical enjoyment, inwardly untransfigured.) In the Lutheran conception—to the truth of which Catholicism does not wholly rise and which the reformed notion does not match—the act of consumption transfigures both the consumed host and the consumer. The "feeling of the presence of God arises," and there is an actual divine presence in the feeling. For the "Spirit and faith" in which "alone God is present" are not the work of a single human activity. They are the work of that double activity which unites the divine giving and the human receiving. They are the work of the Holy Spirit.[50] *

---

morality for which "the highest is infinite process." (See also *Werke*, XI, pp.222 ff. [*Phil. Rel.*, I, pp.228 ff.].) Hegel by no means asserts or implies, however, that even the complete Christian cultic life (of which baptism is merely the beginning) disposes of the need for, or dissipates the reality of, a secular moral action which is, simply by virtue of being such action, eternally incomplete; nor will his philosophy (which will show morality to fall short of the absoluteness of religion) dissipate moral into religious Spirit. On this issue, see above, ch. 3, sects. 4 and 5 and below, ch. 6, sect. 5. For the concept of overreaching (which is vital in this connection) see above, ch. 4, sects. 6 and 7.

* It is perhaps in his interpretation of the sacrament of Holy Communion that Hegel's Lutheran loyalties are most clearly in evidence. In Catholic doctrine (according to which the host is an external thing) "externality is the basis of the whole . . . religion, [and the subject must] accept it passively from

Holy Communion forever completes what in baptism is forever begun. Since the whole life cycle of the church is the work of the Holy Spirit, its totality is *objectively* at one with God. Holy Communion is its climax, in which this oneness becomes a *unio mystica*, a total objective-*subjective* reality. Man, though baptized, has the moral struggle still before him. In Holy Communion he has it behind him; for the double activity of divine Grace and human sacrifice is complete. Grace, psychosomatically present, enters into the psychosomatic individual and transfigures him, requiring of him but the sacrifice of believing acceptance. "There is no sin which cannot be forgiven, if only the natural will is surrendered, except for the sin against the Holy Spirit."[51]

The term *unio mystica* may suggest a divine-human union which —the Divine being infinite and the human, finite—dissipates the human into the Divine. Were this the case, Holy Communion would be an otherworldly experience which fled from rather than transfigured the world; which retroactively destroyed the Creation in which the finite, while dependent on divine Wisdom, is granted independence by divine Goodness; and which (because in so doing it destroyed sin as well), retroactively destroyed the need for a divine death which conquers sin. Such an otherworldly mysticism would be *confined* to the mystical experience; it would not be the climax of a cycle of cultic life. Rather than postmoral it would be amoral if not antimoral. And when it appeared on the scene it would lack all power to move historical realities. Thus Jewish pain and Roman unhappiness both testify to the unre-

---

others." In the Lutheran conception, trans-substantiation is "of the kind in which what is external is absorbed, [and] the presence of God is of a purely spiritual sort, directly connected with the faith of the subject." The reformed conception falls below the Lutheran because for it "God is present . . . only in memory," which is why "the Divine has become lowered to the prose of Enlightenment . . . and expresses a merely moral relationship." (*Werke*, XII, pp.338 ff. [*Phil. Rel.*, III, pp.132 ff.].) *Bln. Schr.*, pp.30–55 is the *locus classicus* of Hegel's position toward Lutheranism. On his position toward Catholicism, see further below, appendix 4 to this chapter, pp.158 ff., and ch. 6, sects. 2(b), 5 and appendix 1.

deemedness of the world; they would remain unmoved by an otherworldly mysticism which merely fled from it.

But it is of the utmost importance to recognize that the *unio mystica* of Hegel's Christian is not of this kind. It is the climax of a cultic life which repeats man's divorce from God as well as his union with Him, *and whose own reality encompasses both*. It neither excludes the divorce, nor is itself one pole of a whole of life which alternates meaninglessly between divorce and union. It rather *redeems* the divorce, and it can do so only by both recognizing and negating it. Indeed, it *is* this negating. The Christian God who has already redeemed death had first to suffer death. *Christian cult can perpetually repeat the death of death only by repeating, as well, the divine death itself.* Christian life includes the agony of Good Friday, even though the bliss of Easter overreaches it. Only thus can Christian life remain in the world and yet redeem it, transfiguring both Roman unhappiness and Jewish pain. Only thus can the comprehensive Truth asserted be *all*-comprehensive—of future possibilities as well as past actualities. Christian life possesses such a Truth because it recognizes the Divine in the extreme of its infinity and the human in the extreme of its finiteness, because it does not flee from but suffers the total agony of the divorce between them, and because in this very agony it both is given and accepts the Truth which heals it.

9. *Theological Thought and the Double Trinity*

However, Christian life, comprehensive in the dimension of the cultic, is still lacking in comprehensiveness so long as it remains confined to that dimension. It is in two crucial respects incomplete.

Hegel's Christian was seen to be initially in the world but not of it: in the world because unlike Stoics and Skeptics he does not flee from it but rather inverts all its values; he is not of the world because the world is not yet *actually* inverted, but inverted only in the life of his faith. According to Hegel's Christian (who thus emerges as both a Protestant and a modern man), this process of transfiguring the actual world (begun with the rise of Christian faith) has remained in principle arrested throughout the entire Middle Ages, during which the divine image in man was recognized in the sight of God but not in that of feudal princes, and during which Christian faith was left in Catholic other-worldliness. Only in the modern world has the divine image become a secular reality, and the Catholic heaven, a Protestant earth.

The process of transfiguring the world, lengthy in one sense, is endless in another. For the Truth forever repeated *complete* in the Christian religious life is in secular life forever yet *to be* completed, even after it has become a modern reality. This difference, far from accidental and temporary, is of the essence of the respective forms of religiosity and secularity. The form of the one is human faith receptive *of* the Divine; that of the other, a divine self-activity manifest *in* the human. The one is complete because the divine gift is complete and need but be humanly received. The other is forever yet to be completed even though the self-activity too is divine, for it becomes actual in an activity which remains bound to the limits of humanity.

But how can modern Protestant faith view its relation to modern secular self-activity? Is this latter reduced by faith to the means by which it conquers the external world? Or is, on the contrary, faith and its inner world conquered by secular self-activity? This latter possibility would not be without precedent. Roman self-confidence destroyed the finite pagan gods: is it the case that modern secular self-confidence must seek to destroy the infinite and therefore final Christian God, and thus inaugurate a radically post-religious era? If so, it would produce a truly devastating challenge. For while Christian faith might confront it with implacable hostility, this stance in itself would amount to defeat—for a Truth which claims not to flee from the world but rather to comprehend and transfigure it.

These are questions of the utmost seriousness. But they cannot at present be answered or even fully stated; for Christian faith—and it is *its* standpoint we are presently describing—is, as Hegel sees it, only beginning to answer them in his own time; its answers, moreover, are one-sided because they require corresponding answers from the standpoint of modern secular self-activity. Not until we have reenacted Hegel's philosophical comprehension of *both* these standpoints—and *only* philosophy can fully comprehend both—can the questions just raised be answered.[52]

So much, for the present, for the one main challenge to the comprehensiveness of Christian Truth. The other—if anything still more serious—has long been dealt with in Christian life. Or rather it has been dealt with in part, for its final disposal will come only from the Hegelian philosophy. This challenge comes from speculative thought.

Conceivably Hegel's Christian might simply reject the ancient philosophic claim to speculative truth (although this might jeopardize his own claim to comprehensive truth). His actual position (already glimpsed in his attitude toward the Greek-Roman world) is quite otherwise. The claimed rise of pagan thought to Divinity was an actual rise, and with or without the help of preexisting pagan philosophy,* Hegel's Christian himself at length accomplishes such a rise in the speculative dogma produced by theological thought and embraced by the church. Christian existence, which is the cultic repetition of the divine incursion *into* time, at length assumes a dimension of thought rising *above* time, to the Deity dwelling in eternity. Here we see the last main characteristic still missing in the description of Hegel's genuine Christianity.**

---

* It is certain that according to Hegel (i) pre-Christian philosophy can rise to the preworldly Trinity, see ch. 6, sect. 2(a) and (b); (ii) Christian faith too accomplishes this rise. What the texts make difficult for us to decide is whether, as he confronts the Greek-Roman world, Hegel's Christian *requires* the Neoplatonic rise to the preworldly Trinity (which is already accomplished in the pagan world) in order himself to rise to that Trinity, i.e., to theological thought.

** See appendix 4 to this chapter, pp.158 ff.

It is one of the utmost importance. Conceivably the Christian God might conceal as well as reveal Himself, confining His disclosure to the human to what He *does*. For Hegel's Christian, the revelation includes what God *is* and is therefore *total*. As far back as in Plato and Aristotle, the God even of pagan philosophy was so lacking in "envy" as to disclose His nature—or some of it—to human thought.[53] The Christian God who is Love can do no less. As will be seen, He does far more.

Having risen to theological thought, what does Christian faith apprehend of the God who dwells in eternity? He is the infinite One of Judaism, but He is no longer an abstract One, empty except in contrast with a manifold world outside Him and yet requiring that world for His own lordship. His unity is self-complete and alive. Its self-complete life is a blessed play of Love, in which Son separates from Father only to be reunited as Spirit. And the theological thought which contemplates the play participates in the bliss.[54] *

But as Christian theological thought rises to the eternal Trinity it comes upon a crucial dilemma. Does the eternal trinitarian Life achieve its playful bliss by indifference to the worldly and human? But then the divine incursion *into* the worldly and human is, after all, a mere myth, believed only by those incapable of theological thought, and there is redemption, not for man who exists in the world but only for his thought as it rises above it. Or is the divine playful bliss achieved by a divine self-movement *through* the world? But then the seriousness with which man takes the divine worldly incursion is, from the standpoint of divine playfulness,

---

* It must be added (and this gives further precision to the points made in appendix 4 to this chapter) that, strictly speaking, theological thought has two poles, corresponding to the two Trinities—one speculative and the other historical. (Catholicism has been prone to subordinate the speculative to the historical [See below, ch. 6, sect. 2(b).], whereas Protestantism has been prone to suffer the loss of the speculative.) *The Hegelian philosophy of religion will have to preserve both these poles.*

mere appearance. In either case theological thought would be forced retroactively to destroy the whole reality of Christian faith, back to its believing acceptance of Creation. For that faith has accepted that finite man and his finite world, while dependent on the divine Infinity by virtue of divine Wisdom, are nevertheless granted *actual* independence by virtue of divine Goodness. But divine Love cannot destroy either divine Wisdom or divine Goodness. It must rather comprehend and complete both.

It is by virtue of an ultimate affirmation of an ultimate Love of the divine Infinity *for finite humanity* that Hegel's Christian rejects the dilemma. What would be a divine Love whose playful bliss depended on indifference to the worldly and human? And what would it be if it passed through both only in order to achieve this bliss, lacking it without such a passage? In either case, the Love would be a divine *self*-love only. Pagan thought at its highest could get no further. Christian faith (reinforced and completed by theological thought) makes the ultimate affirmation of a *total* and *gratuitous* divine Love *for the human*: a total identification with the human, by a Divinity *which does not need it*. Hegel's Christian, then, affirms *two* Trinities: the pre-worldly trinitarian play eternally complete apart from the world, and the real trinitarian incursion into the world, which can forever conquer death only by forever suffering it. But the bond between the two Trinities is Love.*

In the life with these two Trinities Christian life finds at length its redemptive comprehensiveness. Without a cultic aspect it would be confined to a sphere of thought beyond time, leaving existence in time unredeemed. Without a thought-aspect its cultic life with what God has done and does would comprehend and

---

* Here lies not only the innermost center of the comprehensive truth of Christian existence but also—as will be seen—the innermost secret which enables the entire Hegelian philosophy to preserve its "middle" from fragmentation. See ch. 6, sects. 4–6 and appendices 3, pp.218 ff, and 4, pp.220 ff.

redeem all past forms of human life, but its comprehensiveness would fall short of totality since it lacked access to what God *is*. All philosophic thought which claims just such an access would already fall outside it. And what would already be true of present philosophic thought might still come to be true as well of future forms of religious life.* But against these possibilities, the Christianity of Hegel's Christian does claim total comprehensiveness. For it is a life whose cult-pole with the trinitarian incursion into time points to a thought-pole which rises to the divine trinitarian Life above time, and whose thought-pole above time yet turns back to the cult-pole in time. It turns back because it recognizes a divine Goodness which has created man, and a divine Love which has become one with him in his humanity.

Appendix 1

The Concept of Religious Representation (*Vorstellung*)

(*See pp.122 ff.*)

We render Hegel's term *Vorstellung* with the conventional but obscure and artificial "representation" because all more natural terms have false connotations. (In this case, artificiality would appear to have its uses.) Thus "notion" (Walter Kaufmann) and "idea" (in the translation of *Philosophy of Religion* by E. B. Speirs and J. B. Sanderson) suggest subjectivism, and "picture-thinking" (J. N. Findlay) is inadequate because the "picture" may be a merely finite, nonreligious *Bild*, and because the "thinking" would have to refer, not only to the thinking

---

* It may be mentioned in passing that Hegel's treatment of Islam—historically post-Christian but dialectically pre-Christian—must be viewed as quite absurdly prejudiced, indeed, as little more than a caricature, unless that treatment is understood as presupposing and encompassing that comprehensive Christian truth which this chapter has endeavoured to reproduce.

aspect of religious existence but also to religious existence as a whole. (This objection would apply also to "symbolic thinking," although less strongly so.)

Hegel subscribes to the following doctrines:

1. Religious *Vorstellung* refers to the Infinite, in contrast with the merely finite "picture" (*Bild*); thus "world" is a *Vorstellung* whereas "winged horse" is a mere *Bild*. (*Werke*, XI, p.138 [*Phil. Rel.*, I, p.142].)

2. Religious *Vorstellung* refers to the Infinite in a finite way, e.g., by using analogies from natural life, by employing externally connecting terms such as "and" and "also," and—above all!—by taking the Infinite referred to as external to the human person who does the referring (*Werke*, XI, p.143 [*Phil. Rel.*, I, pp.147 ff.]; *Einl. Gesch. Phil.*, pp.166 ff.; see further, ch. 6, sects. 1 and 3).

3. Because of the last-named characteristic, the represented is accepted by the representing person, at least to begin with, as *given*. (*Werke*, XI, p.146 [*Phil. Rel.*, I, pp.150 ff.].)

4. Even while it remains *Vorstellung*, however, *Vorstellung* is capable of expressing its own fundamental inadequacy, i.e., the inadequacy of finitely referring to the Infinite; and when it assumes such an expression it becomes dialectical. (*Werke*, XI, pp.153 ff. [*Phil. Rel.*, pp.157 ff.] On this point, see especially sect. 5 of this chapter.)

5. Even though to begin with the represented is accepted as given, both the represented and representation itself are in every genuine religion part of a spiritual God-man relation in which mere external givenness is transcended. (*Werke*, XI, pp.146 ff. [*Phil. Rel.*, I, pp.150 ff.] On this point, see especially sects. 7 and 8 of this chapter.)

In the above brief account, one decisive characteristic is not mentioned—that religious representation moves toward, but fails to reach, the universality of speculative thought. This is because any present treatment of this characteristic would be wholly premature. (See all of ch. 6.) We may presently only say, negatively, that the thought in question is not finite reflection, and that it does not expose religious representation as a mere human projection and illusion as it reflects on it. Careless readers have always mistaken it for such a reflection, and they have therefore viewed Hegel as a demythologizing enemy of religious faith. In fact, however, Hegel regards a thought of this kind as inferior to religious representation and declares himself to be in alliance with Christian orthodoxy against it. (e.g., *Werke*, XI, pp.28 ff.; XII, pp.350 ff. [*Phil. Rel.*, I, pp.27 ff., III, pp.145 ff.].)

Appendix 2

The Role of Authority in Genuine Religion

(*See p.128.*)

The *Early Theological Writings* remain with an unresolved dualism between a positive religion of the letter—subservience to authority—and a true religion of the Spirit. In contrast, the *Philosophy of Religion* states:

Doctrine and content receive positive form, they . . . are valid in society. All law, . . . whatever is valid, has this form, of being something existing, and as such is essential for everyone, valid and binding. But only the form is positive, the content must be true Spirit. The Bible has this form of positivity; but it is one of its own sayings that the letter killeth whereas the Spirit maketh alive. . . . The grasp is here not passive receptivity; the grasp by Spirit is at the same time its activity. . . . Spirit thus begins with the positive but is essentially present; it is to be the . . . Holy Spirit which grasps and knows the Divine, this content, *as* divine . . . Some have no awareness that they are active in this receptivity." (*Werke*, XII, p.206 [*Phil. Rel.*, II, p.344].)

Obviously Hegel has here found a legitimate albeit subordinate place for "positivity" *within* genuine religion, and this is the case already in the *Phenomenology*. (See ch. 3, sect. 4.) Idolizers of the *Early Theological Writings*—and not only these—see in this a reactionary betrayal of Hegel's early revolutionary conception. In fact his early position toward "positivity" (which goes little if anything beyond Kant) is a thought fragment superseded by but contained in the comprehending position of his maturity; and this development in his philosophy of religion is but part of the development of his entire philosophy. We have already shown, in ch. 4, that the middle of Hegel's mature thought seeks to overreach the external and contingent, rather than flee from it "in monkish fashion," and we shall presently show that in Christianity, as understood in Hegel's mature thought, the Divine suffers and redeems externality rather than, "keeping itself free from death," leaving externality unredeemed. To charge the mature Hegel with a reactionary surrender to "positivity" is to fail to recognize that positivity is far more radically disposed of when, rather than externally opposed, it is absorbed and transfigured.

Appendix 3

Jewish, Greek, and Roman Religion

(*See p.133.*)

The account here begun, and subsequently to be further developed, of the meeting of the Jewish East and the Greek-Roman West departs radically from all standard accounts which simply summarize the dialectical sequence of "religions of spiritual individuality" found in the original text of the *Philosophy of Religion*: Jewish "religion of sublimity," Greek "religion of beauty," Roman "religion of utility." (*Werke*, XII, pp.3–188 [*Phil. Rel.*, II, pp.122–323].) These summaries (particularly when they imply that the dialectically later is *ipso facto* spiritually superior) require the suppression of much conflicting evidence. (i) In his Berlin lectures of 1824 and 1831 Hegel followed the cited sequence, but in 1827 he reversed it, proceeding from Greek through Jewish to Roman religion. (ii) Hegel exalts Greek beauty above Judaism because it "reconciles significance with natural material" whereas Judaism "explicitly recognizes the natural material as inadequate." At the same time, and precisely because Jewish holiness involves a demythologizing (*Entgoettlichung*) of nature, Judaism is *religiously* superior, and far closer to a truth acceptable to modern man who "cannot believe in a Ganges, a cow, a sea, *an Indian or Greek god.*" (*Vorlesungen ueber die Philosophie der Religion*, ed. Georg Lasson [Leipzig: Meiner, 1925–30], vol. II, pt. II, pp.71, 68 ff., 250 ff., 57; italics added. See the additional comment further below.) (iii) At least as regards its religious quality Hegel places Roman religion far below *both* Jewish and Greek religion: "Dying was the only virtue which the noble Roman could practise, and this he shared with slaves and criminals condemned to death." (*Werke*, XII, p.180 [*Phil. Rel.*, II, p.315].) (iv) From the standpoint of Christianity—which the Hegelian philosophy presupposes and encompasses—the relation between the three religions appears as a "meeting" in which Jewish East is on a par with Greek-Roman West. (*Werke*, XII, pp.187 ff., 273 ff., 125 [*Phil. Rel.*, II, pp.322 ff.; III, 62 ff.; II, pp.255].)

The above four points should suffice to demonstrate that any account confined to an ascending Jewish-Greek-Roman sequence presents Hegel as far more anti-Judaic and pro-Greek (as well as pro-Roman) than he actually is (particularly in his mature thought). This practice has a long history in the German Hegelian schools (left as well as right), which are infected with a pronounced anti-Judaic bias. Why is the phrase "Indian or Greek god," cited under (ii), missing from the original edition of Hegel's works? (*Werke*, XII, p.59 [*Phil. Rel.*, II, p.185].) And why does Hermann Glockner's *Hegel-Lexikon* (first published in Germany in 1935!) cite, under "Jewish religion," only negative but no laudatory passages? To give but one example, Glockner quotes Hegel's phrase concerning Jewish "fanaticism of stubbornness" but not the statement (which is part of the same sentence!) that this fanaticism represents "admirable firmness." (*HL*, p.1180; *Werke*, XII, p.85 [*Phil. Rel.*, II, p.212].)

The interpretation we shall give will attempt to take into account all the above aspects of Hegelian doctrine, and it will rely on two main factors: (i) the distinction (made and held fast to throughout chs. 5 and 6) between Christian faith and its reenactment in Hegelian philosophy: for the former standpoint, Jewish East and Greek-Roman West will be seen to be equal in significance; (ii) the fact that the Greek and Roman religions do, and the Jewish religion does not, give rise to philosophy: this is what *makes* Greek-Roman West equal to the Jewish East for the Christian standpoint (when otherwise it would be inferior), and it is also what makes both Greek and Roman religion superior to the Jewish from the standpoint of the Hegelian philosophy.

This whole subject will be dealt with further throughout ch. 6, see especially pp.171 n., 179 n., and 198 ff. n.

Appendix 4

The Role of Theological Thought in Medieval Catholicism and Modern Protestantism

(See p.151.)

This characteristic must be left deliberately vague at this point. (i) Hegel clearly holds that Christian existence and self-understanding—both Catholic and Protestant—remain incomplete without access in theological thought to the preworldly Trinity. (ii) This access must therefore be distinguished from the philosophical—not only from that of pagan Neoplatonism which is without Christian existence and, indeed, divorced from all existence (See below, ch. 6, sect. 2[a].), but also (at least in the first instance) from the Hegelian access; for this latter is not *part* of Christian existence and self-understanding but rather their speculative transfiguration. (iii) But the section of the *Philosophy of Religion* titled, "The Kingdom of the Father," (*Werke*, XII, pp.223–47 [*Phil. Rel.*, III, pp.7–33].) already gives the first phase of the Hegelian transfiguration. We cannot therefore hold that Hegel's Christian (whose representational existence we have seen move from the "Kingdom of the Son" to the "Kingdom of the Spirit" which in speculative transfiguration come, respectively, second and third) at length gains *total* access in theological thought to the "Kingdom of the Father" which in speculative reenactment comes first: for this would make his theological thought already speculative, and the Hegelian speculative thought a redundancy. (In fact, this latter is not a redundancy, and it requires all of modern secular life and all of modern philosophical thought, *in addition to* the life of Christian faith, in order to do its work, see all of ch. 6.) At the same time, one cannot hold that Christian theological thought has *no* access at all to the "Kingdom of the Father": this would be directly at odds with the doctrine stated in (i). (iv) For the purposes of this chapter, the completeness Hegel finds in Christian faith is indicated sufficiently in the doctrine— common to Catholicism and Protestantism—of a double Trinity, of which one aspect is accessible in the life of Christian cult, and the other, in Christian theological thought. (v) The further expansion of the notion of Christian completeness, undertaken in the next chapter, will show the following general results. Catholic theology has access to the true preworldly trinitarian "content," but is confined to unfree subjection in "form" to ecclesiastical authority, and Catholic cultic life too is so subject. (See ch. 6, sect. 2[b].) As for Protestantism, its cultic life-pole is emancipated from Catholic "unfreedom"; but it has on the whole been unable to hold fast, in its theological thought-pole, to the preworldly trinitarian content; indeed, challenged as it is by anti-religious modern philosophy, this loss has been very nearly inevitable. (See ch. 6, sect. 2[c] and appendix 1.) All these assertions are directly related to the claim of the Hegelian philosophy to being the final theology. And this claim is in turn intimately related to the climactic philosophical goal of "making peace" with Christianity. This peace will become intelligible only toward the end of ch. 6.

CHAPTER SIX

The Transfiguration
of Faith into Philosophy

The absolute Idea may be compared to the old
man, who utters the same religious doctrines
as the child, but for whom they signify his
entire life. The child in contrast may understand
the religious content. But all of life and
the whole world still exist outside it.

Enz., sect. 237 *Zus.* (*Werke*, VI, p.409).*

For the Understanding, to be sure, the mysteries
of Christianity are an impenetrable secret. But
because they are speculative in nature Reason can grasp
them. Nor are they secret: for they are revealed.

Werke, XV, p.77 (*Hist. Phil.*, II, p.448).

We have to consider . . . the transition from
faith to knowledge, the alteration, the transfiguration
of faith in philosophy.

Werke, XIII, p.316 (*Phil. Rel.*, III, p.108).

1. *Introduction*

We have now completed our reconstruction of "religion . . . [as
it] exist[s] without philosophy." Our remaining task—and it is the
climactic task—is to understand why "philosophy cannot exist without religion, . . . [and how it comes to] encompass religion in its
own being."[1] More specifically, the task is to understand Hegel's
oft-repeated formula that the true content, already existing in the

---

* Abbreviations are listed on pp.245 ff.

Christian religion in the form of representation, is given in his own philosophy the true form of speculative thought.[2]

This formula is more easily cited than understood. How can philosophical thought emancipate itself from the religious form and yet recognize, preserve, and indeed itself presuppose the truth of the religious content? Not, first, if it reduces what religious representation takes for an *actual* divine-human relationship to the solitary disport of the soul with its own unrecognized products. In that case, religion would be as false in content as it is in form, and philosophy would then destroy its own hopes to grasp the true content even as it exposes the religious failure to grasp it. The divine worship which is philosophy collapses with the divine worship which is religion.*

Philosophy cannot, next, accept a divine presence in the religious relation and yet *simply* reject religious representation. The religious content, while true, would then reduce itself to the emptiest of truths—a sheer empty Presence manifest in or to a sheer feeling equally empty. In Hegel's time as in ours, demythologizing philosophies sought simply to destroy myth and symbol. Hegel's own philosophy is not among these. In his view, myth and symbol do not cover but rather uncover religious Truth.[3] They express content, and the content is inseparable from the form of expression. Philosophic thought, to be sure, aims to rise above religious representation. But if in so doing it simply destroyed this latter it would reduce itself to emptiness. Hegelian philosophy of religion is not demythologizing or antisymbolic. It is transmythological and trans-symbolic.

It cannot, thirdly, possess this last-named character unless it

---

* "Philosophy itself is worship." (*Werke*, XI, p.21 [*Phil. Rel.*, I, p.21]; also *Einl. Gesch. Phil.*, p.169.) For faith, God is not a mere subjective postulate: "God is, and is for us; He has from His side a relationship to us," and this relationship is the object of the philosophical proofs of God as well. (*Werke*, XII, pp.396 ff. [*Phil. Rel.*, III, pp.192 ff.].) This is because in absolute knowledge, as much as in religious faith, the question is not "how man reaches God" but rather "how God reaches man." (*Bln. Schr.*, p.314.)

can rise to infinity. A thought confined to finitude might reflect on religious representation and recognize myth and symbol for what they are. But if while doing so it accepted a divine Presence in religious representation, it could not rise above representation to a higher form of truth. Demythologizing would lead back to re-mythologizing, reflection upon religious life, into immediate religious life itself.*

Hegelian thought, then, can achieve its transrepresentational goals only if it is not finite and human but rather infinite and divine. But how can it achieve its goals even then? The dilemmas just rejected are not Hegel's. The dilemma now to be considered is at the heart of his own philosophy, and it is no very great exaggeration to say that his whole *Philosophy of Religion*—and, indirectly, his whole philosophy—is haunted by it. *Either the representational form of religion is essential to its content, and this is why philosophy requires religion (and the absolute philosophy the Christian religion) as necessary presupposition. But then how can philosophy transcend or transfigure the representational form without loss of the religious content? Or else philosophy does indeed achieve its unprecedented feat: but then was not the representational form all along unessential to the religious content? And does not then philosophy presuppose religion, if at all, only* per accidens?

What is here at stake becomes fully clear through the decisive criterion which distinguishes religious representation from speculative thought. The religiously represented remains *other than* the representing activity; speculative thought, in contrast, is a sheer, infinite self-productivity which has surpassed and vanquished all otherness: "the represented ceases to be such, and ceases to be alien to the knowledge of it, only because the Self has produced it."[4]

---

* See *Werke*, XI, 147 (*Phil. Rel.*, I, pp.157 ff.): "The experience . . . that I cannot help myself by means of reflection, that I cannot, in fact, take my stand upon myself at all, and the circumstance that I still crave something that stands firm—all this forces me back from reflection and leads me to adhere to the content in the form in which it is given . . . ." This is implicitly recognized by religious apologetics "whose chief ground is authority, namely, divine authority—that God has revealed to man what is to be represented."

Religion, then, remains a relation *between* the human and the Divine, but speculative thought is a human activity at one with the Divine.

The Hegelian dilemma may therefore be restated as follows. *Either God is ultimately other than man,* as is the religious testimony of the believer who stands in relation with Him. *But then religion is true in form as well as in content, and philosophic thought must* recognize both as well as itself *remain finite reflection. Or philosophic thought can become an absolute, all-encompassing self-activity. But then it discloses the illusoriness of the gap between the Divine and the human, and hence that—in the decisive respect—religion is false in content no less than in form.* Christian life, in that case, dissipates itself into mere appearance: the sin of man and the death of God are both, after all, not serious realities but mere aspects of a divine play. As for philosophic thought, it is the enjoyment of the play.

This dilemma haunts Hegel's *Philosophy of Religion.* But it is present, as well, in his philosophy as a whole which (as Hegel himself insists) both presupposes and transfigures Christianity. It is no accident that our preceding account of the Hegelian philosophy has wrestled with, but not yet answered, these two questions: how can philosophic thought claim absoluteness over against standpoints of life which themselves claim to fall outside it;[5] and how, having made this claim, can it both encompass the actual world and yet not, as such, destroy it?[6] It has previously emerged that Hegel's philosophy requires an infinite divine-human Life to mediate between finite life and infinite Thought, and that this, for Hegel, is Christian life.[7] What emerges now is that Christianity cannot fulfil this mediating function if a final conflict erupts which is itself incapable of mediation—between it and philosophic thought. It is Hegel's goal to bring about a final "peace" between the final religion and the final philosophy.[8] It would appear that unless he can achieve this peace, his whole philosophy falls into fragments.

This peace is the subject of the present chapter. The manner in which it will be concluded may preliminarily be summed up as follows. The final philosophy presupposes the final religion: unless the absolute content were present in Christian life, philosophic thought could not, in its own right, hope to attain it. But in attaining that content it transfigures its form: for whereas the Christian (and indeed every) religion is a divine-human relation the final (and indeed every) philosophy is a oneness of thought with Divinity. The final philosophy produces peace with the final religion, in that it rises in thought to the divine side of that divine-human relation at whose human side the final religion remains; and having so risen, by reenacting that relation in thought.

Such a philosophic enterprise will produce peace with Christianity only if it can satisfy two crucial conditions. It must be able to rise to the divine side of the Christian divine-human relation, even though Christian faith itself remains at the human, and, having so risen, it must be able to reenact the Christian divine-human relation in thought and yet not destroy or dissipate its representational existence in human life. Whether Hegel's thought can or does supply either of these conditions is, to be sure, questionable. That he seeks to supply them is not. This must be stressed in particular concerning the second condition on which in the *Philosophy of Religion* the main weight rests. The critics have always noted that the Hegelian philosopher "walks on his head," but only rarely that he does so "for a change only"[9]—because he is a man as well. They have seen that his philosophy is a speculative "Sunday [during which man], uniting himself with the Divine, makes his individuality and activity vanish in the Divine";[10] but not that this Sunday is connected with the workaday week "during which man stands on his own feet, is master in his own house, and pursues his own interests."[11] But philosophy, in fact, *is* that connection. The critics, in short, have paid insufficient heed to the fact that nothing is further from Hegel's intentions than the dissipation of human life—life in general and religious life in particular—into philosophical thought.

The general execution of Hegel's intentions in his philosophy as a whole has been discussed in a previous chapter. We then watched the extreme care with which his thought seeks a middle between right- and left-wing extremes, of which one would destroy the actual world and the other, philosophical thought. In the present chapter, we shall have occasion to watch Hegel's speculative transfiguration of Christianity give equal care to seeking a middle which would preserve Christianity against two extremes equally destructive of it. One of these is a speculative pantheism which would dissipate the human into the Divine. The other is an atheistic humanism which would reduce the Divine to the human.[12]

2. *Christianity and the History of Philosophy*

Can Hegel's thought rise from the human to the divine side of the Christian divine-human relation? This question obliges us to introduce (possibly very belatedly) a crucial Hegelian doctrine. *The rise of thought to Infinity or Divinity is by no means an achievement confined to Hegelian philosophy: it is, whether or not it is recognized as such, actual in all philosophy worthy of the name.* Since Parmenides philosophic thought has been "elevated to the realm of the ideal"; as Aristotle first consciously recognized, it has been a "thought thinking itself" which is not finite or human but infinite or divine.[13] Such expressly finite forms of thought as empiricism are one-sided protests against infinite forms of Thought which latter, because abstractly infinite, are themselves one-sided: and both the protest and its object are part of a larger, concrete infinity. According to our exposition thus far it may have seemed that the Hegelian project of rising to infinite Thought is in its self-understanding without precedent, and that it presupposes Christianity. Now it seems that it is as ancient as philosophy itself and (since ancient philosophy is pagan) in no need of Christianity at all.

But it is one of the chief objectives of Hegel's *History of Phi-*

losophy to define the exact relation of Hegelian philosophy both to all prior philosophy and to Christianity.* The definition emerges from the periods into which the history of philosophy is divided. Greek thought, though a "free" rise to Divinity, is in principle limited by the fact that it is pre-Christian. This limitation is transcended by medieval philosophy, which is rooted in the Christian faith. This rootedness, however, robs it of the freedom essential to philosophy, which is why medieval philosophy is not a genuine philosophic period in its own right but rather a time of "fermentation and preparation"[14] of the modern period. Finally, modern philosophy reconquers the ancient freedom, and indeed expands it to infinity. But precisely for this reason it is in its pre-Hegelian forms hostile to the very Christian background to which it owes its power of self-expansion. Only the final modern philosophy—Hegel's own—can *recognize* that modern speculative thought presupposes the Christian faith which it was previously bound to oppose, and that the opposition between the two is relative rather than absolute: and this recognition transmutes total warfare into total peace.

We see that thought moves, to begin with [i.e., in the Middle Ages] . . . , within Christianity, accepting it as absolute presupposition. Later, when the wings of thought have grown strong [i.e., in the modern world] philosophy rises to the sun like a young eagle, a bird of prey which strikes religion down. But it is the last development of speculative thought to do justice to faith and make peace with religion.[15]

(a) *Ancient Philosophy*

This interpretation of the history of philosophy must now be sketched in some detail.[16] And we must begin with Hegel's extraordinary esteem for ancient Greece and all its works which, romantically excessive in his youth, still survives in his mature thought. Thus the *History of Philosophy* devotes more space to

---

* It need hardly be said that the following account treats the *History of Philosophy* only from this point of view, and is forced to leave it otherwise unconsidered.

Greek thought than to all the remainder, and the *Encyclopedia*, albeit a work said to be possible only in the modern Christian world, nevertheless closes with a famous passage from Aristotle's *Metaphysics*.*

However, mature Hegelian thought keeps esteem for Greece within clear and reasonably well-disciplined limits. Modern man may feel at home in Greece; yet he cannot return to it or wish to do so, for his world is Christian. Modern philosophy may "recognize . . . [the ancient as] satisfying at its stage of development," but it satisfies at its stage *only*, which modern philosophy has surpassed. Greek philosophy is an indispensable aspect of the complete philosophy, but it is no more.[17]

From its beginnings in Thales to its end in Neoplatonism, Greek thought is never without the freedom which is of the philosophic essence. For it is at one with a Divinity which is no alien Beyond but rather an immanent Presence. Moreover, as ancient thought develops it grows in richness and content. The abstract Being of Parmenides quickly yields to the dialectical Becoming of Heraclitus which in turn soon emerges—in the *Nous* of Anaxagoras—as a free, self-determining universality. Against the objective universality in which hitherto thought has lost itself subjective reflection then makes its claims, *viz.*, in the sophists and Socrates. This, to be sure, is immediately a mere human—finite—subjectivity, asserted against the objective universality. But Plato and Aristotle raise

* Although Hegel's regard for all things Greek can here be treated only in the present brief section we must stress that its importance can hardly be exaggerated. It has a decisive effect, not only on the Hegelian system as a whole and on such of its parts as the history of philosophy, the philosophy of art (virtually by-passed in this volume) and the philosophy of history but also—for our present purpose still more important—on his philosophical reenactment of religion. Thus Hegel considers the revealed Christian religion, not as an extension of the revealed Jewish religion, but much rather as the comprehensive truth of all religions, and it is doubtful if this would be possible except for the exalted place assigned to Greek religion. We have already expressed our view that the inadequacies even of the mature Hegelian treatment of Judaism are much more due to a pro-Greek than to an anti-Judaic bias, ch. 5, sect. 6; see further, pp.171 n., 198 ff. n., and n. 18.

this, itself, to universality, thus reaching an ideal world alive at
once *as* divine Thought and *in* human thought. Mankind did not
have to wait for Christianity in order to learn that God is not
envious. For this was known, already, to these two greatest of all
pagan philosophers. Indeed, "there is no higher idealism" than
that of Aristotle, even in the modern world.[18]

And yet, this is neither the highest nor the last stage even of
ancient philosophy. The Platonic Idea qua pure thought may "contain everything." It is, however, "abstract": internally complete, it
fails to encompass what is *not* ideal, as well as the subject qua not
thinking; and this failure is reflected in the failures of the Platonic
state. Nor does Aristotle succeed where Plato fails. He does, indeed, recognize the particular and seeks to unite it with the
universal. But he does not find the unity he seeks. Universal and
sense particulars remain beside each other, and the subject qua
thinker and qua human individual fall apart. The comprehensiveness sought remains an unfulfilled need.[19]

Hence classical gives way to postclassical Greek thought, even
though this latter cannot either maintain or recapture the classical
speculative power. In Stoicism and Epicureanism isolated subjectivity, hitherto left outside and uncomprehended, asserts itself,
and in making itself the criterion of all truth this self-assertion is
absolute. By itself, to be sure, this is an arid individualistic, subjectivist, dogmatism. But it *shows* its aridity by a display of its
internal emptiness, and as this emptiness assumes—in Skepticism—
conscious recognition, it annihilates all dogmatic claims of every
isolated subjectivity, those of Skepticism itself included. And this
self-annihilation has a positive power. Ancient Skepticism points
beyond a self-enclosed subjectivity cut off from objective reality,
and to a renewal, within the sphere of inwardness, of an objective
world.

This renewal—the climactic achievement of ancient thought—
is accomplished in Alexandrinian Neoplatonism. Unlike original
Platonism, because it has passed through the destructive subjec-

tivism of the Stoic, Epicurean, and Skeptical phases, Neoplatonism is "left with no other Essence than its own self-consciousness," and this is why it can rebuild the ideal world within this sphere only. As so rebuilt, however, this world is by no means the mere finite product of a merely finite subjectivity. It is an infinite world produced by a subjectivity which, dialectically ruined by Skepticism in its finite claims, has raised itself to infinity on these very ruins. This total "internalization of infinite subjectivity . . . [in which] self-consciousness knows itself to be, in its thinking, the Absolute" is the final standpoint achieved in the ancient world. And of this Hegel asserts that it is "closely connected with the revolution brought about by Christianity in the world."[20]

Nevertheless, the Christian revolution will mark the end of all ancient pagan thought, the Neoplatonic included. True, that most decisive "jolt" in all of history which is Christianity is not wholly confined to Christianity. For Neoplatonic thought shares with Christian faith the "revelation" of a God at once living—trinitarian and "not alien"—in and for subjectivity rather than external to it. In the case of Neoplatonism, however, there is a high price to be paid for this revelation, one too high for survival. The Stoic, Epicurean, and Skeptical assertion of finite subjective thought has been accompanied by a progressive alienation from the external, objective world. This breach is by no means healed by the Neoplatonic rise to infinity. The inward world of thought attained, to be sure, is a complete world, in which Spirit can dwell in self-sufficiency, and while Stoics, Epicureans, and even Skeptics must seek compensation for their empty inward freedom in an external world which, however unfree, is not at any rate empty, Neoplatonic mystics do not need such compensation: for their inward life is rich and internally complete. But this very richness, far from healing the breach between the inward and outward worlds, makes it complete.[21]

The origins of this alienation hark back virtually to the beginnings of Greek philosophy. As early as in Anaxagoras philosophy demythologizes (*entgoettlicht*) nature, thereby threatening that "unity with nature, that beautiful faith, that innocent spirit and childlike purity" which are characteristic of early Greek life. As for the Socratic "freedom of self-consciousness," it may initiate a reversal of the whole "Spirit of the world." At the same time, the critical morality which it produces is also at odds with uncritical Greek custom, externally sanctioned by the gods: thus it poses, at the very time of the "greatest flowering of Greek life," the "threat of disaster." The conflict between Socrates and his Athenian judges is not one between good and evil. It is a tragic collision.[22]

This split the Platonic state cannot heal but only disclose, and it progressively widens as the pagan world moves toward its internal disintegration. Stoic, Epicurean, and Skeptical free thought becomes progressively divorced from an external world which, under Rome, becomes increasingly oppressive, and the nemesis of this flight from the world is an increasing inward emptiness. Neoplatonic thought does create a whole inward world on this empty and barren soil, but because it remains in flight from the external world, its inward creation reflects this flight. Neoplatonism does not tackle the "absolute breach" of an "infinite subjectivity" which permeates both the external and the internal; it seeks escape from that breach. Hence the "totality" in which it comes to dwell, however "concrete," is not a final consummation of the old world but rather a longing for a new.[23]

This result of ancient thought corresponds to a result in the ancient world; for this too ends in longing. There is, however, a significant difference between the two. The Roman world may end with a state of unhappy longing, but it does not transcend this condition, and salvation, when it comes, comes simply from without. Neoplatonic philosophy, in contrast, transcends its pagan limitations sufficiently to recognize them *as* limitations, which is why it has some readiness *of* thought for a Truth which cannot and will not come *from* mere thought. As St. Augustine was to put it, the Neoplatonists may not know the road to the country in which man henceforth is to dwell. But they at least perceive it, albeit dimly and as if through a veil.[24]

(b) *Medieval Philosophy*

Medieval thought exposes itself to Christian faith, and in so doing suffers loss of that freedom which is of the philosophic essence, but just in this lies its greatness and world-historical significance.* As has just been noted, philosophic thought is not wholly unprepared for the Christian reality, which is why it can survive and in some respects even grow under its impact. At the same time, it is not and cannot be *wholly* prepared for it, and this is why it loses its freedom beyond recovery. Or rather, if and when thought reconquers freedom the medieval world will have ended, and the modern world will have arrived.

To achieve its unique greatness medieval thought was bound, to begin with, to resist certain Christian heresies. The Pelagian denial of original sin, the Arian rejection of God incarnate in Christ, Manichean allegorizing concerning the crucifixion, Gnostic dissipation of the historical element in Christianity: these doctrines, had they been accepted by medieval thought, would have left it in its pagan condition—an anachronism in the new, Christian world. For this new world is not made new by the rise of thought to the preworldly Trinity (already achieved in pagan Neoplatonism); nor by the appearance of a perfect Christian man (different

---

* It is worth noting that medieval Muslim and Jewish philosophy have no real place in the Hegelian scheme and are disposed of in ten pages. Of the two, Jewish philosophy poses the greater difficulty. (On Islam, see ch. 5, p.154 n.) For, essentially preoccupied with the divine covenant with Israel, it can less readily be classified with an "East [which] purified itself of all that was individual and definite, while the West descended into the depth and actual presence of Spirit." (*Werke*, XV, p.110 [*Hist. Phil.*, III, p.26].) Hegel seeks to "do justice" to the Christian scandal of particularity but can do none to the Jewish. Hence Maimonides (a genuine philosopher of the Jewish covenant) is disposed of in less than a page. But Spinoza (who rejects Judaism and is rejected by the Jewish community) is given immense and respectful attention, as expressing the Jewish principle in philosophy. See further p.179 n.

from a pagan counterpart such as Socrates, if at all, only in degree); nor again by the mere belief in that "tremendous composition of opposites"—the incursion by the Divine in the extreme of its infinite power into the human in the extreme of its human impotence, i.e., death. Free philosophic thought would dispose of such a mere human *belief* as a mere myth. The new world is made new by nothing less than the *actual event* of divine incursion into human flesh. Nothing less could have cured the contradictions of the ancient world, manifest in both their Roman and Jewish forms.[25] And in fact the cure occurred when the time was ripe for it. But once it had come, philosophic thought was bound to reverse the flight from the external world toward which Greek thought had been driven, and to become reconciled with the event which had reconciled the external world. It is no wonder that, in its self-exposure to such an event, philosophic thought should have lost its freedom, and have remained bound throughout the entire medieval period to an "absolute presupposition of faith." The wonder is much rather that it survived at all.[26]

Medieval thought was established by the Church fathers. These resisted at once two temptations. On the one hand (as already stated), they opposed heretical dissipations of the historical into a speculative dimension, forthrightly paying the price of philosophic unfreedom. On the other hand, they opposed the reduction of the speculative and eternal to a pure history devoid of eternity, thereby saving philosophic thought from destruction. For to their world-historical credit they recognized—as many modern Protestant theologians do not—that the sensuously present, historical Christ can *remain* present for faith only if, having disappeared *as* sensuous and historical, he is "received into the realm of representation": that an inward spiritual relation—as distinct from a mere external historical one—can exist only with a Christ who "sits at the right hand of God." The Neoplatonic timeless Trinity, then, at once remains timeless and yet actually enters into history. And Patristic thought is at once speculative in content and subservient to Church authority.[27] *

Medieval thought cannot regain the freedom here surrendered even in its highest achievements, brought about by the labor of scholastic thought. While this later contains the "deepest speculations of Aristotle and the Neoplatonists . . . [often in] simpler and purer form," these speculations have now a Christian, no longer a pagan basis. And whereas for pagan Greece, nature and self were a solid foundation for a rise of free thought to Divinity, they have now lost their self-sufficient reality. Nature and human self have now reality only through a divine Self which, beyond both, is accessible only through revelation: but revelation itself must be *passively received.*

This, to be sure, requires the testimony of Spirit, and in this testimony my inmost self is present. The testimony, however, remains concealed. It does not develop so as to produce its own content: thus it remains receptive. Moreover, the Spirit which testifies remains distinct from me as individual; . . . and there remains for me only the empty shell of passivity. It is within this intractable standpoint that philosophy must reemerge.

The standpoint is intractable indeed: for philosophy is activity, but the medieval access to the revealed Christian God remains receptive. Thus God has become remote for philosophic thought. Nor can scholastic thought for all its labor succeed in making the intractable tractable. Pagan Greek thought had achieved a living unity with Divinity. Christian scholastic thought merely points to God and is itself finite. Hence this thought (for which God is remote) remains subservient to faith; for this latter possesses the divine presence. "Scholastic philosophy has the same want of independence as thought among the Church Fathers."[28]

To this limitation of medieval Christian thought corresponds a limitation of medieval Christian life. The Divine, while received

---

* See appendix 1 to this chapter, pp.216 ff.

by the believer's sanctified heart, does not permeate his worldly activities; these remain unsanctified. A divorce thus erupts between the sacred and the secular. The believer, free in the sight of God, remains free in His sight *only*, and unfree on earth: salvation becomes a mere other-worldly hope. Moreover, the Church—the repository of the sacred—cannot forever maintain itself *beside* the profane. Existing *in* the world it becomes in due course infected by its worldliness. Its "world of life" which is beyond earth becomes afflicted by the sickness of the "world of death" which *is* earth. And this sickness in the end provokes a radical revolt against the dualism which is its cause: a this-worldly revolt which wants to find—and establish—heaven on earth. In the midst of this revolt modern thought will discover its own essence. Scholastic thought has degenerated into a "god-forsaken" thought—one which seeks with finite means to grasp an Infinity beyond these means. Modern thought will boldly assert itself as an infinite power, immanent in the human mind.[29]

But just as ancient thought at its highest transcends the limits of the ancient world so medieval thought at its highest transcends the limits of medieval Christendom. The proofs for the existence of God—a "wholly new phenomenon" in the Middle Ages—to be sure, are one and all invalid in form, and this reflects their medieval limitations. (The form is that of a finite thought which demonstrates conclusions from fixed premises, and the conclusions do not follow from the premises.) However, their content, which consists of truths of faith, shatters these limitations. This content is the elevation of the finite and human to the Infinite and Divine and—in the case of the ontological argument, richest and uniquely Christian in content—of finite spirit to infinite Spirit. And in the arguments (which are inadequate thought but thought nonetheless) thought has moved toward the appropriation of the religious content, by means of self-elevation to infinity.[30]

That this is a self-elevation is a truth, to be sure, which thought does not here recognize, and indeed this recognition transcends the limits of medieval power. Thus the ontological argument takes itself as moving from a mere subjective—and hence finite and human—idea of God, left in subjective fixity, to an objective divine Being left equally fixed. Still, it requires but one step—albeit one so vast as to be a veritable leap—to give the true content of the ontological argument its true form, that is, for thought to *move* so as to dissolve its own finiteness, to cancel the mere subjectivity of its God-idea, and thus to elevate itself to Infinity. And this elevation is among the ripest fruits of the final philosophy. It is no accident that in the very last year of his life Hegel composed a lecture which transfigured the medieval ontological argument into a final modern speculative truth.[31]

(c) *Modern Philosophy*

The modern world begins with a renaissance of Greek this-worldly freedom. However, this now expands itself, in various, and at first sight unrelated, ways into infinity. Greek man shuns the world of the barbarians; modern man discovers America. Greek states recognize some men as free; truly modern states recognize all men as free simply because they are human. Greek science grasps order and is stopped short by chaos; modern science seeks to penetrate and conquer the infinitude of contingent facts. In short, modern man, like the Greek, has a "joy in the earth," and is convinced that there is "right and understanding [in his] occupation with it." But unlike for the Greek what now invites and indeed demands such occupation is the *whole* earth.[32] *

Modern philosophy too acquires an infinite dimension. Ancient and modern philosophic thought are both free. But whereas the one is "naively" geared to Being, the other is "reflexively" turned on the relation between Thought and Being. The one is free because it is simply at one with the divine Being—a union above all

---

* Hegel's famous reference to America as the land of the future (*Werke*, IX, pp.100 ff. [*Phil. Hist.*, pp.80 ff.].) is wholly in line with his conception of the modern world. See sect. 5 and appendix 4.

nonunion. The other faces up to an "opposition" between Being and Thought so radical as to fragment both into finitude; and it achieves its freedom, not by means of escape from this condition, but rather by means of its gradual conquest. It is in the movement toward this conquest that the infinity of modern philosophic thought consists.

Modern freedom does not simply take over where the Greek left off, with the medieval world as a mere barren interlude between them. If modern science gives "due honor" to the empirical, if modern states recognize the human individual qua individual and human, if modern philosophic thought confronts a gulf between Thought and Being so wide as to reduce it to finiteness and yet shows a justified self-confidence in its own infinitude, all these achievements, impossible among the ancients, would have remained equally impossible in the modern world except for the medieval world which preceded it. For the antimedieval revolt which produces the modern world has positive as well as negative significance. The modern world negates the medieval divorce between the secular present and the sacred beyond, which had left empirical facts without "honor," human individuals worthless except in the sight of God, and philosophic thought bereft of its native freedom. And in this negating process it appropriates what had originally caused the medieval divorce—that "unheard of composition" of an infinite God with a finite man which has produced the Christian world. But in the modern appropriation, that composition descends from a medieval heaven to a modern earth.[33] *

This descent, however, is by no means a one-sided secularization

---

* Hegel writes:

Whole continents . . . did not possess this idea [of freedom] . . . . This idea has come into the world through Christianity, in which the individual as such is of infinite value. For he is object and purpose of divine Love, and destined to have a relation to God as Spirit, to have this Spirit dwell in him. Once man knows, in religion as such, that his essence lies in his relation to the absolute Spirit, he has the presence of the divine Spirit, as well, in the sphere of worldly existence, as being the substance of state, family etc. . . . (*Enz.*, sect. 482.)

of what was formerly sacred. The modern world negates both the sacred and the secular in their medieval divorce and opposition, and it affirms both in their mutually supporting relation. That "worldly judging of worldly things" which is modern science would be fragmented and without direction unless it were the secular aspect of a life whose religious aspect "sanctified" it. The human rights in the modern secular state would remain groundless unless these states in their very secularity were permeated by a religious Spirit. In short, the Christian religion is not a medieval reality only, which in the modern appropriation is as such destroyed. It becomes a modern reality as well—when a heart "appropriating Eternity" does away with monks, priests, and an other-worldly life, and transforms the medieval hope in a beyond into a present, inward experience. The modern world does not destroy Christianity. It produces the Protestant Reformation.[34]

In the modern world, then, the sacred does not reduce itself to the secular even though their medieval divorce has become an anachronism. Neither does it dissipate itself into modern philosophy, and this despite the fact that modern philosophy must (at least to begin with) turn radically against it.

Modern philosophic thought cannot be one aspect of a life of which faith is another. For the very claim to infinity which makes it modern makes it hostile to all claims external to it. Greek thought, falling short of the modern infiinity, left room for an historical-religious Truth external to it, as is illustrated by the medieval use of Greek philosophy.* Modern philosophic thought— whose freedom is infinite—can allow no such room; for its range must include—not remain indifferent to—the finite and historical. Doubtless subservience to a free Protestant heart would be less intolerable for modern philosophic thought than subservience to unfree ecclesiastical authorities.[35] But they are both impossible.

---

* Precisely because Greek philosophy does not conquer the contingent the divine incursion *into* the contingent falls outside it. This at once allows Greek thought to survive in medieval theology and forces it to become subservient to ecclesiastical authority.

It is thus no accident that modern philosophy (unlike philosophy in any previous age) achieves radical emancipation from theology, and indeed, that in achieving it it is not neutral but hostile to theology. Yet in the end the very totality of this warfare will bring about total peace; the very radicalism with which philosophic thought asserts its autonomy—and hence its independence from theology—will finally make it and theology identical. And when this goal is reached the whole history of philosophy has reached its end.*

The reflexive turn of modern philosophic thought begins with the Cartesian *Cogito*, which, recognizing the opposition of Thought and Being, also gives the first, abstract assertion of their identity, "accepting as true [only] . . . what has inner evidence in consciousness." Spinoza exhausts this first assertion. For Parmenides, Thought is naively at one with Being. Spinoza—a Jew who yet is essentially a modern philosopher in a Christian world—takes "Thinking and Being as opposed as well as identical." The Parmenidian Being is an abstract unity, and multiplicity falls outside it. The Spinozistic Substance asserts itself as a unity encompassing the many as well as the one—even at the price of an "acosmic" denial of the many *as* many, and of the finite as finite. This loss of the finite world, to be sure, is a defeat for autonomous Thought. But in the modern world such defeats are met, not by the surrender of the claim to autonomy made by Thought, but

---

* Hegel asserts that "God plays a far greater role in modern philosophy than in the ancient, because the comprehension of the absolute opposition of Thought and Being is now the main demand." (*Werke*, XV, p.425 [*Hist. Phil.*, p.347].) In naive ancient theology, the object is God; hence He is—for philosophy as a whole if not for the theology which is part of it—one object among others. In reflexive modern theology, the object is, or ought to be, the religious divine-human relation, and this is *not* one relation among others. Not until it is all-inclusive—of all opposition as well as of all union—is it wholly actual, and not until it has grasped it as all-inclusive has modern theology reached its final goal. This goal is identical with the goal of reflexive modern philosophy, whose object is the relation between Thought and Being, in their opposition as well as their union. (See, e.g., *Werke*, XI, pp.98 ff [*Phil. Rel.*, I, pp.101 ff.].)

rather by opposite forms of Thought with equal claims to auton-omy. The Spinozistic identity of infinite Thought and infinite Sub-stance is countered by Locke's "metaphysical empiricism" which asserts an absolute opposition of Thought and Being, reducing both to finitude. But just as Spinoza's reflexive thought cannot maintain the simple identity of Thought and Being so Locke's equally reflexive thought cannot maintain their simple opposition. The "a priori idealism" of the one—which begins with a pure uni-versal abstraction—willy-nilly points to particularity and concrete-ness. The "a posteriori realism" of the other moves willy-nilly from the empirically given particular to a universal Substance, posited by Thought alone. Both are one-sided phases of a thinking which, on the one hand, accepts the opposition between Thought and Being and the attendant fragmentation of thought into finiteness and yet, on the other, moves toward the overcoming of both. That they are one-sided is a truth manifesting itself in the Leibnizian monad, which is "internally differentiated and yet remains one and simple." Thus abstract infinity is united with the finite given.[36] *

The Leibnizian monad completes the first period of modern philosophy. But it also discloses its limitations. Leibnizian monads are external to each other, and hence finite and cut off from God.

---

* We cannot here consider ot length the complex relation between Spinoza and Greek philosophy; we can only briefly state what is relevant, which, inci-dentally, corroborates our interpretation of the relation between Jewish East and Greek West. (See ch. 5, sect. 6 and sect. 4 of this chapter.) The Hegelian system is a modern restatement of Aristotelianism: thus the Greeks are higher than the Jews. Yet it cannot *become* such a restatement without Spinozism which destroys philosophical paganism and inaugurates philosoph-ical modernity: thus the Jews are higher than the Greeks. The *religious* sig-nificance of Jews and Greeks for the absolute *religion* is equal, if indeed Judaism does not have the edge, for not until its beauty is destroyed in Roman religion does Greek religion achieve equal significance. It is in their *philosophical* significance for the absolute *philosophy* that the Greeks have the edge, for they attain "freedom" and hence philosophical thought on their own ancient soil whereas the Jews—whose religion does not as such give rise to philosophic thought at all—must be transplanted on to modern Christian soil to achieve Spinozism. See p.171 n.; also *Enz.*, sect. 112; *Werke*, XII, p.60 (*Phil. Rel.*, II, p.186).

"As far as thought reaches, just so far and no further reaches the universe, and where comprehension ceases the universe ceases, and God begins." Thus abstractness has given way to concreteness only at the price of surrender of that claim to infinity which, boldly asserted by Spinoza, is the essential beginning of modern philosophy; and not until modern thought will have reemerged from self-immersion in concrete finitude as a Thought at once infinite and concrete—not until it will have "brought back through Thought" the God it is about to lose—will its goal be reached.[37]

The thought of the period just sketched is "metaphysical" because—whether Spinozistic unity with infinite Substance, Lockean opposition to finite object, or Leibnizian synthesis of the two—it asserts the reality of an objective Being. It is, however, a "metaphysics of the Understanding" only because this Being is merely *asserted;* it is not *developed* by the activity of a *self*-developing Thought. Hence in the period now following, Thought must let go of all such merely asserted dogmas, even at the price of lapse into subjectivist finitude. However, it cannot remain with *sheer* finitude. The period now beginning will turn out to be merely transitional.

On the British scene, finite subjectivist thought remains theoretical, and reduced to a "singular consciousness" divorced from both other singular consciousness and the objective world, it issues in Hume's idealistic skepticism. On the French scene, finite subjectivist thought turns practical, thereby both overcoming isolation and giving skepticism a positive turn. It negates what is, but it does so in the light of an ideal which ought to be, and it realizes the ideal by revolutionizing the social consciousness and the world in which it exists. Thought in both its British and French forms puts a creative product of its own making into the place left empty by the loss of the metaphysical object. This latter object had been possessed by a fixed thought, and the subjective movement of thinking had been a mere "method external to its object." This movement has now become Thought's essential object. Hence for all his skepticism Hume holds fast to the idealistic certainty of self-conscious-

ness, and this latter is activity and movement. Among the French—
who can boast of the greater achievement—the movement of subjective thought becomes *overtly* active in the practical, external
world—so much so as to create a whole world in its image. This
"world of truth," to be sure, is only finite and "external to God,"
for what produces it is a merely *human* freedom falsely made
absolute. But it is a world of truth all the same. And the French
revolution, which is initiated by it, is nothing short of the secular
equivalent of the religious revolution initiated by Luther. There
remains but the need for one final revolution. This will reconcile
the God of Lutheran faith with the activity of finite subjectivist
thought, and it will accomplish its goal by raising subjectivist
thought to an infinity already implicit in it. This revolution is
brought about by German speculative thought.[38]

This revolution begins with Kant, who may be viewed as the
Socrates of the modern world. Like Socrates, Kant asserts the
free thinking subject against the authority of the external world.
But unlike Socrates he has passed through the radical opposition
between Thought and Being which fragments both into finitude.
Hence the freedom he asserts is infinite, i.e., not simply opposed
to the external but inclusive of it: it is an infinitude inclusive of
finiteness. This freedom is "absolutely ultimate . . . [because]
within the finite and in connexion with it an absolute standpoint
arises . . . which *unites the finite* and leads on to infinity." What in
British thought is an absolute given becomes relatively given only,
subject to the dictates of regulative Reason. And what in French
life is an absolute human freedom becomes subject to the imperative of a practical Reason which is more than human.[39]

Kantian freedom renews in the modern context the Socratic
opposition to external deities. For theoretical consciousness, God
is found neither in outward nor in inward experience: thus He
becomes an empty Beyond. For practical freedom He becomes a
mere extrapolated Ideal. In both respects, Kant shrinks from a
radicalism which, fully asserting Thought's appropriating power,

would destroy both the empty theoretical Beyond and the extra-
polation of moral self-activity. But only foolish or faithless Christian theologians will seek refuge in the Kantian inconsistency. For
instead of the "knowledge of God [which is] the essence of revealed religion" they are here left with mere emptiness which con-
ceals—as it does in Kantianism itself—a hidden yearning.[40]

This yearning discloses itself in Fichtean thought because
Fichte, unlike Kant, is a radical. It is Fichte, not Kant, who does
away with things-in-themselves and extrapolated deities, and
demonstrates the great truth which Kant has the courage only to
assert: the *developing* power of a subjective Thought which, being
infinite, is wholly *self*-developing. Hence Fichtean philosophy is
the first fully to explicate that speculative power which has been
implicit in modern thought ever since Descartes. In Descartes and
Spinoza, thinking subjectivity remains unmoving. In Hume and
Rousseau it moves but within the limits of a finiteness in which it
has become absorbed. It is the Fichtean Ego which first discloses
itself as an infinite self-realizing subjectivity—truly infinite because
the finite is part of the self-realizing process. Hence the object is
replaced by self-objectivation; and the Kantian Divinity-beyond,
by a subjectivity whose movement is itself divine—the "moral order
of the world." Here the modern "war" of autonomous philosophic
Reason on the Christian faith has reached its climax.[41]

But in this very climax it comes upon its crisis. For the subjectivist Fichtean Deity is, after all, a mere self-deification, and it
reveals itself as such by lapsing into contradiction. The infinity
striven for is also unattainable: for the subjectivist Deity has reality in the process of striving only. It therefore becomes a yearning,
which in turn becomes a yearning for yearning's sake. This, however, is a lapse into fraudulence which has surrendered its serious
infinite aim in order to rest "comfortably" in its own finite aiming.
Nor is there an escape from such vanity in a mere subjectivist detachment from it—that romantic irony which "finds the Divine in
the recognition of the vanity of all finite things," its own yearning

for infinity included. For this irony is infected with the very vanity from which it seeks detachment: it deifies the finite subject in its ironic self-detachment.[42]

It is precisely in the radical assertion of its claim to infinity, then, that subjective thought comes upon an ultimate finiteness of its own: *subjectivity itself*. And this discloses the need for a final "liberation"—one which does not destroy thought but rather cures it of its subjectivist one-sidedness. In the beginnings of the modern period, Spinoza has sought to surrender subjective thought to an objective Substance which yet cannot absorb it. Since then, philosophy has been asserting the claims of subjective thought, first by surrendering all given objectivity, and at length by raising thought to infinity in its own subjective sphere. The need of the hour now—and it is the final hour of philosophy—is to "bring back" the objective God, through the activity of a subjective thought which shows its supreme freedom by divesting itself of its subjectivist one-sidedness.

This need is in principle filled by Schelling, whose thought is "concerned with that deep speculative content" which has preoccupied the whole history of philosophy. Like ancient thought—Platonism, Aristotelianism, and Neoplatonism—it is in living unity with an objective ideal world. But like all modern thought, it has confronted that opposition between Thought and Being which fragments both into finitude. Like Spinozism, it asserts the unity of Thought and the Divine Being despite their opposition. But unlike Spinozism it is no acosmic denial of fragmentation and finitude but rather encompasses the finite—in both its subjective and objective forms—in an all-encompassing infinity.[43]

But Schelling only *asserts* this final standpoint. He does not *develop* it, and hence he does not *demonstrate* its finality. Rather than a "restless Ego" which establishes its absoluteness and *is* this establishing, his thought remains in mere "intuitive repose." Hence, contrary to its own innermost intentions, it lapses into a sheer, acosmic Spinozistic infinity which is now long superseded, and the finitude which after all falls outside it is left for an empiricism far cruder even than that of Locke. Schelling's thought calls for the labor of the final philosophy. But it does not itself furnish it.[44]

For this reason, too, it fails to bring about peace between philosophy and faith. The true peace will be produced by a philosophic labor which presupposes, recognizes, and appropriates the long-existing Christian faith. Schelling's laborless thought merely sets itself up as its esoteric rival. It is a pseudoaesthetic "accidental faculty possessed by the few" who, in intuitive oneness with the Divine, scorn the faith of the "unfavored" many—those whose God remains other-than-human only because they are unfavored. Such a laborless oneness with the Divine is simply devoid of finitude, a mere flight from finitude—as romanticizing and lacking in seriousness as the subjectivist self-deification which it seeks to replace.[45]

In the preceding chapter, we saw that Christian life can have seriousness and reality only because, while at one with the Divine through divine Love, it continues to bear the burden of human finitude. From the sketch of the *History of Philosophy* now completed emerges the conclusion that Hegel cannot reach his final goals—which are the goals of the entire history of philosophy as he understands it—unless he can make peace with this Christian life *so as to preserve its seriousness and reality*: that is, unless his thought can encompass the finite in a union of thought that stays with, rather than flees from, that nonunion of life by virtue of which the human remains confined to humanity.

3. *Religious Representation and Speculative Thought*

If the account just given is correct, the *History of Philosophy* points to and demands a final peace between the final religion and the final philosophy. Yet it is a virtually universally held view that Hegel's philosophy makes true peace between any religion and any philosophy in principle impossible. Moreover, the *History of Philosophy* may well seem to confirm that view.

This is a view which is inevitable if one considers the respective forms of religion and philosophy in total abstraction from all content. Religion exists in the form of representation, in which the Divine that is represented remains other than the human who does the representing; free philosophy exists in the form of speculative thought which has denied this otherness and has risen to oneness with Divinity. Hence surely their respective forms make all religion incompatible with all philosophy, and surely this general view finds specific confirmation in the *History of Philosophy*. According to that work, Greek philosophy can achieve freedom only by destroying Greek religion, medieval philosophy can recognize the Christian religion only at the price of surrendering the freedom which is of the philosophic essence, and pre-Hegelian modern philosophy can reconquer the lost freedom only by waging total war upon faith. Does it not seem that the Hegelian philosophy could make peace with Christianity only by reenacting the medieval surrender—a step not seriously to be contemplated in the free modern world? And does it not seem that it can complete the modern philosophic enterprise, if at all, only by carrying the modern philosophic war upon faith to the finish?

But the Hegelian forms of religious representation and speculative thought cannot be understood adequately in abstraction from content, and there is not in the final analysis any such thing as an abstract Hegelian doctrine concerning the relation between religion-in-general and philosophy-in-general.* According to Hegel, *all* religion differs by virtue of its form from all philosophy; yet *some* religions—the Greek and the Christian[46]—make possible the rise, respectively, of ancient and modern philosophy. Of these two philosophies—there are no others—the first destroys the basis

* Those inclined to dispute this assertion are reminded that *Enz.*, sects. 564–71 deals with revealed religion, not with religion-in-general, and they are further referred to sect. 4, in which it will be argued that the first part of the *Philosophy of Religion*, "The Notion of Religion," deals, not with general characteristics abstracted by finite thought from all existing religions but rather with a Power finding different explication in each religion, and accessible as such—apart from these explications—only to a Thought at one with divine self-activity.

which makes it possible, i.e., Greek religion.[47] In contrast, Christianity is not destroyed by the philosophy to which it gives rise. This latter culminates in a process which transfigures and reinstates its religious basis, and only thus does it reach its own completeness. No account of the Hegelian doctrine concerning religious representation and speculative thought is adequate if it does not grasp these fundamental assertions. Our present account must be entirely confined to them.

For religious self-understanding, religion is a relation *between* the Divine and the human, in which the Divine is both *other* than the human and yet *inwardly related* to it.[48] If the Divine were not other than the human there would be no relation; and if it were not inwardly related to the human the relation would not be religious. Cult without union is dead and external; without nonunion it is a flight into unreality which lacks the seriousness of labor.[49] The aspects of nonunion and union permeate the whole of representational existence, and *this latter is, therefore, accepted by the religious self-understanding, as a form of truth.*

This much is true of all genuine religions, from the lowest to the highest. Even the nature-worshiper *worships*, not external nature, but the Divine represented as natural.[50] Even the Christian incarnate God is other than His human worshiper. An *actual* man suffering actual death is closer than, say, the Greek deities which are idealized human representations.[51] But he is also more remote, for he *exists*—or rather, *has* existed—outside the spirit of the worshiper; he is not merely *represented* as externally existing. Hence Christian faith necessarily "wavers" between the extremes of a devotional and sacramental unity with the "indwelling Christ," and an historical representation which "sends him back two thousand years into Palestine."[52] *The form of representation, essential to all other religious existence, is essential to Christianity as well.*

If all philosophic thought presupposes religion, then the final philosophy (which recognizes this fact) must first of all *accept the reality of the religious relationship.* That is, it must accept the aspect of inwardness without which religions would be mere external worship, and it must accept the otherness of the Divine without which religious cult would lack its real and serious labor. If it denied either aspect, the final philosophy would not recognize the religious basis required by all philosophic thought. It would rather destroy that basis.

But if in *all* religions the Divine remains other than the human, how can *some* religions (Greek and Christian) make possible for humans a philosophic thought at one with Divinity? Judaism cannot give rise to such philosophic freedom even though, like Greek religion, it recognizes the divine Infinity. For the infinite God worshiped remains wholly other (transcendent Lord) and the aspect of inwardness is confined to an unfree recognition of his lordship.[53] If Greek religion makes possible what Judaism does not, it is because it is the creation of poets. The divine Infinity is immanent in a free and creative worship, and the aspect of divine otherness is confined to its created products. Because of the former, Greek philosophic thought can explicate an Infinity already implicit, by rising to pure unity with the Divine. But because of the latter, it pays a double price for this achievement: it destroys the otherness of the Greek gods (and hence these gods themselves); and it is itself forced to flee from a world which, now demythologized (*entgoettlicht*), yet remains other than the Divinity to which thought has risen.[54]

But if Greek philosophy can rise to freedom only by destroying its Greek religious presupposition, how can the final modern philosophy hope to achieve freedom and yet recognize and make peace with its Christian presupposition? And—another aspect of the same question—how can it hope to stay with and comprehend the world when Greek thought was forced into flight from it? What is the unique relation between Christian representational existence and the final philosophy which brings such goals within reach?

First, the Christian God-man is an actual man external to human representation, as much other-than-human worship as the Lord of Judaism. Christianity is therefore no creation of poets, and Christian, like Jewish, worship has an essential aspect of receptivity. Why then does Christianity, like Greek religion, make philosophic thought possible, rather than, like Judaism, impossible?

This is because, secondly, the Christian God-man does not *remain* transcendent to human worship. He is other than the worshiper and yet, *because He has revealed Himself*, same. Christian worship is *of* Christ. It is worship *in* Christ as well. The Christ is *received*, as externally, historically existent. But He is also *appropriated* by a free representation. *And the human freedom manifest in this appropriation is itself a gift of divine Grace.*[55]

As a result, *the divine-human relation*—in all other religious representation composed of *two* activities, respectively divine and human—*is in Christian representation* one double *activity*.[56] It is *double* because it remains a religious relationship between a Grace which is divine and a freedom which is human. But it is *one* because the freedom is itself represented and experienced as a gift of the Divine. The Jewish commanding Lord remains other than, and over against, an obedience which, human only, remains unfree. Greek worship is free because it is more than human, yet it remains limited in that it accepts, as other, gods on which it has itself conferred this otherness. Christian Grace is at once *actually* other than the human freedom which receives it, and yet it is *in* this freedom *because* it is Grace.

This double activity "gets Christian representation into difficulties."[57] An infinite divine Grace seems to leave no room for a freedom outside it, which is yet needed if it is to be mine and human. And a human freedom seems to leave no room for a divine Grace which, outside it, must be humanly *received*. (This is true at least if such freedom demands, as in modern times it does, infinite scope, and here lies the reason why pre-Hegelian modern thought fails to recognize its Christian presupposition and indeed is hostile to all faith.) Yet Christian representation must *express* these difficulties. It cannot seek refuge from its double activity in a single activity which—whether it dissipates the human into the Divine or the Divine into the human—would destroy the reality of the Christian God-man relationship. And the difficulties—or rather, paradoxes—which flow from this double activity are of the Christian essence.*

It is precisely this double activity of Christian representational existence which enables the final modern philosophy, like the Greek, to achieve oneness of thought with Divinity and yet, unlike the Greek, to recognize, preserve, and comprehend rather than destroy the religion which has made this achievement possible. According to the *History of Philosophy*, in turning against the medieval subservience to Christian faith and against Christian faith itself, modern philosophy has claimed an infinity which, unlike the Greek, is inclusive of finiteness. The final modern philos-

---

* There is an "antinomy" in the Christian rebirth in that, on the one hand, it is "free Grace" which effects it and, on the other hand, the self "has a share in the matter and is left with free will. . . . [However,] firm remaining in this relationship" [i.e., with the *fixed* distinction] is unspiritual, and Lutheranism dissolves such unspirituality (*Werke*, XII, pp.336 ff. [*Phil. Rel.*, III, pp.130 ff.].) This dissolution remains with the representational antinomy, but makes it possible for speculative thought to rise above it. Hegel finds a representational antinomy already between the concepts of divine Goodness and Justice, and their primordial expression in the belief in Creation. (*Werke*, XI, p.153 [*Phil. Rel.*, I, pp.157 ff.]; see ch. 5, sect. 5.) But while he cannot doubt the existence of that belief in Judaism, he cannot admit that it functions, in Jewish as well as in Christian representation, as part of one double activity, and hence as productive of a representational antinomy. For in his view the Divine in Judaism is One only, which is why the Creation falls outside the Divine. (*Werke*, XII, p.51 [*Phil. Rel.*, II, p.176].) In contrast, the Christian trinitarian God creates His own Son. (*Werke*, XII, pp.51, 53, 64 [*Phil. Rel.*, II, pp.176, 178, 189]; also *Enz.*, sect. 161.)
It might be mentioned in passing that Martin Buber's Jewish-inspired *I and Thou* arrives at the same antinomy as Hegel, and at the same view that the fixity of the distinction between Divine Grace and human freedom is unspiritual. (See *I and Thou* [New York: Scribner, 1958], p.96: "I know that 'I am given over for disposal' and know at the same time that 'It depends on myself' . . . . I am compelled to take both to myself, to be lived together, and in being lived together they are one." Also *Between Man and Man* [Boston: Beacon Press, 1955], p.69: "Certainly in my answering I am given into the power of His Grace, but I cannot measure Heaven's share in it.") The fundamental difference is that whereas for Hegel and Buber the antinomy is lived in religious existence, for Hegel it can be transcended by speculative thought, but for Buber it cannot.

ophy now recognizes that the infinity claimed presupposes the faith against which it is directed, and that its negation of that faith has positive as well as negative significance. In recognizing this truth it ceases to oppose faith and instead undertakes to comprehend and transfigure it.*

This task can be accomplished only on two conditions. One is that Christian faith is no longer a merely finite human testimony, in nonunion with a Divinity other-than-human. The other is that the final philosophy is not, once again, a union with the Divine achieved through flight from finiteness and nonunion. *Both* must be "testimonies of spirit to Spirit,"[58] i.e., testimonies of the Divine *in* the human, to a Divinity which, though other than the testifying spirit, is yet manifest in it. And, the testimony of speculative thought will be possible only because the testimony of Christian faith is already actual.

They differ in that thought and speculation will grasp as one single activity what in faith and representation remains double.**
How is this possible? *Religious spirit—the heart—exists on the hu-*

---

* The truth to be comprehended by the final modern thought Hegel describes as follows:

I am to make myself fit for the indwelling of the Spirit . . . This is my labor, the labor of man; but the same is also the labor of God, regarded from His side. He moves toward man and is in man through the act of raising him. What seems my act is thus God's and, conversely, what seems His is mine. This, to be sure, runs counter to the merely moral standpoint of Kant and Fichte; there the Good always remains something yet to be produced . . . , something that ought to be, as if it were not already essentially there. A world outside me remains, God-forsaken, waiting for me to bring purpose and goodness into it. But the sphere of moral action is limited. In religion the Good and reconciliation are absolutely complete and existing on their own account. The divine unity of the spiritual and natural world is presupposed—the particular self-consciousness belongs to the latter—and the question is only, concerning me and over against me, that I should lay aside my subjectivity and take and have a share in the work which eternally completes itself. The Good is not something which merely ought to be but divine Power and eternal Truth. (*Werke*, XI, pp.222 ff. [*Phil. Rel.*, I, p.228].)

** "Grace enlightens the heart of man, it is the divine Spirit in man, so that man may be represented as passive in relation to its activity; i.e., it is not his own activity. In the Notion, however, this double activity must be grasped as single." (*Werke*, XII, p.117 ff. [*Phil. Rel.*, II, p.247].)

*man side of the divine-human relationship. Philosophic spirit—
speculative thought—rises to its divine side. What for Christian
faith is free reception of the Divine by the human is for speculative
thought divine activity in the human.**

This rise has in principle already been achieved in Schellingian
thought; however, it does not recognize itself as such, i.e., as a
philosophical testimony of spirit to Spirit made possible by the
Christian testimony. The last philosophy to wage war on faith,
Schelling's philosophy sets itself up as an esoteric rival faith, and
the nemesis it suffers for such rivalry is dissipation into unreal
abstractions. The final modern philosophy now recognizes itself as
a rise to the divine side of a divine-human relation already actual.
Thus it comes to perceive a task which, if completed, will have
saved it from the Schellingian fate. The one double activity which
is Christian faith *is* double because it is for the heart, which exists
on the human side of the divine-human relationship. The speculative thought which has risen to its divine side must *preserve* the
heart, i.e., the human, in the divine-human relationship. This is
the crucial task of the *Philosophy of Religion*. And on its successful
execution depend both the peace between Christianity and the
final philosophy, and the claim of the final philosophy to *be* final,
i.e., to be a thought comprehensive of reality rather than just another flight from it.

But doubt as to the possibility of this peace must arise even
before its actual execution is considered. For all its Protestant
freedom, the heart, after all, remains *receptive* of divine Grace
and human for precisely this reason.** If this receptivity is
ontologically ultimate how can speculative thought grasp the double activity of faith as single? And if it can do so how can it
recognize the heart *as* heart, i.e., in its human receptivity? It is all-

---

* See appendix 2 to this chapter, pp.217 ff.
** The free heart has enlarged itself through love, abandoning that
"narrow-heartedness . . . [for which] the particular self is object and end."
But it has done so through *"the reception* of the love of God." (*Werke*, XII,
p.390 [*Phil. Rel.*, III, p.184]. Italics added.)

too-obvious that the basic dilemma of Hegel's entire thought—now given a new and indeed its ultimate form—is still unresolved.

To resolve it is, at any rate, Hegel's clearly avowed purpose. According to unequivocal Hegelian statements, the religious heart may be close to speculative thought, far closer than intellectual abstractions; it remains nevertheless clearly distinct from it. Speculative thought may comprehend and transfigure the heart; it must also as such preserve it.

The heart is close to speculative thought because it is not random feeling, or even random religious feeling, but rather permanent character geared to the Divine; because this being-geared is permeated with self-activity which—especially in cult—raises the whole being; and because in this raising activity there is thought. Yet the heart remains clearly distinct from *speculative* thought because it is *mine*—that of an "I" which remains finite and human. Its thinking (*Denken*) is devotion (*Andacht*)—not divine self-activity *in* the human but human contact *with* the Divine. Permeated with self-activity, it is shot through with receptivity as well. And its cultic labor has two aspects, not one aspect only: it is both a rise of the human and a being-raised by the Divine.[59]

As philosophic thought will grasp the double activity of Christian faith as single it will comprehend and transfigure the heart. Yet in so doing it must not destroy but rather reinstate the heart. For, Hegel declares, "a philosophy without heart . . . [is as abstract as a] faith without understanding; . . . philosophic thought and religious faith are part of a living whole, each fragmentary by itself."* A thought which reduced the heart to a mere ghost would itself become ghostly.[60]

---

* *Bln. Schr.*, pp.325, 328. These statements occur in a remarkable review of a book written by a Christian Hegelian. In his book, C. F. Goeschel writes as follows:

To be perfectly frank, the realm of pure speculation has given me on more than one occasion a disembodied, weird, ghostlike feeling, so much so as to produce a longing for persons, and the desire to seek refuge in Holy Writ,

4. *The Speculative Comprehension of Christian Faith*

The *Philosophy of Religion* claims two main achievements on behalf of Christian faith. Christian faith *confronts* non-Christian religions, although it is certain to have found what they seek; philosophic thought *moves through* these religions, and shows them to be partial truths absorbed by the complete Christian truth. Christian faith *finds* the Christian totality; philosophic thought *demonstrates* its totality and transforms representational fact into speculative necessity. If it can attain these two goals—which Christian faith itself cannot—it is because, having risen from the human to the divine side of the religious relationship, it grasps as one single activity what to faith remains double.*

The first attainment of the *Philosophy of Religion* is the *Notion of religion.* This is not, as the term might suggest, the mere work

---

which then, often in a single passage, revived my very bones. I am sensuous enough not to wish to lose, for the sake of comprehension, what I can grasp with my hands.

Hegel comments: ". . . the author here demands that . . . the transition from representation to Notion *and from Notion to representation, which is present in philosophical mediation,* should also find literary expression." Having defended his literary practice, Hegel then makes his crucial statement:

The language of representation differs from the language of the Notion. Further, man not only to begin with knows Truth by the name of representation. *He is also, as a living man, at home with it alone.* The task of philosophic science, however, is not to write its figurations into . . . abstract realms only. *It is also to show . . . their existence in actual Spirit. But that existence is representation.* (*Bln. Schr.*, pp.318 ff., italics added.)

See also appendix 2 to this chapter. On Hegel's review of Goeschel, see *Hegels Leben*, pp.400 ff.

* The following account must confine itself to these two goals in a manner which involves the almost total neglect (except for Jewish, Greek, and Roman religions) of Hegel's speculative reenactment of non-Christian religions. A useful account of these is H. J. Schoeps, "Die ausserchristlichen Religionen bei Hegel," *Zeitschrift fuer Religions- und Geistesgeschichte*, VII, 1955, 1–34.

of the finite understanding. This latter must ignore or reject the human claim to a religious relation with the Divine and regard religion as mere human fact, from which it will then seek to abstract such features as all religions may have in common. Philosophic or infinite Thought begins by accepting the reality of the divine-human relation to which all religions lay claim, and it becomes infinite by reenacting as single what in and for them remains double. The first truth brought to light by such a reenactment is a unity in *all* religious divine-human relationships despite all the conflict between them. The Notion of religion is a single divine-human activity present *in* all existing religions, but not recognized by them *as* this activity because they *are* religions.*

The Notion of religion, however, is no separate reality, and becomes separate only for the thought which reenacts it. It is a mere implicit Power, which requires existing religions for its self-explication. Hence the philosophic thought which grasps the Notion of religion cannot remain in splendid isolation. It is, rather, midway between two confrontations with existing religion. It is preceded by an acceptance of existing religion, as an actual rather than an illusory divine-human relation. (For without this acceptance the Notion of religion would be a mere arbitrary and unreal thought-product.) It is followed by the comprehension of existing religion in terms of the Notion which has been attained—as its self-explication. This second confrontation, however, does not *remain* a confrontation. For the thought which comprehends existing religion absorbs and transfigures it.**

* This is true even of the Christian religion which is the total self-explication of the Notion of religion. For while it is the complete true content it remains, because it is a religion, representational in form. See, e.g., *Werke*, XV, p.275 (*Hist. Phil.*, III, p.194).

** By itself, the Notion of religion is only for philosophical thought. (*Werke*, XI, pp.223, 255 [*Phil. Rel.*, I, pp.229, 261].) And it must first have existing embodiment if it is to *be* for philosophic thought. For "philosophy comprehends what *is*, what has already prior actuality." (*Werke*, XII, p.319 [*Phil. Rel.*, III, pp.111 ff.].)

The Notion of religion, present in all religions, is not however equally present in every religion. Religious claims differ and conflict. Philosophic comprehension preserves the difference but removes the conflict. For it comprehends mutually conflicting divine-human relations as different stages of the self-explication of the Notion of religion. The process of self-explication, however, does not go on in infinitum: it is complete in Christianity. Only because it *is* complete in *this* religion can philosophic thought comprehend *any* religion. For only if the Notion of religion *exists* wholly explicated in the one double activity of Christian faith can philosophic thought *grasp* it *as* Notion—by reenacting as single what to all faith remains double. The grasp of the Notion of religion, then, stands midway between two confrontations, not with existing religion-in-general, but rather with existing Christianity. And the conditions in existing religious life which make it possible for the *Philosophy of Religion* to begin its work also make it mandatory for it to complete it—in the comprehension of the Christian religion as the total self-explication of the Notion of religion.[61] *

So much for the program of the *Philosophy of Religion*. A brief sketch of essentials must suffice for its execution. First, what of the Notion of religion? All genuine religions are totalities of feeling, representation, and cult geared to the Divine, and the totalities differ as does the Divine to which they are geared. Philosophic comprehension grasps as single what in every religion remains double, and it grasps one Power explicated in all different religions. For religious consciousness, the totalities of feeling, representation, and cult are geared *to* the Divine, and are themselves human; and the totalities and Divinities differ and indeed are in mutual conflict. Philosophic comprehension sees the Divine *in* these human totali-

---

* Because the Christian religion is the total self-explication of the Notion of religion it is the absolute religion. (*Werke*, XI, p.83; XII, pp.191 ff. [*Phil. Rel.*, I, p.84; II, pp.327 ff.].)

ties; and the implicit divine-human Power which is in them is in them all.*

This result—the Notion of religion—next produces the task of comprehending existing religions. For these latter the Divine, inwardly related to the human, still remains other-than-human. Philosophic comprehension can neither simply accept this otherness nor simply repudiate it. It cannot accept it: this would retroactively destroy both the Notion of religion and the possibility of comprehending existing religions. It cannot repudiate it: repudiation would dissipate the existing religious reality which philosophy is to comprehend and which is indeed presupposed by this comprehension. What in existing religion is otherness—the Divine being other-than-human and the human, other-than-Divine—is for the philosophic comprehension of religion a Divine *self-othering in* the human.[62]

For this reason, philosophic comprehension can *move through* non-Christian religions when Christian faith, despite its comprehensive Truth, can only *confront* them. Certain to have found what they seek, Christian faith must nevertheless oppose what *they* have found as simple falsehood. And the falsehood opposed, left unabsorbed, can continue to assert itself as truth. Philosophic comprehension has transcended all such mutual opposing. Non-Christian religions are true self-explications of the Notion of religion; thus a justice is done them which Christian faith itself denies them. But they are only partial self-explications of the Notion of religion, whereas Christianity is complete; thus their truths are absorbed and superseded. In this way philosophic comprehension, and it alone, "reconciles the true religion with the false."[63]

---

* See our more extensive account, ch. 5, sects. 2 and 3, which, however, could not yet grasp the Notion of religion *as* Notion. A general account of religion was then needed, but the account remained obscure in status. For it could not be given by a merely finite thought "observing" religious phenomena (*Werke*, XI, pp.167 ff. [*Phil. Rel.*, I, pp.172 ff.].), and the infinite Thought which, rather than observe such phenomena, reenacts the religious divine-human relation was then as yet unavailable.

Even nature religions demand such justice. For Christian faith, these may be sheer idolatry—the worship of a fallen nature in place of its Creator and Redeemer. In the light of the Notion of religion, philosophic comprehension finds a degree of truth even in this idolatrous falsehood. For it sees the human self, born into natural-ness, passing through nature-worship before it can rise and be raised above it; it also sees the Divine, by itself complete apart from the human, as passing through self-externalization *in* nature and finite spirit—non-religious man—before it can *manifest* itself *as* divine *to* a spirit no longer finite only—religious man. It sees the necessity of such passing if the Notion of religion is to encom-pass otherness in its unity so as to become explicit in existing religion. For Christianity, the comprehensive Truth which it ac-cepts on faith, drops from heaven. For philosophic comprehension, it is the end of a process which must begin with the lowest if it is to reach the highest.*

Moreover, it cannot reach the highest straightway from the lowest. Even Christian faith itself views Jewish and Greek-Roman religions[64]—in which the "higher sun of Spirit has caused the natural light to fade"[65]—as partial anticipations of its Truth. Philo-sophic comprehension *demonstrates* this Christian view—that these religions are necessary for, and absorbed in, the development of Christianity.

In the Christian view the Jew, risen above idolatry, worships the infinite God; but, infinite only, this God remains inaccessible. The Greek, though in idolatrous worship of finite gods, worships a Beauty above the human, not a nature below it, and in this Beauty to which he is inwardly related infinity is present—a pres-ence which makes possible eventual philosophic access to the preworldly Trinity. But although recognizing truth in these re-

---

* "Nature religion is the most difficult to comprehend because it lies fur-thest from our [i.e., Christian] representation." But while we can no longer "enter into an experience of it" we *can* comprehend it. (*Werke*, XII, p. 3; XI, p.281 [*Phil. Rel.*, II, p.122; I, pp.288 ff.].)

ligions Christian faith nevertheless confronts them, as anticipations of the total Truth *only*, and false in their claim to finality. These religions, on their part, can do their own confronting of Christianity. The Jew can reject the stumbling block of Christ despite the pain into which he is finally driven. And the Greek may reject him as folly even though at length forced into the choice between Roman unhappiness in a godless world and a philosophic flight to a worldless God. Christian faith can bear witness against both Jew and Greek; but it can do no more.[66]

Philosophic comprehension, in contrast, can do a great deal more. It will not, first, view either the Jewish Lord as simply-infinite and transcendent, or Jewish worship as simply-finite and human: the Divine in Judaism is humanly accessible if only in that it is—at length—*known* to be inaccessible. As confronted by Christian faith, Judaism has wholly one Truth (the transcendent Lord) and wholly lacks the other (His immanence in and presence to the human). As comprehended in the light of the Notion of religion, Judaism is in partial possession of the whole Truth. Jewish worship negates its own finiteness even as it affirms the divine Infinity, and the Jewish God—who is *in* the worship as well as its object— has become immanent even while He remains transcendent. Judaism has the *one* Truth; it has this Truth partially only because it remains in unresolved internal contradiction.

The same is true, albeit oppositely, of Greek, or Greek-Roman, religion. For Christian faith (as Hegel understands it), this too has one truth and one falsehood. Its falsehood is its idolatrous worship of finite gods. Its truth is its celebration of human worth,*

* Greek religion is "a religion of humanity . . . [in which] confidence in the gods is at the same time human self-confidence," and the humanity of the Greek gods is "the defective and yet attractive element" in Greek religion. (*Werke*, XII, p.127 [*Phil. Rel.*, II, p.257].) This must be taken *both* as Hegel's own philosophical appraisal and as one he attributes to Christianity. Hegel's Christian at once condemns the Greek idolatry of the human and himself testifies to the redemption of the human, by a God who by His incarnation, death, and resurrection has raised the human above finitude. The Christian testimony—which is to "the crucifixion of sensuous existence"—

and because this latter truth is conjoined with the former falsehood, it discloses at length the whole misery and grandeur of human power. Its misery is manifest in the absolute enslavement of
man to man, in a godless Roman world deified and made infinite.
Its grandeur is the rise of philosophic thought to infinity and
hence above humanity, to the true albeit worldless trinitarian God.
For Christian faith, then, Jew and Greek each has what the other
lacks, and one must take Hegel to mean that they have equal
value. Neoplatonic thought, to be sure, can rise to oneness with the
trinitarian Presence when Jewish worship can only serve a Lord
who remains distant. But it has fled from a world of which it is
forced to despair, whereas Jewish worship serves *in* the world a
God who is Lord *of* it.*

For philosophic comprehension, the Greek-Roman world culminates, not with the total possession of one Truth (the pre-
worldly Trinity) and the total lack of the other (its worldly incursion). It culminates with the partial possession of the whole Truth,
and this indeed is implicit in this world from its first and wholly
idolatrous beginnings. Even Greek mythological religion reflects
this one Truth: the divine Infinity is *in* the Greek celebration of its
finite but beautiful products.** Because of this presence Infinity

---

preserves and transfigures both "the Jewish representation that God is essentially for thought only and the sensuality of the Greek beautiful shape."
(*Werke*, XII, p.125 [*Phil. Rel.*, II, p.244].)

* Our account admittedly fails to do full justice to the Hegelian view of
the superiority of Rome over Judaea. (*Werke*, XII, pp.157 ff. [*Phil. Rel.*,
II, p.289].) Yet in the end this is not a *religious* superiority but merely that of
a universalizing discipline destructive of religious realities. Religiously (as
we have already noted in ch. 5, appendix 3, p.157), "the noble Roman could
practice only one virtue, namely, dying; and this he shared with slaves and
criminals condemned to death." (*Werke*, XII, p.180 [*Phil. Rel.*, II, p.315].)

** Greek religious consciousness itself

. . . feels this defect of art, when . . . art is the highest religious manifestation,
namely, that the god is fashioned by man. And it attempts to remedy the
defect . . . but only in a subjective way. Images of the god are conse-
crated . . . . that is, the divine Spirit is put into them by means of a process
of conjuration. (*Werke*, XI, p.452 [*Phil. Rel.*, II, p.118].)

can enter—for better and worse—into consciousness. For better: Neoplatonic thought finds speculative access to the trinitarian absolute Infinity. For worse: Roman emperor worship bestows infinity on a mere human ruler, thus making human slavery absolute. For better *and* worse: the very absoluteness of Roman slavery produces a longing for absolute salvation, and the very absoluteness of the Neoplatonic flight from the world discloses that the world is humanly inescapable. The Roman conflict between a godless world and a worldless God—between a human existence wholly enslaved and a wholly free thought fled from human existence—is an internal conflict: it is the partial possession of the whole Truth.

Jewish East and Greek-Roman West, moreover, are themselves internally related; and the complete self-explication of the Notion of religion emerges from their conflict. Philosophic comprehension sees the Jewish world cling stubbornly both to an infinite God and a finite world, trying but failing to bridge the gulf between them. And it sees the Greek-Roman world stay with a divine Infinity immanent in the finite, at the cost of eventual self-disruption into deification of a godless world and flight to a worldless God. The Notion of religion is wholly explicated when there is at once total recognition of the otherness of the Divine—that distance between the Infinite and the finite which makes the Infinite divine and leaves the finite worldly and human—and yet a total presence of the Divine, not for a thought only which has fled from the world, but rather for existing man who remains in it. For Christian faith, the ripeness of the time for Christ, brought about by the meeting

---

This Greek consciousness must be distinguished from the Christian consciousness which recognizes in the Greek "feeling of defect" the presentiment of a higher truth but condemns as simply idolatrous the "process of conjuration" which is to remedy the defect. And the Christian consciousness must in turn be distinguished from philosophical comprehension which recognizes that the subjective Greek remedy is not subjective *only*.

of Jewish East and Greek-Roman West, is a contingent fact. For speculative thought, it is an inner, self-developing necessity.[67]

So much for the one major task of the *Philosophy of Religion*, "the reconciliation of the true religion with the false."[68] It remains in principle fragmentary without the other, the speculative comprehension of Christianity itself. Without this latter both Jew and Greek could persist in defiance not only, as already shown, of Christianity, but also of any philosophical attempt to reconcile them with Christianity. Jewish worldly service of a transcendent Lord, however painful; Neoplatonic union of thought with a pre-worldly Trinity, however escapist; Roman emperor worship in a godless world, however unhappy: these could each assert its absoluteness (as well as resist all attempts to be reconciled to each other). And any such absolute self-asserting in life would expose as a mere arbitrary and lifeless thought a Notion of religion which contradicted it. The *Philosophy of Religion* must *demonstrate* that this Notion is neither arbitrary nor lifeless, and it can do so only by showing that it is wholly explicated in an existing religion. Hegel's work therefore culminates in the transfiguration of the Christian comprehensive Truth, accepted as fact by faith, into speculative necessity. And the whole enterprise stands or falls with this climactic task.

Christian faith, like all faith, remains at the human side of the divine-human relation, and hence humanly receptive of fact. But it knows itself to be one double activity, not one of two activities only: hence the fact received is thoroughly dialectical. Thus the Creation, while accepted as fact, is at once other than the Creator and wholly dependent on Him. Thus also the creature-created-in-the-divine-image, while *self*-accepted as fact, is by nature both good and evil. Though accepting his nature as God-given, he cannot remain in his naturalness, and for this reason the act of self-emancipation from naturalness is both anti-divine—a fall—and divinely willed and necessary. This togetherness of contingent facticity and dialectic explodes into paradox in the supreme fact of the Christian faith. Christ is indeed a "tremendous composition" of the Divine and the human. For here the Divine in the extreme of its infinity enters into the human in the extreme of its finitude and, what is more, into one contingent human in a contingent place and time. Yet this incursion into the finite redeems the finite: and it occurs when *all* history is ripe for it.

Christian faith remains with facticity and paradox even as in the Christian community worship *of* Christ becomes explicitly worship *in* Christ as well. For the communal testimony to Spirit, while itself Spirit, remains in the form of receptive faith, and the Christ present *in* this testifying Spirit remains historical fact *for* it as well. Nor does Christian faith rise above facticity and paradox as—with or without Neoplatonic aid—it attains to theological thought. For the pre-worldly Trinity attained by such thought remains distinct from its worldly incursion, and the thought which has risen to the former remains but one pole of Christian communal life, while the other is existence *in* the world, *with* the trinitarian incursion *into* it. These two poles, however—and this is crucial—are not in conflict or mutually destructive. They point to each other and indeed become the absolutely comprehensive form of religious life. This is because of the supreme mystery implicitly accepted by every religious faith but wholly explicit only in the Christian faith: that the Divine which needs no relation to the human nevertheless stands in relation to the human, without yet suffering loss of its divinity. The final mystery of Christian faith is neither the pre-worldly Trinity nor its worldly incursion. It is the final paradoxical fact that they are and remain *two* Trinities even while they are united: *It is Divine Love.*[69]

Christian faith, then, remains with received paradoxical fact. Philosophic comprehension transfigures it into speculative necessity, and it does so by rising in reenacting thought to the divine side of the Christian divine-human relationship. In this reenactment, what for Christian faith is the thought-pole of life and last in time to emerge *becomes the absolute point of departure.** The pre-worldly Trinity—that divine play in which Son separates from Father only to become one with Him in Spirit—*emerges as the absolute Notion of religion*: it is that divine-human unity which is in various degrees explicated in every existing religion.[70]

The worldly incursion of that Trinity emerges as the total self-explication of the Notion of religion. For what to faith remains human life-pole irreducible to theological thought-pole is over-reached by *speculative* thought which, having risen to Divinity, reenacts it. For the life-pole of faith, the Divine remains other-than-human, and the human, other-than-Divine. For the specula-tive thought which reenacts Divinity the human other is a divine *self*-othering; the diremption *between* the Divine and the human, a divine *self*-diremption; and the divine reconciliation *with* the human, a divine *self*-reconciliation. The total self-explication of the absolute Notion of religion is a single whole of divine Life com-posed of the "Kingdom of the Father" (the inward life of the preworldly Trinity), the "Kingdom of the Son" (the divine self-othering in nature, finite spirit, up to its climax in the divine Incar-nation in nature and finite spirit), and the "Kingdom of Spirit" (that divine self-reconciliation in the Christian community mani-fest in a worship which is both in and of Christ). This total process is necessary in that the divine self-othering is required if the abso-lute Notion of religion is to find total self-explication, and in that the divine self-reconciliation is possible only when the process of divine self-othering and self-diremption has reached a stage at

---

* This is clearly stated in a crucial passage already cited in ch. 5, sect. 5. Since that passage has had a decisive influence on our entire approach to the exposition of Christianity in both the preceding and the present chapters, it should here again be cited: "The Idea was first in the element of thought; this is the foundation and we have begun with it. In philosophical science the universal and more abstract must come first. . . . *In fact, however, it is later in existence.*" (*Werke*, XII, p.247 [*Phil. Rel.*, III, pp.33 ff.]; italics added.)

which the time has become ripe for it. Such, in the briefest of outlines, is the Hegelian comprehension of the Christian faith.*

Can it make peace with the faith it comprehends? Or only be
hostile to it? At first sight, the Hegelian comprehension seems confronted with but two choices, both hostile to faith. Either the pre-
worldly trinitarian play emerges as inherently complete; but then
its worldly manifestation merely repeats the play: and the seriousness with which faith receives that manifestation is a mere illusion,
due to receptivity and hence to faith itself. Or else the worldly
manifestation of the Trinity is as serious as faith takes it to be,
but then its significance is other than faith sees it. For Christian
faith, it is a free gift of Love, unneeded by the Divine, to its human
other. For philosophic comprehension, it is an act of divine self-
love, needed by a Divinity incomplete without it. It is obvious
that a comprehension of either kind would be radically hostile to
Christian faith—indeed far more hostile than those pre-Hegelian
modern philosophies which, rather than comprehend the Christian
content, could only wage war upon it.

But a comprehension of either sort—by a thought reenacting
Divinity—would be protested against too loudly, by a faith insisting on remaining human. And a thought which claimed to encompass life would in fact fail to encompass this protest made in and
by life. Philosophizing man, "walking on his head," would thus dissipate rather than confirm the life of faith in which man "stands on
his feet"; and this would suffice to invalidate the claims made by
the absolute philosophy. In short, the dilemma arrived at threatens
not only the peace between Christian faith and Hegelian philosophy. It threatens, too, the absolute standpoint required by Hegel's
thought as a whole.

It threatens, as well, the middle sought by the entire Hegelian
philosophy. For the philosophical dilemma vis-à-vis the double

---

* In view of our extensive descriptive account of Christianity in ch. 5,
sects. 4–9 we may be brief in our present account of its speculative reenactment.

Trinity of Christian faith merely specifies the general dilemma of the Hegelian middle. We have long rejected a right-wing dissipation of the actual world into the logical realm: this would be specified by the dissipation of the worldly trinitarian incursion into a timeless trinitarian play, and we have also rejected a left-wing reduction of Idea and Spirit to worldly finitude: this would be specified by the reduction of the worldly trinitarian incursion to a divine self-realization which, bereft of a pre-worldly Trinity to sustain it, could never be complete.*

But just as the problems of Hegel's entire philosophy come to a head in its relation to Christian faith so does their solution. For Hegel rejects the dilemma which has just been posed, both of whose horns would be destructive of Christian faith. The pre-worldly trinitarian play is complete, apart from its worldly manifestation; yet this latter—no mere repetition of the play—is as real for philosophic comprehension as it is for Christian faith. The trinitarian God is wholly real apart from the world and wholly real in it, and only because of His preworldly reality can His worldly manifestation be complete. *The two Trinities of Christian faith, then, do not reduce themselves, in one of two opposite ways, to one: they remain two, for philosophic thought as much as for Christian faith. And philosophy accepts what faith has asserted: that their relation is Love.*

This Love, then, remains in one decisive respect unchanged in nature by the philosophical transfiguration. For faith, divine Love is a gift to the human other unneeded by the divine Giver. For philosophic thought, divine Love *remains* such a gift even though it is a divine self-othering. This Love does not shrink into a divine unconcern with the worldly and human, nor into a concern necessitated by divine need. Divine Love, therefore, is the ultimate *fact* of faith *which remains fact even for the final philosophy, and only*

* Theologians in particular have time and again accused Hegel of either pantheism or atheistic humanism. On Hegel's own reaction to these two charges, see *Enz.*, sect. 573.

because philosophy accepts this fact can it attain absolute finality.*

Here lies the ultimate condition on which Hegel's philosophy can make peace with Christian faith. A thought which reduced the Christian God to an unworldly trinitarian play would leave the world unredeemed, and itself reenact the Neoplatonic flight from it. A thought which transformed Him into a self-realizing worldly reality would deny the comprehensiveness of Christian faith and reduce itself to finitude. A thought which *recognizes* the divine Love of Christian faith forever *begins as* faith, humanly receptive of the divine gift; forever *rises above* such human receptivity, by reenacting the divine gift to the human other as a divine self-othering; and forever *reinstates* human faith as a phase in its own rise above humanity. Only a thought of this kind can be divine and yet a possibility for thinkers who are, and remain, human.

5. *The Final Secular-Religious World and the Final Philosophy*

But how can religious faith, once thus comprehended, survive *as* faith? Comprehension may save its content. (For it preserves as double the Trinity which for Christian faith is double.) Can it save its form? Or must it, in *reenacting* as divine *self*-othering what human faith *receives* as *Other* expose such receptivity as mere appearance, reflecting human limitations which are now transcended? Such an exposure would surely end the life of faith. And it would end, as well, a thought which, rather than simply dwell with the Divine, is perpetually to reenact its rise *to* It. It seems that Hegel's peace between the final philosophy and Christian faith must become—for *both* religion and philosophy—a peace of death.

Yet that this is contrary to Hegel's innermost intentions has been the recurrent theme of the entire preceding exposition. The *Phenomenology* can maintain its absolute standpoint of thought

---

* See appendix 3 to this chapter, pp.218 ff.

only if it preserves *some* standpoints of life. The system as a whole can dwell in its middle only if it overreaches rather than dissipates the actual world. And the *Philosophy of Religion* can comprehend the Christian divine-human relation from the divine side only if it both arises from and preserves the faith which lives at its human side. A thought which simply destroyed the representational form of faith would surely call forth a protest from the life of faith. And this protest, falling outside the thought which claimed to encompass it, would reduce this latter to "ghostliness."

But the *Philosophy of Religion* does not end with a rigid opposition between the forms of religious life and speculative thought. It ends, rather, with the mediation between life and speculative thought, the mediation of the ultimate dichotomy. *Its crucial condition is that a conflict which in one sense is yet to be resolved by thought is in another already resolved in life.* Just as the true content is present in modern life (in its religious, Protestant dimension) so is the true form of infinite self-activity (in such secular activities as scientific inquiry, moral consciousness, and perhaps above all, political life).[71] Moreover, true content and true form are not unrelated, let alone in conflict; in modern ethical life (*Sittlichkeit*) "the reconciliation of religion with actuality, with worldliness, is existing and accomplished fact."[72] Here "the mundane . . . realm of fact has discarded its barbarity and unrighteous caprice, while the realm of [religious] truth has abandoned the world of beyond and its arbitrary force."[73] "Actuality as such is reconciled with Spirit, and the state with religious conscience."[74] This inner bond between the free Christian testimony of spirit to Spirit (which remains receptive for all its Protestant freedom) and "free" modern secular self-activity (which by itself remains fragmented for all its infinite self-confidence) is for Hegel the ultimate revelation of Reason in modern life—the ultimate revelation that "the Rational is actual, and the Actual, rational."* *Only*

---

* *Rechtsphil.*, Preface. Hegel's famous dictum does not either absurdly deny the empirical element in common knowledge, or scandalously deify

*on condition of the existence of this Reason in life can there be a
true peace between it and that Reason which is speculative
thought.*

This conclusion might be gathered from our previous exposition
of Hegel's *History of Philosophy*.[75] For in this work we saw *not
one but two* conditions of philosophical thought in life—religion
and secular self-activity. And we also saw the war waged on faith
by that infinite self-activity which is modern philosophy paralleled
by another, waged by that infinite self-activity which makes modern secular life modern. But since its form must ally modern philosophy with modern secular life one might guess that the one war
can turn into peace only if the same is somehow true of the other:
if Protestant conscience, rather than remain in inward unworldly
receptivity, assumes self-active worldly outward expression; and
if secular self-activity recognizes a foundation in religious inwardness which transcends the scope of all secular power.[76] Only if
this double condition is somehow satisfied in life can the time be

---

naked power: "the actual" is not any and all existing fact (which, because of
the impotence of nature and finite spirit [See ch. 4, sect. 7 and p.109 n.] must
include the irrational, contingent and evil) but rather existing fact only
insofar as it manifests rationality. But is Hegel's dictum not then rescued
from scandalousness only at the price of being reduced to an innocuous
tautology? It is in the end because it can see no third alternative that Rudolf
Haym's influential *Hegel und seine Zeit* (Hildesheim: Olms, 1962), pp.357 ff.,
chooses the first alternative and accuses Hegel of "sanctifying the existing
order." Thus arose the still widely current legend of Hegel as the official
philosopher of the Prussian state.

But Hegel is not, as Haym charges, guilty of a "hopeless confusion of two
concepts of the actual." As Franz Rosenzweig has seen, the Hegelian dictum
is meant to apply only "since through Christianity the Idea of the Kingdom
of God on earth has become the ethical demand and the standard of all
human institutions." (*Hegel und der Staat* [Munich and Berlin: Oldenbourg,
1920], II, p.79.) It is neither an apotheosis of naked power nor a tautology
for a Christian believer to assert that "God has revealed Himself, and the
world is the place of His revelation." The Hegelian dictum is this assertion
reenacted in the ultimate philosophical form, and this reenactment has been
made possible and indeed mandatory because—so Hegel believes—in the
modern world the religious form of the divine manifestation has a secular
counterpart, and because the two are implicitly united. On this whole subject,
see further appendix 4.

ripe for the final philosophic thought. It is evident that the entire Hegelian enterprise, first fully conceived in the *Phenomenology*, has now come full circle.

With this conclusion the ultimate question to be asked of the Hegelian philosophy—a question which has emerged again and again throughout these pages, only to be studiously postponed—has now become at length inescapable. It is only on condition of a union of the religious and secular aspects of modern spiritual life—both endowed with a dimension of infinity—that the final philosophy is possible: *what then is the relation between the union which is already actual in modern life and the union which is still to be produced by the final thought?*

On this decisive question Hegel's thinking undergoes, over the decades, a remarkable change. For the early Hegel, the final philosophy will revolutionize a life which still needs revolutionary change. For the mature Hegel, the final philosophy *can* only comprehend life, and *need* only comprehend it: for the final unity is already implicit in life itself. For the early Hegel, philosophy will produce a new religion on the ruins of the old. For the mature Hegel, philosophy comprehends the old religion, and this latter is not and cannot be ruined.

In an early manuscript Hegel writes as follows:

. . . Protestantism has freed itself from alien consecration. Hence Spirit can now consecrate itself as Spirit, in its own proper form; and it can dare to *produce* its original self-reconciliation in *a new religion*, in which the infinite grief and whole gravity of its discord is acknowledged, but at the same time serenely and purely dissolved. It can do so, that is, if there will be a free people, and if Reason will have given birth again to its reality as ethical Spirit (*Sittlichkeit*), a Spirit bold enough to take unto itself its *pure shape, on its own soil and in autonomous majesty* . . . . To embrace the whole energy of the suffering and discord which has controlled the world and all its forms of culture for several thousand years, *and also to rise above it—this can be done by philosophy alone.*[77]

The central point of this remarkable passage is the prognostication that philosophy will, can, and must produce a religion, i.e., a form of life. The early Hegel believes that philosophy *must* initiate a new form of life. (For life is still in principle fragmented, and the old religion, while free, is yet lacking "Spirit's own proper form.")[78] And he also believes that it *can* initiate it. As late as in 1808 he still writes: "I am more convinced every day that theoretical labor accomplishes more in the world than practical. Once the realm of representation is revolutionized the actual world cannot bear up."[79] Philosophy, then, will give a "philosophical *existence* . . . [to the] feeling . . . [of the] religion of modern times . . . [that] God is dead [thus producing a] speculative Good Friday," and in *that* existence absolute discord is absolutely redeemed, in the "highest Totality" which has assumed the shape of "serenest freedom."[80]

But how would the life of this new religion have to be understood? In the old religion, grief and discord may be resolved, but only in a cultic life which, first, continues to recognize persisting sin even as it receives the Grace which redeems it, and which, secondly, acknowledges a secular realm outside the cultic marked, not by a divine reconciliation eternally accomplished but rather by a reconciliation eternally *to be* accomplished—by human self-active labor. For this double reason, in the old religion the human, while rising and raised to oneness with Divinity, can *remain* human. Can it remain so in the new religion projected by early Hegelian philosophy? Certainly not, for it must become divine. A Spirit which in "autonomous majesty" *purely* dissolved discord would fuse into *simple* identity religious union-with-Divinity and secular self-activity, abolishing the receptive form of the one and superseding the finite and hence discordant content of the other. Such a religion would be either a post-Christian and post-secular rational mysticism which dissolved the human into the Divine, or else a post-religious humanism which dissipated Divinity into an eternal goal to be realized by a projected self-deification of the human. This new religion would wrench Hegelian thought from its middle and force it into one of the extremes.

But Hegel's mature thought has turned sharply from this early conception of a new religion to be produced by philosophy. The "grey in grey" of philosophy cannot rejuvenate but only comprehend a "shape of life." It reenacts the old religion in thought; it can produce no new religion to replace the old. It is not the cock which heralds a new morning but rather—in one of Hegel's most celebrated passages—the "owl of Minerva [which] rises to flight with the coming of dusk."[81]

Popular opinion here takes Hegel as reducing philosophy to the reflective self-consciousness of civilization, there being—potentially—as many philosophies as there are civilizations, each arising toward the end and hastening death. This interpretation is radically mistaken. In Hegel's view, only some civilizations can be productive of a philosophy. Moreover, his own philosophy is in principle the final philosophy, comprehensive of the civilization which—by virtue of its religious and secular aspects, both endowed with a dimension of infinity—is itself in principle complete. Finally —and this is the decisive thesis—the comprehension which is in principle complete does not weaken or end the life which is in principle complete. "Only natural old age is weakness; the old age of Spirit is that complete maturity in which Spirit goes back, as Spirit, into unity."[82]

Hegel's decisive thesis, however, gives rise to a decisive question concerning the conditions on which it can be maintained. Life must still be divided if the unification which is philosophic thought is to be needed, and yet it must already be united if that unification is not to destroy it. This is in fact the mature Hegel position. Philosophy—which *can* only comprehend life—*need* only comprehend it: for modern life is already in principle united. Yet because it *is* life its unity must *remain creative diversity*: the Spirit which goes back into *simple* unity is philosophic thought *only*. Such a thought does not replace a life which remains creatively diversified: *it calls for continued participation in it.*

What has at length emerged, then, is Hegel's *faith in the modern world, and this is the ultimate condition in life of the possibility of his entire philosophic thought.* If the mature Hegel can accept the modern world as in principle final, it is because, first, he shares the double faith which in his view constitutes it. The Christian "Kingdom of God [is] founded forever . . . [and] the very gates of hell cannot prevail against it."[83] Equally indestructible is the infinite modern self-confidence which is manifest in free secular self-activity: the idea of freedom, once in principle actual, cannot be dislodged.[84] But secondly, Hegel can take this world as final—as continuing to persist after philosophy has united it in thought—only because he takes it as already *being* one world; *no less indestructible than the two dimensions which constitute the modern world is the inner bond which unites them:* "their opposition has implicitly lost its marrow."[85] It is this last-named faith which in the end is decisive. *Only on the assumption of an actual—and, in principle, final—secular-Protestant synthesis in modern life can Hegel both venture that final synthesis which is his philosophic thought and yet maintain that it will not end the life which has made it possible.*

This faith, and the philosophical comprehension which arises from it, may certainly be called conservative in contrast to the early Hegelian revolutionary expectations. But neither his faith nor his philosophic comprehension has any truck with a conservatism which would freeze the early nineteenth century European world into permanence. For the opposition between the religious and secular aspects of that world has "lost its marrow *implicitly*"[86] only. The secular idea of freedom, in principle actual, is actual in principle and as idea only, and because it is infinite the task of realizing it is unending. Protestant faith, on its part, though *freely* receptive, can always again lapse into that *sheer* receptivity and unworldly lassitude which is the danger of all religious faith. Only the inner bond between secular freedom and Protestant faith can produce the dynamic which frees the one from being fettered to some finite status quo and the other from inactive unworldliness. The bond is dynamic because it keeps what it has permanently united, at the same time, in permanent creative tension. The modern world, then, which is made one by this bond, is in principle final, but it is final in principle only. And the precise characteristics in it which make revolution both impossible and unnecessary render it capable of infinite internal reforms which will meet all future needs. There is no conflict between Hegel's faith in the finality of modern European-Christian civilization and his references—deliberately kept few, sparse, and enigmatic—to an American future.*

Nor is there a conflict between a final philosophic comprehension of the final form of life and a faith in the continued reality of the life comprehended. If man, though human, can rise in the final thought to the absolute divine self-activity, it is in the last analysis because the man who is an infinitely self-confident, modern, secular agent and the man who is a free, modern Protestant worshiper are *one* man. At the same time, because this man *remains* human, he can rise to divine self-activity in thought *only*: in life the two aspects, though inwardly united, must *remain* two. Hence qua worshiper man remains receptive of a Truth wholly actual without his doing, and yet he remains qua secular agent productive in the world of a Truth which requires his doing. Philosophy—which is the union of "wisdom of the world" and the "knowledge of God"[87]—has risen above this dichotomy in thought. But it would itself be a ghostly abstraction unless it demanded continued participation in a life which continues to have both these aspects in creative diversity. The *Philosophy of Religion* stubbornly insists that it is not the foe but true friend and protector of Christian

---

* See appendix 4 to this chapter, pp.220 ff.

life, and Hegel ends his *History of Philosophy* with a plea to his
listeners to "give ear . . . [to] the urgency" of Spirit and to help
"make it actual."[88]

6. *"Knowledge of God" and "Wisdom of the World"*

Hegel describes philosophy as "wisdom of the world"[89] and also
as "knowledge of God."[90] In its completely developed form—i.e.,
Hegel's own—it is the total unification of these two aspects. This
must be our inevitable conclusion if we relate the results of the
present chapter, devoted to the *Philosophy of Religion*, to those
of an earlier chapter (ch. 4) devoted to the middle of the system
as a whole. For the earlier chapter had shown that the middle of
the Hegelian system must remain fragmented unless Divinity is
wholly present in the actual world, and unless philosophy is capable of comprehending this presence. And the present chapter
has shown that, unless Divinity has a *worldly* presence, speculative
thought cannot hope to "transfigure faith into philosophy."[91] The
system, then, requires the *Philosophy of Religion*, as an indispensable and indeed its central part, and the *Philosophy of Religion is*
part of the system, not a philosophical enterprise which stands
apart.

Philosophical knowledge of God and wisdom of the world both
arise from nonphilosophical human life. The first arises from religious representational existence, and in its complete form from
Christian existence. The second presupposes "the awakening of
the wisdom of the world in the spirit of governments and nations,
i.e., wisdom concerning what is . . . right and rational in the actual
world."[92] Such wisdom is manifest wherever there is right and law,
and hence recognition of human freedom, and it is at least in principle completely manifest in the modern secular idea that all men
are free, simply because they are human.

Philosophical knowledge of God and wisdom of the world must

seek each other from the start. Cut off from the former, philosophical wisdom of the world would remain as finite as the secular existence from which it arises, and the knowledge of God—both the religious and the philosophical—would fall outside it. Philosophical knowledge of God, on its part, must from the start seek philosophical wisdom of the world. For "the content of philosophy and religion is identical [only] *except for the more specific content of external nature and finite spirit which does not fall into the sphere of religion.*"[93] This "more specific content" may not fall into the sphere of religion. It does fall, however, into the sphere of philosophy. An unworldly philosophical theology which simply ignored this more specific content would be opposed by a wisdom of the world which aimed at the conquest of externality in life, as well as by a *philosophical* wisdom of the world which aimed at such a conquest in the realm of thought. Taken as a single whole, then, philosophical cognition aims at comprehending "the relation of religion to the remainder of man's *Weltanschauung.*"[94]

The Hegelian philosophy claims to have completed the unification of philosophical knowledge of God and wisdom of the world. On the one hand, it raises the "more specific content of external nature and finite spirit" above finitude by "altering the categories,"[95] and it can do so because the knowledge of God, already existing in the form of religious representation, is ready to be transfigured into the form of speculative thought. On the other hand, it unites the God of both Christian faith and all past speculative thought so thoroughly with a speculatively transfigured world as to produce a total union in thought of what remains creatively diversified in life.

Hegel sums up all these conclusions in a remarkable statement. He writes:

The absolute Idea may be compared to the old man, who utters the same religious doctrines as the child, but for whom they signify his entire life. The child in contrast may understand the religious content. But all of life and the whole world still exist outside it.[96]

Appendix 1

Medieval Catholic and
Modern Protestant Theology

(*See p.173.*)

According to Hegel,

the general relation of the first Christian church to philosophy . . . [is that] on the one hand, the philosophic Idea has been transplanted into this religion [and that, on the other] this moment in the Idea—according to which this latter breaks up within itself into Wisdom, the active Logos, the Son of God, etc.—has been brought to a culmination in subjectivity, and further in the sensuous immediate individuality and present existence of a human individual appearing in space and time. (*Werke*, XV, pp.100 ff [*Hist. Phil.*, III, p.16].)

Hegel thus clearly holds that to have insisted on these *two* aspects— rather than to have permitted the reduction of either to the other—is the great achievement of Patristic thought: it is by no means a defect in it. And since this insistence implies unfree subservience to ecclesiastical authority this willingness to become subservient, too, is an achievement rather than a defect.

Still, this subservience *is* a defect, and it marks, in Hegel's view, the inferiority of medieval Catholicism to modern Protestantism. As will be seen, whereas medieval Catholicism is other-worldly and subservient to authority, for modern Protestantism salvation has descended from a distant heaven into a present free heart. Despite this, however, medieval Catholic *theology* is on the whole superior to most if not all of modern Protestant theology. In the former, authority directs the speculative grasp of the preworldly Trinity to the divine incursion into history, and this limits speculative freedom, and it directs believing acceptance of the historical Jesus, resting on authority, to the eternal trinitarian God incarnate in Him: thus it gives limited range to speculative freedom. In contrast, Protestant thought all too often (as in romanticism) dissipates the divine eternal Presence into sheer feeling, both devoid of objective content and divorced from history, or (as in Deism) it removes it to a mere remote object of abstract thought, or else again it loses both Divinity and eternity in a fruitless search for the historical Jesus.

These are no mere accidental aberrations. Medieval theology makes philosophy subservient to church authority and preserves it within these limits. Such compromises are destroyed in the modern world, by the radicalism of both modern secular life and modern philosophy. (See this chapter, sect. 2[c].) Because of this radicalism, Protestant apologetics has become hostile to all philosophy. But this hostility is self-defeating, and the true need of Protestant faith is quite otherwise. It requires a thought which (like medieval thought) grasps the two Trinities as present rather than beyond, hence with a freedom wholly emancipated from medieval authoritarianism. Precisely such a grasp is the task of Hegel's *Philosophy of Religion*, which therefore claims to be the final modern theology. (On this whole issue, see *Werke*, XI, pp.212, 220 ff.; XII, pp.194 ff., 354 [*Phil. Rel:*, I, pp.217, 225 ff.; II, pp.330 ff.; III, p.149]; *Werke*, XV, pp.233 ff. [*Hist. Phil.*, III, pp.151 ff.]; *HL*, pp.1234 ff., 1924 ff., 2448 ff.; sects. 4–6 of this chapter.)

Appendix 2

The Speculative Rise from the Human to the Divine Side of the Divine-Human Relation

(*See p.191.*)

This interpretation is central to this chapter and, indeed, to our whole account of Hegel's thought. (For the other two central theses advanced in this chapter, see appendices 3 and 4.) But it is at variance with the standard interpretation which, in effect, concludes that Hegel dissolves the Christian religion into a speculative pantheism, and that he regards its representational form as merely exoteric and devoid of truth and reality.

We have already argued that the standard interpretation (which we consider radically mistaken) derives from the failure to distinguish between Hegel's view of Christian existence and self-understanding and his attempt speculatively to reenact it. (See ch. 5, sect. 1.) It may here be added that it springs from a careless reading of the texts as well. Hegel explicitly states that the religious heart remains permeated by receptivity in its free Protestant form as well as in its Catholic form. (See the texts referred to on pp.191 n. and 192 ff. n., and in n. 59.) Moreover, this receptivity is by no means mere appearance, simply disposed of by the speculative reenactment of the religious God-man-relationship. That the Hegelian reenactment *means* to reinstate rather than dissipate the religious relationship is shown by statements such as the following: "God is God only insofar as He knows Himself. His self-knowledge is, *further, man's self-consciousness and the human knowledge of* God, which moves on *so as to become man's self-knowledge in* God." (*Enz.*, sect. 564, italics added.) Man's self-knowledge *in* God does not dissipate the reality of his knowledge *of* God.

Appendix 3

The Preservation of the Double Trinity in Speculative Thought

(*See p.206.*)

This is one of the three crucial points in which the interpretation given in this chapter differs from the conventional. (For the other two, see appendices 2 and 4.) Of these three it is the most important, for if our account is correct, Hegel here takes the decisive (though by itself still inconclusive, see sect. 5 of this chapter and ch. 7, sects. 3 and 4) step toward (i) reinstating rather than dissipating Christian representational existence and (ii) supplying the element still needed by the middle of his entire thought. (See above, ch. 4, sect. 8.)

But *is* our account correct or even tenable, in view of Hegel's assertion that philosophy "knows the content [of Christianity] *according to its necessity?*" (*Werke*, XII, p.351 [*Phil. Rel.*, III, p.146]; italics added.) Three points must be borne in mind in the interpretation of this necessity: (i) "The Notion *produces* the Truth (this is subjective freedom) but at the same time *recognizes* its content as *not* produced," i.e., as already actual in Christianity, and it is by doing both that it "justifies religion and in particular the Christian or true religion." (Ibid.) (ii) This activity (which is at once a producing and a recognizing) must grasp *both* "God [*and*] . . . His relation to the world" (*Enz.*, sect. 573.), a grasp which encompasses the entire Hegelian philosophy. (iii) As speculative grasp of Christianity, it must reenact the trinitarian God *both* as a "Love . . . [which is a] play of differentiation which is not serious" (*Werke*, XII, p.227 [*Phil. Rel.*, III, p.11].), *and also* as the conquest of an infinite pain which is all too serious; that is, as a reconciliation which is actual despite the "otherness, finiteness, weakness, and frailty of human nature." (*Werke*, XII, pp. 279 ff. [*Phil. Rel.*, III, p.69 ff.].)

These three assertions (which must be understood together) cannot be understood at all unless for philosophical thought as well as for Christian faith the two Trinities of Christian faith *remain* two, and unless the Love which connects them is a *philosophically recognized fact*. And as this philosophical recognition expands itself, so as to encompass the nonreligious aspects of the human *Weltanschauung* as well as the realities of Christian faith (See sect. 6 of this chapter.), it connects the two circles of the entire Hegelian philosophy, of which one is the *Logic*, and the other, the system as a whole.

But then in what sense does the Notion *produce* the recognized Christian content "according to its necessity" in the *Philosophy of Religion*? And in what sense does the *Encyclopedia demonstrate* that "the Idea," once self-complete, *must* "freely release itself into Nature?" (See above, ch. 4, sect. 7.) *In no other sense than by grasping all otherness as a divine self-othering.* Thus the *Philosophy of Religion* can see the world as *both* actual in its finitude—other than the pure play of the divine trinitarian Love—*and also* as overreached by a God othering Himself in it. (The Notion grasps both aspects when it comprehends God as Spirit.) Thus too the *Enzyklopädie* grasps Nature as other than the Idea in its logical purity, *and also* as the self-externalization of the Idea; it does both when it grasps Spirit as presupposing Nature (hence actual in its finitude) and also as presupposed by Nature (hence infinite). And, as we saw above (Ch. 4, sects. 6–8.), it accomplishes this double grasp when it recognizes overreaching power in both Idea and Spirit.

The Modern Secular-Protestant World

(*See p.213.*)

That modern secular self-activity and modern Christian faith must remain in creative diversity rather than become a simple unity is our third major departure in this chapter from commonly accepted accounts. (For the other two, see appendices 2 and 3.) Issues of great importance are here at stake. My account immediately rejects Hegel's supposed "deification of the Prussian state" (and indeed, of *any* state) as well as the possibility that in Hegel's view any state, or any *form* of state (taken in its full empirical concreteness), can ever be final or endorsed as final by philosophy.

A full defense of my interpretation is wholly beyond the scope of this work. (This would have to examine the *Philosophy of Right* in detail, and it would probably have to concede that the work does not always live up to its own thesis [sect. 3] that positive right inevitably limits the scope of philosophy—an application of the general thesis that philosophical thought must recognize the contingent *as* contingent even while overreaching it.) All we can presently do is (i) outline the conditions on which a creatively diversified modern secular-Christian life could become a *simple* unity, (ii) reject any such unity as un-Hegelian, and (iii) consider the implications of this rejection.

One possible simple unity would be a modern Christian state. But this (advocated by not a few of Hegel's contemporaries on the left as well as the right) is bitterly attacked by Hegel as worse than an anachronism. A medieval Catholic state (whose religious basis was other-worldly and authoritarian) could give at least limited and disciplined recognition to secular right and law. A state ruled by the modern Protestant "heart" (which is freed of external authorities and has descended from heaven to earth) could give no such recognition. It would give "free scope to caprice, tyranny and oppression." (*Werke*, XI, pp.242 ff. [*Phil. Rel.*, I, p.248].) In his assault on the idea of a modern Christian state, Hegel does not remain in the realm of abstraction. Thus he defends (*Rechtsphil.*, sect. 270) the emancipation of the Jews (still much embattled in the German states of his time), not only against Metternich-style reactionaries but also against that romantic-revolutionary "German-Christian" nationalism which had emerged during the war of liberation. This latter is often naively mistaken for a Western-style liberalism. (See, e.g., Karl Popper's ignorant but influential *The Open Society and its Enemies* [London: Routledge, Kegan & Paul, 1963], II, pp.56 ff. Knowledgeable accounts are G. E. Müller, *Hegel: Denkgeschichte eines Lebendigen* [Bern and Munich: Francke, 1959], pp.309–15; and Herbert Marcuse, *Reason and Revolution* [New York: Oxford, 1941], pp. 178 ff.) In fact, it is the earliest precursor of Nazi German–Christianity. The Heidelberg philosopher J. F. Fries (attacked by Hegel in the preface to the *Philosophy of Right*, though not for his antisemitism but rather for exalting the "mush of the heart, friendship and enthusiasm") published in 1812 a pamphlet demanding that Jews be limited in their right to marry and trade, expelled from villages, and forced to wear a Jewish badge.

The alternative simply unified form of modern life would be one in which the secular aspect had so totally appropriated the religious (the Divine already having descended from heaven into a "heart" on earth) as to produce the death of God and become itself divine— whether in the form of one particular actually existing order or in the form of an actually existing historical movement from one such order to another. But this possibility (subsequently embraced by left-wing Hegelians) is repudiated by Hegel himself. For him, the distinction between the "true" and the actually existing state remains, as does that between state and religion, even though their root is one. (*Werke*, IX, pp.537 ff. [*Phil. Hist.*, p.449].) For, first, "the ethical life (*Sittlichkeit*) of the state and religious spirituality are *mutually* warranting" (*Enz.*, sect. 552, italics added); i.e., the state cannot *be* "ethical" if, appropriating the religious dimension, it becomes totalitarian. And, secondly (and still more significantly), the religious dimension is not confined to interaction with the political because, whereas the realm of the political remains forever fragmentary, the religious realm possesses an absoluteness shared only by art and philosophy. (Karl Löwith rightly attacks Marxist and fascist interpreters who view the Hegelian recognition of the right of the individual in the state as a mere reflection of bourgeois half-heartedness. Hegel's "individualism . . . rests on the Christian principle of the 'right of absolute subjectivity,' of the infinitely free personality of the individual, which did not find expression in the 'merely substantial' state of the ancient world." (*Gesammelte Abhandlungen* [Stuttgart: Kohlhammer, 1960], p.114.)

Two further points may be made in support of our interpretation. First, *The Philosophy of Right* ends, not with a form of state (let alone an actual state), but rather with an account of a history which is in idea complete and yet remains as actuality open-ended. On one occasion, Hegel actually contrasts a possible future "American living rationality" with a present European "imprisonment" (*Werke*, X 3, pp.354 ff.), and whereas he exalts Lutheranism and German philosophy Hegel has no high opinion of German political self-activity: "we have all sorts of commotion in and on top of our heads; but through it all the German head quietly keeps its night-cap on and carries on as usual." (*Werke*, XV, p.501 [*Hist. Phil.*, III, p.425].)

The second point is perhaps most important of all. Our account alone is consistent with the middle sought by the entire Hegelian philosophy. It would be wrenched from this middle into a right-wing extreme by the absurd view which would make all history end with a present actual state and into a left-wing extreme by a view which, leaving history *simply* open-ended because simply secular, would fragment all spirit—philosophy included—into eternal finitude.

CHAPTER SEVEN

Conclusion:
The Crisis of
the Hegelian Middle

Is it possible to speak here of perishing
when the Kingdom of God is founded forever
and the Holy Spirit is eternally alive in its
community, so that the very gates of
hell cannot prevail against the church?
To speak here of a passing away would be
to end on a discordant note.

Werke, XII, p.354 (*Phil. Rel.*, III, pp.149 ff.).*

1. *Introduction*

In his inaugural lecture at the University of Berlin, Hegel demanded initially but this of his listeners: "trust in science, belief
in Reason, self-confidence."[1] These initial demands turn out to be
monumental. The self-confidence is in a philosophic thought
which is infinitely self-active. The science to be trusted "opens the
locked up essence of the universe."[2] And the Reason one must believe in is not human only but, in the end, divine. For "there is but
one Reason. There is no second super-human Reason. Reason is the
Divine in man."[3]

Here, in a nutshell, is the presumptuous rationalism—supposedly
presupposed from the start and hence dogmatic and arbitrary—
which has always been widely regarded as so fundamental an of-
fense in the Hegelian philosophy as to make it unworthy of serious

---

* Abbreviations are listed on pp.245 ff.

consideration. But if the preceding investigation has shown any-thing, it is that this philosophy is not arbitrary, and that its doubt-less unprecedented presumptuousness is matched by an equally unprecedented humility. Hegel's "science" can appear on the scene only when the time is ripe for it. Reason is divine only be-cause it has been revealed to be so by history, divine as well as human, philosophical as well as nonphilosophical. And the self-confidence of man is not in man only but in a Divinity at work over against and within him. Hegel's initial demand of his Berlin students, then, is also, and at the same time, the "result" of several millenia of "labor."

But what if Hegel's appraisal of his own age, and hence of all history, were radically mistaken? Or what if epoch-making events were to occur which destroyed all grounds of the Hegelian esti-mate, either of modern secular freedom, or of modern Protestant faith, or of the inner bond between them? Our investigation has left us in no doubt that this would fragment the middle of Hegel's thought, if only because it would shatter his "peace" between faith and philosophy. Nor can anyone be in doubt that this possi-bility has become actual since Hegel's time, if not in his own. In-deed, such are the crises which have befallen the Christian West in the last half century that it may safely be said that, were he alive today, so realistic a philosopher as Hegel would not be a Hegelian.

What contemporary significance, then, attaches to the Hegelian philosophy? One possible answer is: no significance. Thus neo-Thomism seeks to resurrect a premodern peace between faith and philosophy, while Anglo-Saxon thought (its religious aspect included) on the whole simply bypasses Hegel, and indeed all of German idealism. This is not the place for an argument with neo-Thomists, logical positivists, or linguistic philosophers of religion. Only two points can briefly be argued. First, the Hegelian peace between Christian faith and philosophy is unsurpassable, and marks the end of an era: if it fails, no similar effort can hope to succeed. Secondly, if the Hegelian enterprise does fail, it is significant in its very failure. Much, if not most, important religious thought until today is post-Hegelian in essence as well as in time.

2. The Hegelian Philosophy as the Consummation of German Idealism

The first point is best made by an effort thus far deliberately avoided:[4] a summary account of Hegel's place within the whole phenomenon known as German idealism, designed to show that his enterprise is not isolated but rather radicalizes and unites all the major themes of his predecessors.*

What main idealistic themes are radicalized and united in the Hegelian system?

(i) First, the Kantian "have courage to use your own reason"[5] has become absolute in the Hegelian *Logic*.

Even within its Kantian limitations reason is radical enough, far more so than in the Enlightenment thought which has furnished Kant with his motto. Enlightenment reason may not submit to arbitrary external authorities, such as absolute monarchs, priests, and sacred texts exempt from criticism. It *does* submit to the authority of both empirical fact without and sensuous inclination within. Compared to so harmless a rational freedom, the autonomy of Kantian reason is indeed revolutionary. It will recognize in external empirical fact only what it has a priori placed into it. Nor will it allow itself to be a slave determined by passion within: it *is* reason only when it is *self*-determined. Kantian reason rejects *all* submissiveness because it is *self*-activity. Until today one observes, especially in the sphere of religious thought, the contrast between

---

* The following generalizations can be substantiated only in "The God Within," which will also show that it needs two qualifications: the Kantian philosophy does not quite fit into the generalization, and Schelling's "positive" philosophy, not at all. Here we shall not include this latter, unknown in Hegel's lifetime. As for Kant, we shall at least hint at some of the major respects in which he stands apart.

the heirs of Hume and those of Kant. Thus some of the former proclaim the "death" of God for the harmless reason that the word "God" has no empirically verifiable meaning. Some of the latter— Marx, Nietzsche, Sartre, to name but a few—proclaim this death on behalf and for the sake of a radically self-active human freedom. There can be no doubt as to which group of thinkers is more radical or religiously more significant.[6]

Even so, Hegel radicalizes the Kantian reason. This latter remains finite and human; for it is an empty self-activity except when united with a sensuousness which, by itself, is blind. In contrast, the Hegelian *Logic* has "raised" rational self-activity to infinity. This is largely although not exclusively because the Reason in question clearly and unequivocally is—as the Kantian is not— *philosophical* Reason. Only the post-Kantian idealists—not Kant himself—pay due attention to philosophical Reason. They reflect not only on the reason manifest in human experience, and examined by philosophy, but also on the Reason which does the examining.* This reflection results in the discovery that, in recognizing the limits of the examined reason, examining Reason transcends these limits. Hegel's *Logic* completes this philosophical process, which is *doubly*-examining because it attends to *both* the examined *and* the examining Reason. His work both recognizes and indeed presupposes the categories of finite thought, and alters these categories, so as to integrate them into the infinitely self-active thinking which it performs.

(ii) But what would be a free Reason of *any* sort—Kantian or Hegelian—which is a mere philosophical assertion? No more than a groundless dogma and a ghostly abstraction. It is a widespread view that such thinkers as Fichte and Hegel tried to deduce the world by means of pure reason. This is of all the misunderstandings of their thought the most disastrous. In the minds of

---

* As early as in Fichte's works one finds Kant criticized for failing to recognize that, simply by examining theoretical and practical reason, philosophical reason not only distinguishes but also relates them.

Kant and every one of his German idealistic successors, free philosophical Reason must have what may be called an existential matrix, or *Sitz im Leben,* in order to have reality of any kind, and in order to be furnished with what one may term experiential verification.* The recognition of the need for such a matrix is built into every aspect of their thought: the *Sitz im Leben* of philosophic thought is a *second* theme with all these thinkers, additional to that of autonomous Reason. And this second theme is inextricably interwoven with the first.

This assertion cannot here be demonstrated but only illustrated. Kant proves the possibility of moral freedom**—on the grounds of the actuality of moral obligation. Fichte reenacts in philosophic thought the *absolute* Ego, which *posits* the non-Ego: this requires the prior existence of the *moral* Ego which *confronts* the non-Ego, as the "material of its duty rendered sensuous." Schleiermacher asserts a philosophical "realism" that is "higher" than Fichte's moral idealism: he bases it on a religious *feeling* of absolute dependence which discloses an *actual* dependence. Schelling puts forward a philosophical "real-idealism," composed of philosophies of nature and consciousness: this real-idealism but reenacts in conscious thought what is already unconsciously enacted in life, coming to consciousness in the work of art. Of each of these pre-Hegelian thinkers it is true, to use Kantian language, that human life supplies the *ratio cognoscendi* of a truth of philosophic thought, whereas philosophical thought discovers the *ratio essendi* of a truth of nonphilosophic life.†

---

* After what has been shown above (See especially ch. 4, sect. 8.), it need hardly be repeated that this term is not to be understood in an empiricist or positivist sense.

** This implicitly includes—though Kant himself barely attends to or even recognizes this fact—the freedom of philosophical thought as well as that of moral action.

† This theme still dominates such a twentieth-century work as Martin Heidegger's *Sein und Zeit.* See my article, "The Historicity and Transcendence of Philosophic Truth," *Proceedings of the Seventh Inter-American Congress of Philosophy* (Quebec: Laval, 1967), pp.77–92.

(iii) The dimension of life which is the matrix of philosophic thought can hardly fail to be existentially ultimate. For Kant and his idealistic followers this means—and this is the *third* theme they share—that it is *religious* in significance.* Kant takes his stand on a morally justified religious hope, Fichte on a "religion of joyous moral activity," Schleiermacher on one of pious passivity, and Schelling on that unique "revelation" which is art. Philosophical preoccupation with religion is not, therefore, a subsidiary discipline in their respective systems only. Religion is also, and indeed primarily, the experiential basis of their entire philosophic enterprise, and philosophic thought concerning it, a central requirement. This is, of course, not to deny that what *functions* as "religion" may be, in some or all cases, antireligious by certain standards; certainly it is far removed from all orthodoxies. Thus even Kant caused orthodox eyebrows to be raised. And Fichte was embroiled in a notorious controversy over atheism.

The Hegelian philosophy radicalizes not only the Kantian autonomous reason. It radicalizes, as well, the Kantian and post-Kantian search for an existential matrix of philosophic thought. And in this process it is driven into a unique philosophical confrontation with historical Christianity.

Hegel radicalizes the search for the existential matrix in that he seeks *comprehensiveness*. It is no longer adequate to exalt one dimension of life at the expense of all others: this would suffice to infect philosophy with one-sidedness and make it fall short of "science." The required matrix must be *all* of life or "experience": the barbaric as well as the civilized; concrete moral or social action as well as abstract natural science; the life confined to finitude as well as those of its dimensions—art and religion—which transcend it. The pursuit of this requirement has two fundamental, and inter-

---

* In *Sein und Zeit* the existential matrix of philosophical thought is still existentially ultimate but no longer religious, as is borne out, for example, by the work's ostensible religious neutrality. But Heidegger's later thought casts considerable doubt on that neutrality, see Hans Jonas, "Heidegger and Theology," *The Phenomenon of Life* (New York: Harper & Row, 1966), p.235 ff.

related, consequences: a realism comes to be part and parcel of Hegel's mature thought which is wholly lacking in the thought of his predecessors, Kant only excepted; and this occurs precisely as his idealism comes to make all-encompassing demands which are unprecedented.

These consequences, and their interrelation, are most readily seen in the demand in which the entire Hegelian philosophy reaches its climax. Hegel must demand that an *infinitely* free philosophical thought, which is to overcome all dualisms *within* life, must in the end also overcome the dualism *between* it and all of life. That demand cannot be met by the dissipation of life into philosophic thought: this would be a reduction of *both* life and thought to a "night in which all cows are black." Nor can it be met by a surrender of thought to life: this would be the reduction of philosophic thought to finitude. The Hegelian philosophy must be *both* unyieldingly realistic in its acceptance of nonunion *and* unyieldingly idealistic in its assertion and production of union. And it is able to be both only if it can be a thought activity which overreaches life, rather than one which is either destructive of life or shipwrecked by it. Such a thought activity would forever *arise from* a life required as its basis and presupposition, it would *rise above* it and in so doing transfigure it, and—because the result of having risen does not destroy but *is* the process of perpetual rising—it would *reinstate* life even as it transfigures it. In this sense and in this sense alone, the Hegelian philosophy is a form of rationalism. But it is true enough that in this sense it is the most rationalistic philosophy ever conceived, indeed, it is a rationalism which is unsurpassable.

But *can* philosophic thought overreach life if this latter is really *all* of life? This depends on two conditions: on whether life, while indefinitely fragmented into nonunion, also and already moves toward union and thus toward philosophic thought; and on whether philosophic thought can so move toward life as to encompass nonunion rather than merely "shun it . . . in monkish fashion."

The Hegelian idealistic claim to comprehensiveness is radically misunderstood unless seen as united with a realistic self-exposure to the contingencies of the actual world.

That there is in fact such an indissoluble union of realism and idealism may be corroborated by the contrast between Hegel and his predecessors. Precisely because these latter aim at less than comprehensiveness of thought they can exalt the "essential" in life—the matrix of philosophic thought—and, by the same token, underrate or belittle all aspects of life which are not essential. Further, and exactly because of this hard-and-fast distinction, they tend to romanticize the essential: joyous moral activity (Fichte), pious passivity (Schleiermacher), aesthetic creation (Schelling) all come dangerously close to being mere philosophical constructions rather than historical realities. In contrast with such romanticizing, the mature Hegel—the *Early Theological Writings* are still under the spell of romanticism—shows the utmost realism. His thought does not flee from nonunion but confronts and seeks to conquer it. As for union, this must *exist* in life; it cannot be a mere ideal asserted by philosophers. Hegel's predecessors—again Kant only excepted—are all inclined to philosophical homiletics. The mature Hegel repudiates all spurious philosophical homilies,* and instead confronts *existing* religions and their genuine homiletical expressions. Hegel—unless we are mistaken, Hegel alone—seriously confronts the *existing* religions of human history.**

This confrontation results—one might almost say, to Hegel's surprise—in an encounter with historical Christianity, i.e., with a Christianity which is philosophically *un*diluted, *un*demythologized, *un*reconstructed. His predecessors, all Christians of sorts, tend to

---

* "Philosophy must guard against the temptation to wish to be edifying," *Phän.*, p.14 (*Phen.*, p.74).

** An actual exception to this generalization is Schelling's positive philosophy. (See p.225.) Schleiermacher would appear to be only an apparent exception. For his early *On Religion* (New York: Harper, 1958) makes its philosophical case virtually without appeal to historical religious realities, and the great work of his maturity—*The Christian Faith* (Edinburgh: Clark, 1958)—is no longer a *philosophical* confrontation.

refashion the Christian faith in their own philosophic image, and this is true of the *Early Theological Writings* as well. The mature Hegel, taking existing religion and indeed all existence seriously, has made an astounding discovery. The religious life of man did not have to wait for philosophic thought, or for purification by philosophic thought, in order to be redeemed from nonunion, disruption and evil. *In Christian life, this redemption has already occurred.* For Christianity *itself*—not merely the philosophical comprehension of Christianity—is a process of overreaching; it is a "union of union and nonunion" in which sin is both utterly real and yet wholly conquered. Indeed, were it not for this conquest of nonunion already actual in life, philosophy would remain fragmented in its attempt to conquer nonunion in thought. It would, in the end, have to flee from nonunion, and thus from life as a whole. Increasing involvement with historical Christianity is thus no accident in the philosophy of Hegel's maturity, much less a lapse into reaction due to resignation or old age. It is part and parcel of that realism which distinguishes the mature Hegelian idealism from all others.

Nor is this involvement on Hegel's part a betrayal of idealistic Reason or freedom. Orthodox as regards Christian content, Hegel's mature thought is as free as regards form as that of his predecessors or, for that matter, as his own *Early Theological Writings*. Indeed, the claims here made on behalf of rational freedom exceed all others in boldness. For Kant, revelation remains beyond the bounds of reason. His successors can philosophically comprehend Christianity only by either ignoring or denying its claims to revealed status.* Hegel at once accepts the paradoxical revelation of God in Christ and dares comprehend it in philosophical thought.

(iv) For all the preceding reasons taken together, Hegel is forced to *confront history*—the *fourth* major theme all German

---

* This is one of several major issues over which Kant's successors make an immediate break with Kant. Kant never attempted, and could not have attempted, to furnish a critique of revelation. Yet such is the title of Fichte's first work.

idealistic philosophers have in common. History is by no means unessential either for Kant or his successors prior to Hegel, if only because the matrix of philosophical thought must have historical existence.[7] History can nevertheless remain peripheral so long as the matrix of philosophic thought is less than *all* dimensions of human life, and so long as the relation between life and philosophic thought has not become the central issue. Philosophic thought must presumably erupt *somewhere* in life. But so long as life provides the required matrix—Kantian or Fichtean morality, Schleiermacher's religiosity or Schelling's art—there is no real reason why it might not equally erupt anywhere. For Hegel, philosophy *cannot* equally erupt anywhere; indeed, it cannot simply erupt at all.

Philosophy cannot equally erupt anywhere: the whole of life (unlike abstract aspects of it torn out of context) is subject to historical development, and this is true also of the life of the Christian faith. Philosophy cannot simply erupt at all: no unbridgeable chasm may remain between comprehending thought and the comprehended life from which it arises. This is why the rise of Christianity alone does not suffice to make the time ripe for its philosophic comprehension. What must exist prior to such comprehension, in addition to the Christian content, is the form of rational self-activity. Indeed, only when rational form and Christian content are already implicitly united in history can that explicit unification occur which is the final, and hence transhistorical, philosophical thought.

It must, therefore, be said that *the actual existence of one specific historical world is the cardinal condition without which, by its own admission and insistence, the Hegelian philosophy cannot reach its ultimate goal.* This specific world may be called—with reservations—the modern bourgeois Protestant world.* This latter

* In the present critical context we feel free to use the term "bourgeois" which in the previous expository context (See ch. 6, sect. 5.) we have deliberately avoided. The term has nowadays mostly negative connotations, and in

takes itself as in principle final and indestructible, and is accepted as such by Hegel in idea, if not in empirical fact.

What attests to the finality and indestructibility of the modern bourgeois, Protestant world? As regards its religious aspect, it is the faith of a community which bears witness to the indwelling Kingdom of God, which is eternal. As regards its secular aspect, it is the varied manifestations of free modern rationality. These range from modern natural science through modern morality to the modern state, and they are all free or rational because ideally infinite: present and future obstacles are all potential conquests. But the two testimonies—religious and secular—are inadequate so long as they are mutually hostile or indifferent. They become adequate only when they point to each other, i.e., when they make the modern bourgeois, Protestant world *one* world. The Christian salvation has descended from a medieval Catholic heaven into a modern Protestant heart on earth; this remains a worldless pietism unless this heart demands free worldly action as its authentic secular expression. Secular self-activity, on its part, has acquired in the modern world a dimension of infinite ideality which makes it break the bounds of all finite reality and yet leaves it eternally fragmented by reality: thus its free doing of what forever yet remains to be done points to what Divinity has already done, i.e., to a divine acting merely appropriated by a receptive faith.

3. The "Discordant Note"

What if the modern bourgeois, Protestant world were lacking in either spirit or power or, to use Hegelian language, what if it were

any case suggests one finite form of life among others. In Hegel's view, the secular aspect of the modern world is permeated with infinity and, moreover, encompasses a whole *Weltanschauung* which has active expressions in all aspects of secular life, and by no means in its economic, social or political aspects only. For Hegelian and other nineteenth century German thought on the bourgeois Christian world, cf. Karl Löwith's already much-cited *From Hegel to Nietzsche*. At various stages in the present inquiry, we have derived many insights from Löwith's masterly study.

merely existing without being actual? What if its achievements were fragmentary or indeed wholly fraudulent? Hegel did not ignore or shy away from these questions. His realism forced him to confront them, and—as if to confound glib biographers—not only when the high hopes aroused by the French revolution had long become a mere memory and he himself old and resigned, but on various occasions in his career.[8]

Hegel never despaired of the modern bourgeois, Protestant world. Hence he never faced up to the effects of such despair upon his thought. But he did perceive severe strains in his contemporary world. Moreover, on occasion he responded to these with an altogether startling turn of thought.

Although in the *Philosophy of Right* Hegel is certain that in the modern state "the realm of fact has discarded its barbarity and un-righteous caprice, while the realm of truth has abandoned the world of the beyond and its arbitrary force,"[9] he is by no means as certain as is commonly supposed that this unity of truth and fact is—as, after all, it must be—*itself* fact, or that the future will mani-fest what the present does not. The *Philosophy of History* ends with the remark that Spirit, reconciled with the actual world, is re-conciled in thought only—not in life. Most startling, and indeed for all its restraint altogether shattering, is the end of the *Philosophy of Religion.* This is a mournful litany on contemporary Christian decadence. Faith—for which "the very gates of hell cannot prevail against the Kingdom of God"—may reject the "discordant note [of] the spiritual community . . . passing away." Philosophy cannot re-ject it; for it sees faith itself in a state of decay. "The discordant note is actual in real life. Religious unity has vanished from modern life, as much as it did in Imperial Rome . . . when the Divine was profaned." Hence political life—which requires a religious basis and inspiration—is "inactive and without confidence," so much so that all artificial attempts to revive it are foredoomed to failure.[10]

Hegel attributes this decay in large measure to the work of "re-flection." The modern Understanding has fragmented immediate spiritual unity, and it is at work not only in modern science but also, for example, in modern economic relations and—although this was not yet much in evidence in Hegel's time—in modern technology. Many of Hegel's contemporaries responded to these forces with a futile flight into a romanticized past. Hegel accepts them as a modern necessity, and yet believes in the power of Spirit to re-create itself as a new unity beyond fragmentation. But what if the modern bourgeois, Protestant world lacks this power? What will then heal fragmentation? Philosophy, itself a form of spiritual life, can heal fragmentation in the sphere of thought; it cannot otherwise heal it. In life, the discordant note remains. And—so Hegel concludes—philosophic thought has no choice but to become a "separate sanctuary," inhabited by philosophers who are an "isolated order of priests." They cannot "mix with the world, but must leave to the world the task of settling how it might find its way out of its present state of disruption."[11]

What an incredible, what a shattering turn of thought! The entire Hegelian philosophy may be viewed as one vast effort to stay with the modern Christian world, in contrast with Greek-Roman philosophy, which was compelled to flee from the ancient-pagan world. Are we to understand that the Hegelian philosophy too is, in the end, forced into flight?

4. The Crisis of Hegelianism and Post-Hegelian Thought

In the early nineteenth century, this question could still remain marginal. Were Hegel alive today, he would be forced to regard it as central. For our contemporary Christian West, unlike Hegel's own, is characterized by a fragmentation which is all-pervasive and inescapable. On the one hand, the Divine today speaks at most obscurely and intermittently to the believer; and this latter, if he is a Christian, can no longer ignore, or simply seek to convert, a rising world which is non-Western, non-Christian and nonwhite: he exists in a post-Christian world. On the other hand, our secular world too is postmodern; for the old modern Western self-confidence has been shaken to the core in this century. Two world wars have destroyed Europe's spiritual hegemony. The Western culture which has produced the idea of the freedom of all has also unleashed forces which would dehumanize and make slaves of all. And philosophical, sociological, and psychological skepticism articulate, or even aggravate, the widespread failure of nerve. Only in a single sphere—science and scientific technology—the old modern self-confidence still survives, and even here, since Auschwitz and Hiroshima, it is mixed with terror. From so fragmented a world the Hegelian philosophy would be *forced* to flee, as surely as Neoplatonism was forced into flight from Imperial Rome. Only thus could it maintain itself as a serene unity of thought free of fragmentation. Yet, if the preceding investigation has demonstrated anything, it is that, in the light of Hegel's declared central intentions, such a resort to flight would be tantamount to radical failure.

What, then, is the effect of this inevitable failure upon post-Hegelian thought? One possible answer is: there is no essential effect, for the Hegelian philosophy, and indeed the idealistic tradition which it completes, is a mere episode in the history of Western thought—an aberration which deserves to be forgotten. At least in the sphere of religious thought this answer is not convincing, for one can deny neither the existence of a uniquely modern secular-religious problem, nor the significance of the Hegelian attempt to cope with it. Thus it is in vain that the religious believer pretends that the modern secular world is no different from its premodern precursors: he can maintain himself neither in a simple other-worldliness nor in a simple unworldliness, nor can he simply abide in the modern world by premodern, but now undermined, sacred authorities. It is equally in vain that modern secular culture pretends to religious neutrality. It cannot simply let go of the old modern claim to autonomy and hence must—unless it comes to terms with faith and the God of faith—itself make quasi-, pseudo-, or antireligious claims. Again, a philosophic thought which simply bypasses Hegel is apt to bypass, as well, the whole modern secular-religious problem. This is true, for example, of scientific and logical positivism at the one extreme, theological positivism* at the other. For the one merely ignores the challenge of faith while claiming, on the authority of either science or empiricist skepticism, to have disposed of it. And the other takes its stand on pre-modern sacred authorities as if these latter were not, in the modern world, radically questionable. Philosophic thought no less surely bypasses the modern secular-religious problem when it disclaims all competence to contribute to its solution. Thus present-day linguistic philosophy of religion is prone to protest its neutrality toward all substantial issues, and ostensibly confines itself to the mere analysis of religious language. Such a neutralist program, were philosophic thought actually to abide by it, would demand the indiscriminate analysis of any and every religious language— spurious, obscurantist, and anachronistic as well as genuine and alive. Philosophy can never be so neutral, and the humility of much present philosophy is a mere mock-humility, disguising failure of philosophic nerve.

What, then, if the Hegelian philosophy is no mere aberration? In Hegelian language, does a "result" follow from the "process" of its failure? A result certainly follows if, staying close to Hegel's own thought, one dwells on the flight into which, today, it would be forced. This flight must result in a judgment upon either the world or the fleeing thought. Both these possibilities became, after Hegel, historically actual.

The first is actual, for example, in Bradleian idealism. Here philosophic thought flees from the world simply because it *is* the world. The Hegelian difference between the ancient pagan

---

* Dietrich Bonhoeffer criticizes Karl Barth's "positivist doctrine of revelation which says in effect, 'Take it or leave it' . . ." (*Letters and Papers from Prison* [London: SCM Press, 1953], p.126.) This justified criticism, however, is far from disposing of Barth's neoorthodoxy as a whole, as will be indicated in the very few remarks we can here make on this subject.

and the modern Christian world has become, so far as philosophic thought is concerned, after all accidental. History turns out to be, despite all of Hegel's labor, as inessential to philosophic truth as traditional metaphysicians since Plato have asserted: the dualism between the cave of history and eternity is final.

On such grounds, Hegelianism—or rather, what remains of it— reduces itself to but another contender in an essentially unhistorical philosophical arena; moreover, it is not then likely to do well in the battle. Coming, after all, "shot from the pistol," it is open to the charge of dogmatism. Compelled, after all—despite all protestations—to remain with a merely postulated Reality, it will dissipate appearance into another "night in which all cows are black." No wonder even ancient metaphysics and medieval syntheses of faith and reason have shown greater modern vitality than so truncated a Hegelianism; no wonder Platonism and Thomism are still alive while "the Absolute" is dead.

Such a right-wing turn, then, leaves no result except the addition of yet another contender to the philosophical arena. In contrast, a left-wing result transforms the arena itself. This result follows if one holds fast to the Hegelian thesis that the goal of philosophic thought is to stay with the world: that every philosophic flight from the world is the mark of partial or total failure. A left-wing turn on such grounds discloses that philosophic thought stands in need of an existential matrix, and it discloses, as well, that the Kantian philosophy (in which this need first finds radically explicit recognition) is the turning point in the history of Western metaphysics.* As for Hegel's philosophy, its significance is then seen as lying in its very failure. Unlike pre-Kantian metaphysics it seeks to stay with the world; like pre-Kantian metaphysics it seeks to rise to eternity: and it cannot do both. And this failure marks the

---

* In the essay referred to on p.227 I try to show that if the turn of thought here described is taken, it is the Kantian, not the Heideggerian philosophy which emerges as the great dividing point in the history of Western metaphysics.

end of all past metaphysics even as it initiates a new. The new metaphysics is a thought which remains bound to existing man and his world even as it seeks the transcending comprehension of both.

The destiny of philosophic thought under such circumstances depends on the condition of man and his world, and on the philosophic interpretation of that condition. Both may move far from Hegelianism. But two opposite possibilities, both still alive, result immediately from the crisis of Hegel's own thought. Despairing of Hegel's modern bourgeois, Protestant world, philosophic thought may hold fast to his modern secular freedom, or to his modern Protestant faith.

The first has occurred in such left-wing Hegelians as Feuerbach and Marx. For these, like for Hegel himself, the Christian God is the last of all gods who exhausts all religious possibilities. But unlike for Hegel this God does not redeem man but preserves and indeed aggravates his alienation; and this is precisely because He *remains* God, i.e., other-than-human. Hence this last God points to a radically post-religious future, and the bourgeois, Protestant human freedom already actual points to a radically secular freedom which is yet to become actual. Both will be produced by the most decisive of all acts, which is at once the negation of divine otherness by the human and a radical self-affirmation of the human. On the grounds of such a turn of thought, Hegel's secular freedom is preserved and indeed transfigured by the death of God for which it is responsible, and so is free philosophic thought. At the same time, the loss of Hegel's Christian content deprives both this postreligious secular world, and this post-Hegelian philosophic thought, of all hopes to finality. Free secular life becomes infinitely dynamic, hence inherently revolutionary and bourgeois no longer, and philosophic thought becomes the forever fragmented herald of a forever fragmented future.

What of a philosophic thought which holds fast to Hegel's modern Protestant faith? This too is a left-wing post-Hegelian possibility—if the faith is in a God who enters into and stays with the world, not in a God who, indifferent to the world, forces faith into flight from it. This possibility, however, depends on one crucial condition. The God whom faith *represents* as other-than-man and his world must *remain* in this otherness, even while entering into the world, vis-à-vis both modern secular freedom and modern philosophic thought. He is not judged by contemporary secular or religious fragmentation but, on the contrary, judges the contemporary world and all its secular and religious works, as much as any other. Hence the faith confessing such a God must turn against all modern pretensions to infinity, whether those of modern secular freedom or those of modern philosophic thought: these are, in the end, all idolatrous. As for the philosophic thought which stays with such a faith, it must accept this judgment upon modern secularity, as well as, in an act of foundering, repent of its own pretensions to infinity.

Such a philosophic thought, to be sure, recognizes the representational form of faith. But it can no longer hope to rise through this recognition to a higher form of Truth. The time is not ripe for the self-elevation of thought to the divine side of the divine-human relation, for *no* time has *this* kind of ripeness. Hence reflection points to a Kierkegaardian immediacy-after-reflection, and detached thought upon the divine-human relation points to existential participation in it. The God who is other-than-man for religious representation retains His otherness for philosophic thought as well; and the philosopher can only "point to ... [but not] deal with" Him.[12] There is no greater attempt than the Hegelian to unite the God of the philosophers with the God of Abraham, Isaac, and Jacob. The "result" of its failure is that the two fall radically and finally apart.[13]

Must post-Hegelian religious thought remain at these starkly opposed extremes? Recent developments suggest that they represent one-sided protests and temporary necessities, not permanent possibilities.

Thus it is instructive to consider the fate of nineteenth century left-wing Hegelians. Their denial of Hegelian transcendence led these to seek an absoluteness immanent in actual humanity; yet in the process virtually each thinker accused his predecessors of dissipating concrete man into unreal abstractions. This process culminated in Marx and Nietzsche, both left-wing Hegelians in a wider sense. Scorning Feuerbach's merely abstract freedom, and a merely "utopian" socialism, both thinkers found an *actual* humanity *absolutely* free, in the one case, in the future classless society, in the other, in the future "overman." Yet in retrospect Marx' dialectical socialism is far more utopian than that of the utopians; and Nietzsche's Overman is a far more unreal myth—and one infinitely more dangerous—than all past transcendent gods. By the standards of Hegel's own thought, such forms of post-Hegelian atheism are one-sidedly idealistic, and they are appropriately followed by the post-Hegelian atheism of such thinkers as Sartre and Camus, whose realism resists all temptations to make man divine.

No less instructive is what, for want of a better word, may be called post-Hegelian neoorthodoxy. Kierkegaard's protest against the modern world and the modern church is a necessity; yet, were this protest to become frozen, it would turn into an unbiblical unworldliness which is against Kierkegaard's innermost intentions: and, by his own confession, his personal conflict between his two loves—of God and Regina—remains unresolved only because of insufficient faith.[14] Again, Karl Barth *must* say "No" to the word of man in behalf of the Word of God, for the two remain incommensurable. But he cannot remain with a sheer No, lest the God once present in the world now be dissipated into a mere memory. As Martin Buber teaches, the meeting of the Divine and the human occurs, if it occurs at all, not in a separate sphere cut off from the world. It occurs in the world in which men meet each other.

These developments indicate that philosophic thought must move beyond the extremes of partisan commitments, and grope for what may be called a fragmented middle. This is not to suggest a revival of the Hegelian philosophy. But it is to suggest that philosophic thought, however rooted in existential commitments, craves a comprehensiveness which transcends them. To be sure, this craving can no longer expect, or even seek, more than fragmentary satisfaction. Yet it is not doomed to total frustration, and it is unvanquishable. Currently, the metaphysical urge is widely mocked, denied and obscured by a flight into piecemeal philosophizing. But, as Kant wrote, "that the spirit of man should ever wholly abandon metaphysical investigations is as little to be expected as that men, in order not always to breathe impure air, should ever prefer not to breathe at all."[15]

Abbreviations

Hegelian Works

Werke

Werke: Vollständige Ausgabe durch einen Verein von Freunden des Verewigten, 2nd ed. (Berlin: Duncker & Humblot, 1840–47).

JE

Jubilee Edition, *Sämtliche Werke,* ed. Hermann Glockner (Stuttgart: Frommann, 1927–30).

Phän.

Phänomenologie des Geistes, ed. Johannes Hoffmeister (Hamburg: Meiner, 1952).

Phen.

The Phenomenology of Mind, trans. J. B. Baillie (London: Allen & Unwin, 1931).

Logik	*Wissenschaft der Logik*, ed. Georg Lasson, 2nd ed. (Leipzig: Meiner, 1932).
Logic	*Science of Logic*, trans. W. H. Johnston and L. G. Struthers (2nd ed.; London: Allen & Unwin, 1951).
Enz.	*Enzyklopädie der philosophischen Wissenschaften*, ed. Friedhelm Nicolin and Otto Pöggeler (Hamburg: Meiner, 1959).
Zus.	*Zusatz* (Addition) to sections of *Enz.*, as found in *Werke*, VI, VII 1, and VII 2.
Rechtsphil.	*Grundlinien der Philosophie des Rechts*, ed. Georg Lasson (Leipzig: Meiner, 1911).
Th. J. Schr.	*Theologische Jugendschriften*, ed. Hermann Nohl (Tübingen: Mohr, 1907).
E. Th. Wr.	*Early Theological Writings*, trans. T. M. Knox and Richard Kroner (Univ. of Chicago Press, 1948).
Phil. Hist.	*Philosophy of History*, trans. J. Sibree (New York: Colonial Press, 1899).
Hist. Phil.	*History of Philosophy*, trans. E. S. Haldane (London: Kegan Paul, Trench, Trübner & Co., 1892–95).
Einl. Gesch. Phil.	*Vorlesungen über die Geschichte der Philosophie. Einleitung: System und Geschichte der Philosophie*, ed. Johannes Hoffmeister (Leipzig: Meiner, 1944).
Phil. Rel.	*Lectures on the Philosophy of Religion*, trans. E. B. Speirs and J. B. Sanderson (London: Kegan Paul, Trench, Trübner, 1895).
Dokumente	*Dokumente zu Hegels Entwicklung*, ed. Johannes Hoffmeister (Stuttgart: Frommann, 1936).
Bln. Schr.	*Berliner Schriften*, ed. Johannes Hoffmeister (Hamburg: Meiner, 1956).
Briefe	*Briefe von und an Hegel*, ed. Johannes Hoffmeister and Rolf Flechsig (Hamburg: Meiner, 1956–60).

Secondary Sources

Hegels Leben	Karl Rosenkranz, *Hegels Leben, Supplement zu Hegels Werken* (Berlin: Duncker & Humblot, 1844).
HL	*Hegel-Lexikon*, ed. Hermann Glockner (2nd ed.; Stuttgart: Fromann, 1957).
IH	G. R. G. Mure, *An Introduction to Hegel* (Oxford: Clarendon Press, 1940).
Study	G. R. G. Mure, *A Study of Hegel's Logic* (Oxford: Clarendon Press, 1950).
"T. G .W."	"The God Within: The Religious Thought of Kant, Fichte, Schleiermacher and Schelling." (Tentative title of a forthcoming companion volume to the present work.)

For the convenience of the reader, references are given to the available English translations as well as to the original German texts, even though the translations offered are generally my own. This practice is superfluous, however, in the case of *Enz.* (except for the *Zusätze*) and *Rechtsphil.* Here I cite by paragraphs which are identical in German texts and English translations. The best translation of *Rechtsphil.* is Hegel's *Philosophy of Right*, trans. T. M. Knox (Oxford: Clarendon Press, 1945). Of *Enz.* the second part—the *Philosophy of Nature*—has never been translated into English. The first part is *The Logic of Hegel*, trans. William Wallace (Oxford Univ. Press, 1904). The third part is *Hegel's Philosophy of Mind*, trans. William Wallace (Oxford: Clarendon Press, 1894). I have generally used the original edition of the *Vorlesungen über die Philosophie der Religion*, (*Werke*, XI–XII [*Phil. Rel.*]) although Georg Lasson has produced a critical edition (Leipzig: Meiner, 1925–30), because Lasson's text has been out of print and has not been translated into English. Important deviations are noted, however.

Notes

1. *Introduction*

1. *Hegels Leben*, p.xii.

2. *Human Experience and Absolute Thought:*
The Central Problem of Hegel's Philosophy

1. "Differenz des Fichteschen und Schellingschen Systems der Philosophie," *Werke*, I, pp.159 ff.

2. The *Encyclopedia of Philosophical Sciences*. (*Enz.*) On Hegel's conception of the relation of his philosophy to the history of philosophy, see below, ch. 6, sect. 2.

3. Hegel himself uses "science" for the *total* system, and "logic" for what once was "metaphysics." See the whole of ch. 4.

4. On this vital point, see ch. 4, which is wholly devoted to it.

5. *Bln. Schr.*, pp.19 ff.

6. See Dieter Henrich, "Hegels Theorie über den Zufall," *Kant-Studien*, 50 [1958–59], 131 ff. See ch. 4, sect. 8 and appendix 2, which gives as full a discussion of contingency as is possible in these pages.

7. *Werke*, I, p.157. Unlike the Nietzschean death of God, the Hegelian is followed by a divine resurrection, see ch. 5, sects. 7–9; ch. 6, sects. 4 and 5.

8. On this crucial term, see ch. 4, sects. 6, 7, and especially n. 35; further ch. 5, sects. 8 and 9, and ch. 6, sects. 4 and 5.

9. Karl Löwith's outstanding *From Hegel to Nietzsche* (New York: Holt, Rinehart & Winston, 1964) is entirely devoted to the break in post-Hegelian European philosophy.

10. See further ch. 7, sect. 2. We deliberately refrain, at this point, from placing Hegelian thought into an historical setting. (In any case general accounts of this kind are readily available in the histories of philosophy.) To give such an account at this point would in effect be to prejudge that Hegel's philosophy is a mere part of the historical phenomenon of German idealism. But, first, Hegel's philosophy is as much a response to Aristotle and Spinoza as to Kant, Fichte, and Schelling. Second, it claims to encompass the whole history of philosophy. Third, it claims to be, at least in principle, the final philosophical Truth. Not until these claims have been considered can one decide whether Hegel's philosophy may be placed into an historical setting or whether to do so is already to fail to understand it. For the position of Hegel's philosophy within German idealism, see ch. 7, sect. 2.

11. See ch. 3, sects. 1 and 6.

12. See ch. 5, sect. 1; ch. 6, sect. 1.

13. *Th. J. Schr.*, p.348 [*E. Th. Wr.*, p.312], italics added. Richard Kroner rightly calls this formula "the future philosophical system in a nutshell." (*E. Th. Wr.*, p.14.) The mature formula is "The Absolute is . . . the Identity of Identity and Non-Identity." (*Werke*, I, pp.252, 255; *Logik*, I, p.59 [*Logic*, I, p.86].) See also *Werke*, XIV, p.226 (*Hist. Phil.*, II, p.80): "God, the Absolute, is the Identity of the Identical and the non-Identical."

14. That this misunderstanding, in the main a result of positivistic preconceptions, is also shared by Marxists has been shown by G. E. Müller, "The Hegel Legend of 'Thesis, Antithesis and Synthesis,'"

Journal of the History of Ideas, XIX (1958), 411–14. On the relation between "pure" and "applied" logic, see all of ch. 4.

15. *Enz.*, sect. 95.

16. *Ibid.*

17. See below, ch. 4, sects. 2 and 6, and especially Appendix 1.

18. *Phän.*, p.19 (*Phen.*, p.79).

19. *Phän.*, p.48 (*Phen.*, p.116).

20. On Hegel's brief romantic phase, see most conveniently, Richard Kroner's introduction to *E. Th. Wr.*, pp.14. ff. This phase virtually ended as early as 1800.

21. *Phän.*, p.26 (*Phen.*, p.89).

22. See my articles, "Schelling's Conception of Positive Philosophy," *Review of Metaphysics*, VII (1954), 564 ff; and "Schelling's Philosophy of Religion," *University of Toronto Quarterly*, XXII (1952), 1 ff. The subject will also be treated in "T. G. W."

23. This label has been attached to Hegel by Thomists as well as existentialists, see, e.g., Etienne Gilson, *Being and Some Philosophers* (Toronto: Pontifical Institute of Medieval Studies, 1949), ch. 4.

24. See ch. 4, n. 14.

3. The "Ladder" to the Standpoint of Absolute Knowledge

1. *Phän.*, pp.12, 58 (*Phen.*, pp.71, 129).

2. J. G. Fichte, *Werke* (Berlin: Veit, 1845), II, p.324; for Schelling, see his *Darstellung meines Systems der Philosophie* (1801), the first work in which he espoused absolute idealism. Schelling's other major works espousing that philosophy are his *Bruno* (1802) and his *Vorlesungen über die Methode des Akademischen Studiums* (1802).

3. See all of ch. 4.

4. See sect. 6 of this chapter.

5. *Phän.*, pp.25 ff. (*Phen.*, pp.86 ff.).

6. *Phän.*, p.25 (*Phen.*, p.87), cf. *Enz.*, sect. 246 Zus. (*Werke*, VII 1, p.18). See further, ch. 6, sect. 1, especially n. 9.

7. See sect. 6. For the ripeness of the history of philosophy for "science," see ch. 6, sect. 2.

8. *Rechtsphil.*, Preface.

9. All passages referred to in this paragraph are in the *Introduction*, *Phän.*, pp.63–75 (*Phen.*, pp.131–45). The Introduction introduces the

Phen. whereas the much more famous Preface is meant to introduce the whole Hegelian system. For a brilliant but controversial and indeed arbitrary commentary on the Introduction, see Martin Heidegger, "Hegels Begriff der Erfahrung," *Holzwege*, (Frankfurt-am-Main, Ger.: Klostermann, 1950), pp.105–192.

10. *Phän.*, p.26 (*Phen.*, p.88).

11. Useful summaries are given by Herbert Marcuse, *Reason and Revolution* (New York: Oxford Univ. Press, 1941), pt. I, ch. 4, and J. N. Findlay, *Hegel: A Re-examination* (New York: MacMillan, 1958), chs. 4 and 5. More thorough works confined to the *Phenomenology* are Alexandre Kojève, *Introduction à la Lecture de Hegel* (Paris: Gallimard, 1947); Jean Hyppolite, *Genese et Structure de la Phenomenologie de l'Esprit de Hegel* (Paris: Aubier, 1946), and Jacob Loewenberg, *Hegel's Phenomenology: Dialogues on the Life of the Mind* (LaSalle, Ill.: Open Court, 1965).

12. *Enz.*, sect. 140.

13. This section is a preliminary interpretation of the second major section of *Phen.*, "Self-consciousness" (*Phän.*, pp.133–71 [*Phen.*, pp. 215–67].) It is preliminary because it requires subsequent placement into a larger context. We have in places expanded Hegel's own extremely terse exposition. In this we are indebted to Kojève (See n. 11.) but have sought to avoid his one-sided emphases.

14. The summation given in the preceding two paragraphs is based on many texts in addition to *Phen.*, especially *Werke*, IX (*Phil. Hist.*), Intro., pt. I, sect. 1, and pt. IV, sect. 3.

15. For the immediately preceding and immediately following paragraphs, see *Phän.*, pp.133–40 (*Phen.*, pp.218–27). The text is here at its tersest, and most in need of expansion.

16. For the preceding, see *Phän.*, pp.141–46 (*Phen.*, pp.229–34).

17. For the preceding, see *Phän.*, pp.146–54 (*Phen.*, pp.234–40).

18. This is explicitly shown concerning Stoicism, *Phän.*, pp.343, 523 (*Phen.*, pp.502, 752.) In *Enz.*, sect. 432 *Zus.* (*Werke*, VII 2, pp.283 ff.) it is asserted that the life-and-death battle for prestige takes place "only in the state of nature where men are isolated individuals, but it is alien to civic society and the state; for here that which is the result of the battle—recognition—already exists." The similarities to Hobbes are obvious, but so are the differences which in the end are far more important.

19. *Phän.*, p.314 (*Phen.*, p.458).

20. *Phän.*, p.328 (*Phen.*, p.479). "Ethical life" is the conventional but inevitably unsatisfactory rendition of Hegel's *Sittlichkeit*. We hope that the Hegelian meaning will emerge from the context, sufficiently for our present purpose. On the Hegelian distinction between "morality" (*Moralität*) and "ethical life" (*Sittlichkeit*) in the *Philosophy of Right*, see sect. 141 of that work; also ch. 6, sect. 5.

21. On this type of historicism, see my *Metaphysics and Historicity* (Milwaukee: Marquette Univ. Press, 1961), pp.55 ff. Hegel himself is not an historicist, and historicism emerged only with left-wing Hegelianism, see ch. 4, sect. 3.

22. See sect. 6 of this chapter.

23. *Phän.*, pp.473 ff. (*Phen.*, pp.685 ff).

24. Ibid.

25. Ibid.

26. See below, all of chs. 5 and 6, and particularly ch. 6, sects. 1, 3–5.

27. That it is Fichte, not Kant, who first asserts that man is a self-maker (and consequently clashes radically with traditional Christian belief) will be shown in "T. G. W." As regards Hegel's confrontation of this issue, it is not until ch. 6, sect. 5, that we shall have seen the full extent of the tension between Christian faith and free self-activity, and along with it the Hegelian attempt to resolve this tension.

28. See ch. 4, sect. 4; ch. 6, sect. 2(c).

29. In "T. G. W." it will be shown how Schelling himself struggled against the dissipation of the finite at various stages of his career.

30. These doctrines will be discussed fully in "T. G. W." For a brief survey, see ch. 7, sect. 2.

31. *Phän.*, pp.483 ff. (*Phen.*, pp.699 ff.). Hegel would appear to be referring here to both Jewish and Persian religion. Possibly he felt uneasy about identifying these two even then. In any case, in *Phil. Rel.* this identification has wholly disappeared.

32. *Phän.*, p.502 (*Phen.*, p.725).

33. The doctrines sketched above are developed at considerable length in the section titled, "Revealed Religion" (perhaps more accurately "Manifest Religion"), *Phän.*, pp.521–48 (*Phen.*, pp.750–85). We shall treat Christianity at length ch. 5, sects. 4–9; ch. 6, sects. 3–4.

34. On this presupposition, see ch. 5, especially sects. 1, 4–9; ch. 6, sects. 1, 2(b), 3.

35. On this rise, see ch. 6, sects. 1–4.

36. This section focuses attention on "Spirit Certain-of-Itself: Moral-

ity," the last chapter of the major division titled "Spirit." (*Phän.*, pp. 423–72 [*Phen.*, pp.613–79].)

37. *Phän.*, pp.79–129 (*Phen.*, pp.149–213).

38. *Phän.*, p.129 (*Phen.*, p.213).

39. *Phän.*, p.178 (*Phen.*, p.276). The section titled, "Reason," is the second longest in the work (*Phän.*, pp.175–312 [*Phen.*, pp.271–453].) and, as regards its details, both most dated and most obscure. But the overall role of the section in the work as a whole is clear enough.

40. *Phän.*, p.349 (*Phen.*, p.512).

41. Ibid.

42. *Phän.*, p.422 (*Phen.*, pp.609 ff.).

43. *Phän.*, p.429 (*Phen.*, p.620), italics added. Hegel here treats Kantian thought not as philosophy, but as the articulation of the "moral view of the world."

44. The passages referred to in this paragraph are *Phän.*, pp.434, 428–31, 429 (*Phen.*, pp.629, 619–23, 620).

45. We thus render Hegel's *Gewissen* as used in *Phän.*, pp.445–72 (*Phen.*, pp.644–79), to suggest a form of selfhood which is both knowledge and action. (See especially *Phän.*, pp.448–49 [*Phen.*, pp.648–49].) Among other things, Hegel would here seem to grapple with Schelling's *Gewissenhaftigkeit*, a concept which that thinker had formed in 1804. Schelling's concept will be dealt with in "T. G. W."

46. *Phän.*, p.450 (*Phen.*, p.650).

47. *Phän.*, pp.454, 461 (*Phen.*, pp.655, 663 ff.).

48. The passages referred to in this paragraph are *Phän.*, p.462 ff. (*Phen.*, pp.665 ff.). Among other things, Hegel here gives a critique of ethical romanticism. For his critique of religious and philosophical romanticism, see ch. 5, sects. 2 and 4; ch. 6, sect. 2(c).

49. *Phän.*, pp.471 ff (*Phen.*, pp.677 ff.).

50. See ch. 4, sects. 6 and 7.

51. *Phän.*, p.553 (*Phen.*, p.794).

52. *Phän.*, p.554 (*Phen.*, p.795).

53. *Phän.*, p.559 (*Phen.*, p.801).

54. *Phän.*, p.26 (*Phen.*, p.88).

55. See all of chs. 5 and 6.

56. In *Hist. Phil.* The *Phen.* confines itself to brief allusions to the history of modern philosophy, *Phän.*, pp.559–61 (*Phen.*, pp.801–804). See ch. 6, sect. 2.

57. See ch. 7, sects. 3 and 4.

58. In case Hegel's "science" collapses (See ch. 7, sects. 3 and 4.),

the *Phen.* breaks apart into fragments which no longer add up to an "introduction" to science.

59. *Werke*, XI, p.64 (*Phil. Rel.*, I, p.65).

4. The Hegelian Middle

1. *Phän.*, p.184 (*Phen.*, p.282).
2. On this term, see sects. 6, 7, and n. 35 of this chapter; also ch. 5, sects. 8 and 9, and ch. 6, sects. 4 and 5.
3. J. N. Findlay's term, see n. 19.
4. *Logik*, I, p.5 (*Logic*, I, p.35); *Enz.*, sect. 24. Hegel also refers to the *Logic* as "metaphysical theology, which contemplates the Idea of God in the sphere of pure thought." (*Werke*, XII, p.434 [*Phil. Rel.*, III, p.235].)
5. *Enz.*, sect. 24 *Zus.* 2 (*Werke*, VI, p.49).
6. Cf. Schelling, *Werke* (Stuttgart and Augsburg, Ger.: Cotta, 1856–61), VII, p.354: "Dualism . . . is merely a system in which Reason tears itself apart and despairs." For Hegel, see *Enz.*, sect. 60. Cf. also Fichte, *Nachgelassene Werke* (Bonn, Ger.: Marcus, 1834), II, p.147: "The difficulty of every philosophy which did not wish to be dualistic but was in earnest in its search for unity was that either God or we had to perish. We did not want to perish. God was not to be allowed to perish." The connection between the rise to an absolute standpoint and the rise above every dualism was clearly perceived in Kant's *Critique of Judgment*, sects. 76 and 77. This Kantian work Fichte, Schelling and Hegel all held in the highest esteem.
7. S. N. Trubetzkoy, quoted in Iwan Iljin, *Die Philosophie Hegels als Kontemplative Gotteslehre* (Bern, Switz.: A Francke, 1946), p.404.
8. Schelling's doctrine will be treated in "T. G. W." For Hegel, see *Phän.*, pp.17 ff. (*Phen.*, pp.77 ff.), his first open criticism of Schelling, which gradually led to a permanent breach between the erstwhile friends. (See also *Briefe*, I, pp.159 ff., 194.)
9. *Enz.*, sect. 82 *Zus.* (*Werke*, VI, p.160). Hegel's actual words are: ". . . the mystical, as synonymous with the speculative, is the concrete unity of those determinations which the understanding accepts as true only in their separation and opposition." See also *Werke*, XII, p.553 (*Phil. Rel.*, III, p.367); *Einl. Gesch. Phil.*, pp.191, 209 ff.
10. E.g., *Werke*, VII 1, p.30.
11. *Bln. Schr.*, p.424.
12. See, e.g., *Enz.*, sect. 246 (*Werke*, VII 1, p.11):

The origin and development of philosophical science requires empirical physics as its presupposition and condition. But the development and preliminary labors of a science are one thing, that science itself is another. In science itself, these can no longer appear as basis. The basis is here to be the necessity of the Notion.

On this whole issue, see appendices 1 and 2 to this chapter.

13. *Logik* I, p.54 (*Logic* I, p.82); cf. also *Enz.*, sect. 78.

14. *Logik* I, p.41 (*Logic* I, p.69). Possibly Hegel has borrowed this expression from Schiller's *Ideal and Life*, to which he explicitly refers when using the expression in the context of aesthetic discourse. (*Werke*, X 1, p.201.) It would be well worth inquiring into the relation between Hegel's logical realm and those beautiful spirits which owe their beauty to being "freed from the bondage of dependence on external influences and all those perversions and distortions which are connected with finite appearance." (Ibid.) One of the major limitations of our present study is that it must leave Hegel's philosophy of art almost wholly unconsidered.

15. *Rechtsphil.*, sect. 3 must here suffice as evidence that Hegel recognizes the persistence of contingency in the lives of states and, indeed, in history as a whole.

16. *Enz.*, sects. 9, 22, 60, 246, 246 *Zus.* (*Werke*, VII 1, p.19). Hegel credits Schelling with first "having altered the categories according to which thought applied itself to Nature." (*Werke*, XV, pp.607 ff. [*Hist. Phil.*, III, pp.535 ff.].) When Arnold Ruge asserts that the Hegelian *Logic* must be reduced from crypto-theology to "critique of all the sciences" (Karl Löwith, *Die Hegelsche Linke* [Stuttgart: Frommann, 1962], pp.44 ff.), he either fails to face up to, or else rejects, the Hegelian claim to be altering the categories. This is standard left-wing procedure.

17. This crucial point is habitually ignored by left-wing interpreters, such as those criticized by Iljin, pp.404 ff.

18. *Logik* I, p.31 (*Logic* I, p.60). What has been said in the preceding two paragraphs about the logical realm is well summed up in the following passage: "This advance in the determination of the Notion Logic develops in its necessity; each stage through which it passes involves the elevation of a category of finitude to its infinitude." (*Werke*, XII, p.433 [*Phil. Rel.*, III, p.235].)

19. The basic shortcoming of J. N. Findlay's otherwise worthy *Hegel: A Re-examination* (London: Allen & Unwin, 1958) is its failure to

recognize that the immanentist is neither the sole possible nor the correct alternative to the transcendent-metaphysical interpretation. (Findlay's work deserves much credit for undermining the latter, long dominant in the Anglo-Saxon world under British idealist influence.) Hegel does not just "sometimes make use of the transcendent language of religion," nor does he hold—let along make plain—that "the notional diction of philosophy" differs from the imaginative language of religion merely in saying the same thing "more clearly" (in view of the tortuousness of Hegelian language, the opposite is much closer to the truth). Nor again is it his view that time is overcome only in the sense that "we reach levels of thought at which . . . [time] ceases to count at all." (Pp.20 ff.) In view of Hegel's thesis that the Christian religion already is the absolutely true content, one must take seriously Hegel's use of religious language which is frequent and deliberate. And it is simply false that when philosophy gives the true religious content the true form of thought, it merely says the same thing more clearly. Nor is Hegel's Idea, as Findlay asserts, a mere "conceptual blue-print." (P.20.) Finally, Hegel would not credit with overcoming time a thought which is merely indifferent to time. All these points of Hegelian doctrine will be discussed fully in chs. 5 and 6.

20. Ch. 3, especially sect. 2.

21. Fichte's and Schelling's doctrines will be treated in "T. G. W." For a terse Hegelian statement on Fichtean idealism, see *Enz.*, sect. 415.

22. For hints of this criticism, see *Werke*, XV, pp.590 ff., 614 ff. (*Hist. Phil.*, III, pp.517 ff., 542 ff.) One of the incidental purposes of the present section is to expand further the account (Ch. 2, sect. 4.) of Hegel's relation to Schelling. On the one hand, even prior to *Phen.* Hegel was never a mere follower of Schelling, a fact obscured by Hegel's great modesty vis-à-vis Schelling in their early relation but nevertheless beyond doubt, at least since Hermann Nohl's publication of *Th. J. Schr.* in 1907. On the other hand, it is absurd to deny that Hegel's debt to Schelling is fundamental.

23. Nicolai Hartmann simply asserts that Hegel "places before" philosophy of nature a "further fundamental discipline" (i.e., logic) just as Schelling had placed philosophy of nature before Fichte's transcendental philosophy. Since he wholly fails to inquire why either Schelling or Hegel found such a placing-before necessary, he is quick to charge Hegel with a "vast dogmatism" of a simply presupposed and simply self-confirming all-embracing rationalism. (*Die Philosophie des*

Deutschen Idealismus [Berlin: De Gruyter, 1950], p.273; also "Hegel und das Problem der Realdialektik," *Blätter für Deutsche Philosophie*, IX [1935–36], p.12.) Hartmann's charge is thoughtlessly repeated by others. (See, e.g., Wolfgang Albrecht, *Hegels Gottesbeweis* [Berlin: Duncker & Humblot, 1958], p.116.) We shall deal in "T. G. W." with the reasons which forced Schelling to move beyond Fichte's transcendental idealism toward a realistic philosophy of Nature. As for Hegel, he may indeed be *finally forced* into a dogmatism of Reason. He does not, at any rate, *initially leap* into it, by means of "premises" of a "syllogism." (These are Albrecht's terms. See ch. 2, sect. 3.) Indeed, he explicitly condemns "dogmatism, not only . . . the assertion of something determinate—Ego *or* Being, thought *or* sense—as the true, . . . but also the false view that philosophy presupposes a supreme principle from which everything is to be deduced." (*Werke*, XIV, p.508 [*Hist. Phil.*, pp.563 ff.].)

24. See pp.85 ff. n. and sects. 6 and 7 of this chapter.

25. This assault is part of Schelling's turn from absolute idealism to a post-idealistic "positive" philosophy. This will be dealt with in the concluding sections of "T. G. W."; see also my articles cited in ch. 2, n. 22.

26. This must be qualified, however, in the light of the considerations offered in ch. 7, sects. 3 and 4.

27. For a brief account of Hegel's view of pre-Christian (i.e., Greek) philosophy, see sect. 8. For a fuller account, see ch. 6, sect. 2(a).

28. The following is a classical statement of Hegelian idealism:

In Being-for-self enters the category of ideality. Being-then-and-there (*Dasein*), as in the first instance apprehended in its being and affirmation has reality . . . , and thus finitude as well is in the first instance in the determination of reality. But the truth of the finite is its ideality. Similarity, the infinite of understanding, which is set beside the finite, is itself only one of two finites, untrue and a non-substantial element. *This ideality of the finite is the main thesis of philosophy: and for that reason every genuine philosophy is idealism.* (*Enz.*, sect. 95, italics added; see also sect. 96 *Zus.* [*Werke*, VI, pp.189 ff.].)

For the role of finitude, reality, and the understanding within philosophical thought, see also *Enz.* sects. 79–82.

29. *Phän.*, p.87 (*Phen.*, p.159); *Enz.*, sect. 246 *Zus.* (*Werke*, VII 1, p.16); and also *Werke*, XIV, p.476; XV, p.530 (*Hist. Phil.*, II, p.332; III, p.455).

30. Cf. and relate (among many others) these passages: *Logik*, I, pp. 5 ff., 19, 45 ff. (*Logic*, I, pp.35 ff., 48, 74); *Enz.*, sects. 22, 23, 24 *Zus.* 2 (*Werke*, VI, pp.49 ff.); sect. 82 *Zus.* (*Werke*, VI, p.159); sect. 121 *Zus.* (*Werke*, VI, p.245); sects. 214, 238 and *Zus.* (*Werke*, VI, p.411); sect. 420 *Zus.* (*Werke*, VII 2, p.262).

31. Cf. this remarkable passage already cited: "I raise myself in thought to the Absolute . . . thus being infinite consciousness; yet at the same time I am finite consciousness . . . . Both aspects seek each other and flee each other . . . I am the struggle between them." (*Werke*, XI, p.64 [*Phil. Rel.*, I, pp.63 ff.].) As we have said above (ch. 3, sect. 6.), the resolution of this struggle is the ultimate theme of the entire Hegelian philosophy. We have already treated this passage elsewhere (*Metaphysics and Historicity* [Milwaukee: Marquette Univ. Press, 1961], pp.68 ff.), though limitations of space made its treatment in that work wholly inadequate.

32. See ch. 3, sect. 4, and chs. 5 and 6.

33. The passages quoted or referred to in the last four paragraphs are all found in *Enz.*, sect. 246 *Zus.* (*Werke*, VII 1, pp.13, 16, 13).

34. *Phän.*, p.29 (*Phen.*, p.93); see also, e.g., *Enz.*, sect. 382.

35. Among the numerous passages in which this crucial term occurs we may cite *Phän.*, p.124 (*Phen.*, p.207); *Logik*, I, p.41; II, p.242 (*Logic*, I, p.70; II, p.237); *Enz.*, sect. 24 *Zus.* (*Werke*, VI, p.47); *Enz.*, sects. 213–15; *Werke*, XI, pp.179, 192, 202 (*Phil. Rel.*, I, pp.187, 197, 208); *Werke*, XIV, p.473 (*Hist. Phil.*, II, p.329); *Einl. Gesch. Phil.*, p.141. Its universal neglect is illustrated by the fact that it is listed neither in *HL* nor in any Hegel-index I have consulted.

36. *Bln. Schr.*, p.16.

37. See, e.g., *Enz.*, sects. 213 ff., 236 ff., 574; *Logik*, I, p.6 (*Logic*, I, p.36).

38. See sects. 2 and 3 of this chapter. What seemed then a hopeless contradiction has now emerged as a coherent doctrine.

39. For a full discussion of these terms in their religious context, see ch. 5, sect. 5.

40. *Enz.*, sect. 247.

41. *Enz.*, sect. 244; *Logik*, II, p.505 (*Logic*, II, p.486).

42. See especially *Enz.*, sects. 553 ff., 574 ff.

43. *Enz.*, sect. 24 *Zus.* 2 (*Werke*, VI, p.50); also, e.g., *Enz.*, sects. 250 and 314 *Zus.* (*Werke*, VII 1, p.265); *Werke*, IX, p.81 (*Phil. Hist.*, p.65). Additional passages are cited by Iwan Iljin, *Die Philosophie Hegels als Kontemplative Gotteslehre* (Bern, Switz.: Francke, 1946), p.245.

44. See, e.g., *Enz.*, sects. 554 and 574.

45. See ch. 7, sect. 4.

46. The decisive question left unanswered in this chapter will be answered only in ch. 6, sects. 4–6 and appendices 3 and 4 to that chapter. On the crisis of the Hegelian middle, see ch. 7, sects. 3 and 4.

5. *The Religious Basis of the Absolute Philosophy*

1. *Enz.*, second preface (*Werke*, VI, pp.xxi ff.); also *Werke*, XI, p.21 (*Phil. Rel.*, I, p.19).

2. See ch. 2, sect. 3.

3. *Einl. Gesch. Phil.*, p.192.

4. One notable recent exception is Karl Barth, *From Rousseau to Ritschl* (London: SCM Press, 1959), pp.268–305. (Published in the United States as *Protestant Thought from Rousseau to Ritschl* (New York: Harper, 1959).

5. *Werke*, XII, pp.283 ff. (*Phil. Rel.*, I, pp.290 ff.); also *Enz.*, sect. 405.

6. See, e.g., *Werke*, XI, pp.11 ff., 36 ff., 68 ff.; XII, pp.194 ff. (*Phil. Rel.*, I, pp.9 ff., 35 ff., 67 ff.; II, pp.330 ff.). On the positive aspects of romantic subjectivism, see ch. 3, sect. 5, and ch. 6, sect. 2(c).

7. See *Werke*, XI, pp.115 ff.; XII, pp.384 ff. (*Phil. Rel.*, I, pp.118 ff.; III, p.180 ff.).

8. *Werke*, XII, pp.384 ff. (*Phil. Rel.*, III, pp.180 ff.); *Bln. Schr.*, p.74. See also *Werke*, IX, p.355 (*Phil. Hist.*, p.291): "What essentially matters in the case of piety is its content, whereas nowadays it is often maintained that so long as there are pious feelings it does not matter what makes up their content." Whether Hegel does justice to Schleiermacher's actual teaching is a question which will be dealt with in "T. G. W."

9. *Werke*, XI, p.130 (*Phil. Rel.*, I, p.134): "If religion is to exist as feeling *only* it dies away into something devoid of both representation and action, and loses all definite content."

10. *Werke*, XI, pp.137 ff. (*Phil. Rel.*, I, pp.142 ff.) The text here treats intuition (*Anschauung*) separately from representation (*Vorstellung*) whereas Georg Lasson's edition (*Vorlesungen über die Philosophie der Religion* [Leipzig: Meiner, 1925–30], I, p.110.) reduces intuition to representation. We follow Lasson's text, which is doubtless more correct in this instance.

11. E.g., *Werke*, XI, pp.204 ff.; XII, pp.384 ff. (*Phil. Rel.*, I, pp.210 ff.; III, pp.180 ff.).

12. *Werke*, XI, pp.206 ff., 213; XII, p.403 (*Phil. Rel.*, I, pp.211 ff., 218; III, p.200). In a more precise sense "faith" is reserved by Hegel for the Christian religion—where it means the "testimony of spirit to absolute Spirit." (*Werke*, XI, p.206; XII, p.361 [*Phil. Rel.*, I, p.211; III, p.157].) See further sects. 7 and 8 of this chapter.

13. For our treatment of the "Notion of religion," see ch. 6, sect. 4.

14. See ch. 6, sects. 1, 3 and 4.

15. *Enz.*, second preface (*Werke*, VI, pp.xxi ff.).

16. "T. G. W." will contain an essay on Schleiermacher.

17. See ch. 7, p.230 n.

18. See, e.g., *Werke*, XI, pp.39 ff., 167 ff.; XII, pp.344 ff. (*Phil. Rel.*, I, pp.38 ff., 172 ff.; III, pp.139 ff.).

19. *Werke*, XII, pp.50 ff. and especially pp.218 ff., 247 ff. (*Phil. Rel.*, II, pp.175 ff; III, pp.1 ff. and 33 ff.). We use the expression "Power of divine Wisdom" because *Enz.*, sect. 81 *Zus.* (*Werke*, VI, p.155) has "Power" rather than "Wisdom."

20. *Werke*, XII, pp.255 ff. (*Phil. Rel.*, III, pp.42 ff.).

21. *Werke*, XII, pp.265 ff. (*Phil. Rel.*, III, pp.53 ff.). Other representative passages dealing with the fall of Adam include *Enz.*, sects. 24 and 405, and *Werke*, XI, pp.268 ff. (*Phil. Rel.*, I, pp.275 ff.).

22. *Werke*, XII, pp.70, 76 ff. (*Phil. Rel.*, II, pp.197, 204).

23. *Werke*, XII, pp.46 ff., and especially pp.69 ff., 81 ff., 85 ff. (*Phil. Rel.*, II, pp.170 ff., 196 ff., 208 ff., 212 ff.).

24. *Werke*, XII, pp.79 ff. (*Phil. Rel.*, II, pp.206 ff.); also *Enz.*, sect. 112 *Zus.* (*Werke*, VI, pp.226 ff.).

25. *Werke*, XII, p.270, also pp.77, 83 ff. (*Phil. Rel.*, III, p.59; II, pp.204, 210 ff.).

26. *Werke*, XII, p.271 (*Phil. Rel.*, III, p.60).

27. *Werke*, XII, pp.270 ff. (*Phil. Rel.*, III, pp.59 ff.).

28. *Werke*, XII, pp.95 ff., and especially pp.115 ff., 126 ff., 140 ff. (*Phil. Rel.*, II, pp.224 ff., 245 ff., 256 ff., 272 ff.).

29. An account which, while lacking this balance, is otherwise thorough is given by Nathan Rotenstreich, "Hegel's Image of Judaism," *Jewish Social Studies*, XV (1952), 33–52.

30. On the former, see ch. 6, sect. 2(a).

31. *Werke*, XII, p.127 (*Phil. Rel.*, II, p.257).

32. *Werke*, XII, pp.156 ff., 272 ff. (*Phil. Rel.*, II, pp.288 ff.; III, pp.62 ff.).

33. See ch. 6, sect. 2(a) and (b).

34. *Werke*, XII, pp.276, 291 (*Phil. Rel.*, III, pp.66, 82).

35. See below, ch. 6, sect. 2(a).

36. *Werke*, XII, p.124 (*Phil. Rel.*, II, p.255); see ch. 6, sect. 3.

37. *Werke*, XII, p.286 (*Phil. Rel.*, III, pp.77 ff.).

38. *Werke*, XII, pp.287, 295 (*Phil. Rel.*, III, pp.77, 86).

39. *Werke*, XII, pp.295 ff. (*Phil. Rel.*, III, pp.86 ff.).

40. *Werke*, XII, p.300 (*Phil. Rel.*, III, p.91).

41. See ch. 4, sects. 6 and 7.

42. *Werke*, XII, pp.305 ff. (*Phil. Rel.*, III, pp.97 ff.).

43. *Werke*, XII, pp.272 ff., 288 ff., 298 ff. (*Phil. Rel.*, III, pp.62 ff., 79 ff., 89 ff.).

44. "On the Proof of the Spirit and the Power," *Theological Writings*, trans. Henry Chadwick (London: Black, 1956), pp.53 ff. Lessing's question was also dealt with by Schelling and Kierkegaard, see my articles cited in ch. 2, n. 22, and Søren Kierkegaard, *Concluding Unscientific Postscript* (Princeton Univ. Press, 1941), pp.59 ff.

45. *Einl. Gesch. Phil.*, p.180.

46. See sect. 2 of this chapter (especially n. 6) and also ch. 6, sect. 2(c). What is at stake here is above all a critique of modern Christian romanticism.

47. *Einl. Gesch. Phil.*, p.180.

48. *Werke*, XI, pp.221 ff.; XII, pp.308 ff. and especially pp.336 ff. (*Phil. Rel.*, I, pp.226 ff.; III, p.100 ff., 130 ff.). For the crucial philosophical significance of the characteristic of Christian cult just described, see ch. 6, sect. 3.

49. *Werke*, XII, pp.333 ff. (*Phil. Rel.*, III, pp.127 ff.).

50. The passages cited in this paragraph are all found in *Werke*, XII, pp.338 ff. (*Phil. Rel.*, III, pp.132 ff.).

51. *Werke*, XII, pp.338 (*Phil. Rel.*, III, p.132).

52. See ch. 6, sects. 2(c) and especially 5. A preliminary discussion was given above, ch. 3, sects. 5 and 6—preliminary because the Notion was then only asserted and not yet developed.

53. See ch. 6, n. 18.

54. *Werke*, XII, pp.227 ff. (*Phil. Rel.*, III, pp.10 ff.).

6. *The Transfiguration of Faith into Philosophy*

1. *Enz.*, second preface (*Werke*, VI, pp.xxi ff.). Cf. also *Werke*, XI, p.21 (*Phil. Rel.*, I, p.19).

2. See, e.g., *Werke*, XII, pp.352 ff. (*Phil. Rel.*, III, p.148); *Phän.*, pp.532, 554 (*Phen.*, pp.764, 795); *Enz.*, sect. 573; *Einl. Gesch. Phil.*, p.186.

3. *Einl. Gesch. Phil.*, p.57.

4. *Phän.*, p.482 (*Phen.*, p.697). See also *Einl. Gesch. Phil.*, p.186; *Werke*, XV, pp.495 ff. (*Hist. Phil.*, III, pp.419 ff.).

5. See ch. 3, especially sect. 6.

6. See ch. 4, especially sect. 8.

7. See, e.g., *Werke*, XI, p.4 (*Phil. Rel.*, I, p.2): "God is the beginning of all things, and the end of all things . . . . He is also the middle which gives life and quickening to all things . . . . *In religion man places himself into a relation to that middle.*" (Italics added; cf. ch. 4, sect. 8.)

8. See n. 15.

9. *Phän.*, p.25 (*Phen.*, p.87). Cf. *Werke*, IX, p.535 (*Phil. Hist.*, p.447). Hegel changes the meaning of this metaphor when he describes evil as "the perversion of good, which possesses an actuality in its own right, but stood on its head." (*Bln. Schr.*, p.314.) According to this latter meaning, Christian faith and philosophic thought would have to be described as being on their feet. See also ch. 3, sect. 1.

10. *Einl. Gesch. Phil.*, pp.220 ff.

11. Ibid. See also *Werke*, XI, pp.8 ff. (*Phil. Rel.*, I, p.7). Cf. ch. 4, sects. 6 and 7.

12. See, e.g., the careful statement deliberately placed close to the end of *Enz.* (sect. 573).

13. *Werke*, XIII, p.274 (*Hist. Phil.*, I, p.254); *Einl. Gesch. Phil.*, p.217.

14. *Einl. Gesch. Phil.*, p.252; also, e.g., pp. 236 ff.

15. *Einl. Gesch. Phil.*, pp.190 ff.; also *Werke*, XII, pp.350 ff. (*Phil. Rel.*, III, p.148). It would be a "false peace" for religion and philosophy "each to go its own way and to move in separate spheres . . . For the need of philosophy and religion is the same: to fathom the True." (*Einl. Gesch. Phil.*, pp.196 ff.)

16. To avoid unnecessary multiplication of notes in the following sketch of *Hist. Phil.*, references to cited passages and summarized doctrines will not be given individually, but rather at the end of one, two, and sometimes even more paragraphs.

17. *Werke*, IX, p.273 (*Phil. Hist.*, p.223); *Werke*, XIII, pp.167 ff. (*Hist. Phil.*, I, pp.149 ff.); *Werke*, XII, pp.95 ff. (*Phil. Rel.*, II, pp.224 ff.); *Werke*, XV, p.436 (*Hist. Phil.*, III, p.358). On this point, one may contrast Hegel's mature thought with his *E. Th. Wr.*, which are almost wholly subject to what has been called the "tyranny of Greece,"—a tyranny from which many of Hegel's contemporaries never managed to emancipate themselves.

18. *Werke*, XIII, p.345; XIV, p.290 (*Hist. Phil.*, I, p.320; II, p.143). For the important thesis that "God is not envious," see, e.g., *Enz.*, sect.

564; *Werke,* XIV, pp.219, 282 (*Hist. Phil.,* II, pp.73, 135); *Werke,* XII, p.352 (*Phil. Rel.,* III, p.148). There is a significant connection between the Platonic-Aristotelian view that God is not envious and the Christian faith in a God so lacking in envy as to suffer and redeem death.

19. *Werke,* XIV, pp.222, 259 (*Hist. Phil.,* II, pp.76, 113).

20. *Werke,* XIV, p.516; XV, pp.3 ff. (*Hist. Phil.,* II, pp.372 ff.).

21. *Werke,* XV, pp.79 ff. (*Hist. Phil.,* II, pp.450 ff.).

22. *Werke,* XIII, p.352; XIV, pp.41, 62, 78, 63, 102 (*Hist. Phil.,* I, pp.327, 386, 407, 423, 408, 446).

23. *Werke,* XV, p.81 (*Hist. Phil.,* II, p.452). On Neoplatonism, see especially *Einl. Gesch. Phil.,* pp.240, 244.

24. *Werke,* XI, pp.387 ff. (*Phil. Hist.,* pp.318 ff.). Cf. St. Augustine, *De Civ. Dei,* book X, ch. xxix.

25. See, e.g., *Werke,* XII, p.273 (*Phil. Rel.,* III, p.63); also sect. 4.

26. *Werke,* XV, pp.100 ff. (*Hist. Phil.,* pp.15 ff.). On Socrates and Christ, see *Werke,* XII, pp.287, 295, 349 (*Phil. Rel.,* III, pp.77, 86, 144).

27. *Werke,* XV, pp.95 ff., 99 (*Hist. Phil.,* III, pp.10 ff., 15).

28. *Werke,* XV, pp.124 ff., 129 (*Hist. Phil.,* III, pp.40 ff., 45). See also *Einl. Gesch. Phil.,* pp.218 ff.

29. *Werke,* XV, pp.133 ff., 151, 177 ff. (*Hist. Phil.,* III, pp.49 ff., 67, 94 ff.).

30. *Werke,* XV, pp.144 ff. (*Hist. Phil.,* III, pp.61 ff.).

31. *Werke,* XII, pp.546–53 (*Phil. Rel.,* III, pp.360–67). On this whole subject, see Hegel's vitally important and much-neglected *Lectures on the Proofs for the Existence of God, Werke,* XII, pp.359–553 (*Phil. Rel.,* III, pp.155–367). Hegel deals with the ontological argument in particular on many occasions. (*HL,* pp.854–77, 1710). For its role in the theology of the Christian or absolute religion, see especially *Werke,* XII, pp.210 ff. (*Phil. Rel.,* II, pp.349 ff.).

32. *Werke,* XV, pp.239 ff. (*Hist. Phil.,* III, pp.157 ff.).

33. *Werke,* XII, pp.212, 286 (*Phil. Rel.,* II, pp.351 ff.; III, p.76); *Werke,* XV, pp.242 ff. (*Hist. Phil.,* pp.160 ff.).

34. *Werke,* XV, pp.241, 229, 241 (*Hist. Phil.,* III, pp.159, 149, 159).

35. Even this is true only with qualifications, see appendix 4.

36. *Werke,* XV, pp.307, 620, 243 ff., 412 (*Hist. Phil.,* III, pp.227, 549, 161 ff., 334 ff.). (On Parmenides and Spinoza, see also, e.g., *Logik,* I, pp.68 ff.; II, pp.164 ff. [*Logic,* I, pp.95 ff.; II, pp.167 ff.].)

37. *Werke,* XV, pp. 426, 337, 484 (*Hist. Phil.,* III, pp.348, 257, 408).

38. *Werke*, XV, pp.437, 483 (*Hist. Phil.*, III, pp.359 ff., 407 ff.).

39. *Werke*, XV, p.500 (*Hist. Phil.*, III, p.424); italics added.

40. *Werke*, XV, pp.500 ff., 552 ff. (*Hist. Phil.*, III, pp.424 ff., 478).

41. *Werke*, XV, pp.310, 328, 573 (*Hist. Phil.*, III, pp.230, 248, 500); also *Werke*, XI, pp.181 ff. (*Phil. Rel.*, I, pp.187 ff.). Fichte's doctrine will be treated in "T. G. W."

42. *Werke*, XV, pp.571 ff. (*Hist. Phil.*, III, pp.498 ff.).

43. *Werke*, XV, pp.613 ff. (*Hist. Phil.*, III, pp.541 ff.).

44. *Werke*, XV, pp.615 ff. (*Hist. Phil.*, III, p.544).

45. *Werke*, XV, pp.592 ff. (*Hist. Phil.*, III, p.520). Schelling's doctrine will be treated in "T. G. W."

46. See, e.g., *Einl. Gesch. Phil.*, pp.236 ff., 252.

47. See, e.g., *Enz.*, sect. 552. Roman philosophy is essentially Greek insofar as it, too, is made possible by Greek religion.

48. See, e.g., *Werke*, XI, pp.113 ff., 124 ff., 137 ff., 146 ff. (*Phil. Rel.*, I, pp.116 ff., 128 ff., 142 ff., 150 ff.). See ch. 5, sects. 2–4.

49. See, e.g., *Werke*, XI, pp.25, 66 ff., 204 ff., 232 ff. (*Phil. Rel.*, I, pp.23, 65 ff., 210 ff., 237 ff.). See ch. 5, sects. 2–4.

50. Cf. the distinction (already referred to in ch. 5, appendix 1) between "image" or "picture" (*Bild*) and "representation" (*Vorstellung*), *Werke*, XI, pp.137 ff. (*Phil. Rel.*, I, pp.142 ff.). See also *Werke*, XI, pp.80 ff. (*Phil. Rel.*, I, p.81): "'Of no religion can one say that men worship the sun, the sea, nature . . . ; these objects, while still natural, . . . are at the same time represented spiritually." Cf. also *Werke*, XI, pp.279 ff (*Phil. Rel.*, I, pp. 287 ff.).

51. The "main defect" of the Greek gods is not that they are "too anthropomorphic" but that they are "not anthropomorphic enough." (*Werke*, XII, p.124 [*Phil. Rel.*, II, p.255].)

52. *Einl. Gesch. Phil.*, p.180. On the "constant unrest" of religious representation and the "hovering" of religious feeling, see *Werke*, XI, pp.140, 125 (*Phil. Rel.*, I, pp.145, 129).

53. *Werke*, XII, p.60 (*Phil. Rel.*, II, p.186). See above p.179 n.

54. See, e.g., *Einl. Gesch. Phil.*, pp.199 ff., 232 ff., 343 ff.; *Werke*, XII, p.119 (*Phil. Rel.*, II, p.249).

55. *Werke*, XI, p.222; XII, pp.116 ff., 336 ff. (*Phil. Rel.*, I, pp.227 ff.; II, pp. 246 ff.; III, pp.130 ff.).

56. *Werke*, XI, p.222 (*Phil. Rel.*, I, pp.227 ff.).

57. *Werke*, XI, p.222 (*Phil. Rel.*, I, pp.227 ff.).

58. *Werke*, XI, pp.98, 160, 188 ff., 200, 206, 213, 216; XII, pp.201 ff

(*Phil. Rel.*, I, pp.101, 165, 193 ff., 205 ff., 211 ff., 218, 221 ff.; II, pp.338 ff.).

59. See, e.g., *Werke*, XI, pp.121 ff., 206 ff. (*Phil. Rel.*, I, pp.118 ff., 211 ff.).

60. *Werke*, XI, pp.33 ff. (*Phil. Rel.*, I, pp.31 ff.). Hegel insists that "feeling as such is not expelled by philosophy." (*Werke*, XII, p.353 [*Phil. Rel.*, III, p.149].)

61. *Werke*, XI, p.256 (*Phil. Rel.*, I, p.262).

62. *Werke*, XI, pp.192 ff. (*Phil. Rel.*, I, pp.197 ff.).

63. *Werke*, XI, p.76 (*Phil. Rel.*, I, p.77).

64. See ch. 5, appendix 3.

65. *Werke*, XII, p.5 (*Phil. Rel.*, II, p.125).

66. On the contrast between Jewish pain and Roman unhappiness, see, e.g., *Werke*, XII, p.273 (*Phil. Rel.*, III, p.63).

67. *Werke*, XII, pp.187 ff., 276 ff. (*Phil. Rel.*, II, pp.322 ff.; III, pp.66 ff.).

68. *Werke*, XI, p.76 (*Phil. Rel.*, I, p.77).

69. See ch. 5, sect. 9.

70. Compare Hegel's account of the realized Notion of religion (*Werke*, XII, pp.191 ff. [*Phil. Rel.*, II, 327 ff.].) with his account of the Notion of religion. (*Werke*, XI, pp.87 ff. [*Phil. Rel.*, I, pp.89 ff.].)

71. This doctrine is, of course, already present in *Phen.*, see especially *Phän.*, p.553 (*Phen.*, p.793); and also ch. 3, sects. 4 and 5.

72. *Werke*, XII, p.344 (*Phil. Rel.*, III, pp.138 ff.). On Hegel's notion of *Sittlichkeit*, see ch. 3, n. 20.

73. *Rechtsphil.*, sect. 360.

74. *Enz.*, sect. 552.

75. See also ch. 3, sects. 5 and 6.

76. See further, appendix 4 to this chapter.

77. *Hegels Leben*, p.141, italics added. The passage is translated in part in Richard Kroner's introduction to *E. Th. Wr.*, p.38.

78. *Hegels Leben*, p.141; *E. Th. Wr.*, p.38.

79. *Briefe*, I, p.253.

80. "Glauben und Wissen" (1802), *Werke*, I, p.157.

81. *Rechtsphil.*, preface. On the image of the cock, see Karl Löwith, *From Hegel to Nietzsche* (New York: Holt, Rinehart & Winston, 1964), p.65. For our own use of this image, see the end of ch. 1.

82. *Werke*, IX, p.134 (*Phil. Hist.*, pp.108 ff.).

83. *Werke*, XII, p.354 (*Phil. Rel.*, III, pp.149 ff.).

84. See p.210 and n. 79.

85. *Rechtsphil.*, sect. 360.
86. Ibid.
87. See sect. 6 of this chapter.
88. *Werke*, XV, p.624 (*Hist. Phil.*, III, p.553).
89. *Enz.*, sect. 552.
90. See *HL*, pp.877–80.
91. *Werke*, XII, p.316 (*Phil. Rel.*, III, p.108).
92. *Enz.*, sect. 552.
93. *Enz.*, sect. 573, italics added.
94. *Werke*, XI, p.7 (*Phil. Rel.*, I, p.6).
95. See ch. 4, sects. 5–7.
96. *Enz.*, sect. 237 *Zus.* (*Werke*, VI, p.409).

7. Conclusion: The Crisis of the Hegelian Middle

1. *Bln. Schr.*, p.8
2. Ibid.
3. *Einl. Gesch. Phil.*, p.123.
4. See ch. 2, n. 10.
5. Kant, "What is Enlightenment?" *On History*, ed. L. W. Beck (New York-Indianapolis: Library of Liberal Arts, 1963), p.3.
6. A currently fashionable phenomenon known as "death-of-God" theology includes Paul Van Buren's *The Secular Meaning of the Gospel* (New York: Macmillan, 1963) and T. T. J. Altizer's *The Gospel of Christian Atheism* (Philadelphia: Westminster Press, 1966). Except for the atheism and the slogan, these two works have virtually nothing in common; for the one rests on a linguistic-empiricist skepticism and the other, on a Nietzschean self-affirmation.
7. On Kant, see my "Kant's Concept of History," *Kant-Studien* 48, 3 (1956–57), 381 ff.
8. See, e.g., *Dokumente*, pp.358, 371; *Werke*, I, p.174.
9. *Rechtsphil.*, sect. 360.
10. The passages quoted in the last half of this paragraph are all found in *Werke*, XII, pp.354 ff. (*Phil. Rel.*, III, pp.149 ff.).
11. Ibid. It is not accidental that toward the end of *Phil. Rel.* Hegel repeatedly characterizes philosophy as a flight, see *Werke*, XII, pp.350 ff. (*Phil. Rel.*, III, pp.145 ff.); also *Einl. Gesch. Phil.*, pp.151 ff.
12. See Martin Buber, *Eclipse of God* (New York: Harper & Bros., 1952), p.50. This turn is first taken in Schelling's positive philosophy, see my "Schelling's Conception of Positive Philosophy" (*Review of*

Metaphysics, VII [1954], 563 ff.) and "Schelling's Philosophy of Religion" (*University of Toronto Quarterly*, XXII [1952], 1 ff.). This subject will also be dealt with in "T. G. W."

13. A new rapprochement is attempted by Paul Tillich, see, e.g., his *Biblical Religion and the Search for Ultimate Reality* (Chicago: Univ. of Chicago Press, 1955). Our present remarks express the belief that such a rapprochement is possible, if at all, only on the grounds that Hegel's philosophy is but another contender in an essentially unhistorical philosophical arena. Such would appear to be Tillich's view, although it does not seem that he ever reaches total clarity concerning the relation between the human situation, on the one hand, and history and the history of philosophy, on the other.

14. *The Journals of Kierkegaard*, trans. and ed. Alexander Dru (London: Oxford Univ. Press, 1959), p.121; cf. Martin Buber, *Between Man and Man* (Boston: Beacon Press, 1955), p.57.

15. *Prolegomena to Any Future Metaphysics*, trans. Paul Carus (La Salle, Ill.: Open Court, 1947), p.142.

Index